THE INTREPID QUAKER:
ONE MAN'S QUEST FOR PEACE

THE INTREPID QUAKER:
ONE MAN'S QUEST FOR PEACE

Memoirs, Speeches, and Writings
of Stephen G. Cary

Edited by
Alison Anderson and Jack Coleman

PENDLE HILL PUBLICATIONS
338 PLUSH MILL ROAD,
WALLINGFORD, PA 19086

For information please address

Pendle Hill Publications
338 Plush Mill Road,
Wallingford, PA 19086
800-742-3150
www.pendlehill.org
For book orders: bookstore@pendlehill.org

Library of Congress Cataloging-in-Publication Data

Cary, Stephen G.
    The Intrepid Quaker: one man's quest for peace :
memoirs, speeches, and writings of Stephen G. Cary.
    ISBN 0-87574-943-7
    1. Cary, Stephen G. 2. Quakers--United States--Biogra-
phy. 3. Pacifists--United States--Biography. I. Title.

BX7795.C32A3 2003
289.6'092--dc22
[B]
                                        20033062327

For Margaret Morris Cary,
who planted the ideas

and

Elizabeth Summers Cary,
who nourished them.

PERMISSIONS

Pendle Hill is grateful to the following individuals and organizations for their permission to use the material in this collection:

American Friends Service Committee for permission to use photographs from their archives and to reprint: "Address to the Annual Gathering of the American Friends Service Committee, November 17, 1990" and "A Possible Quaker Contribution to the Christian Dialogue Regarding Justice, Peace, and the Integrity of Creation."

Betty Cary for permission to use Cary family archive material, including photographs and background material.

The Haverford College student publication, *Chautaugua*, for permission to reprint "A Quaker Vision for Haverford" (May 1987).

Friends Publishing Corporation for permission to reprint the following articles from *Friends Journal:* "A Response to September Eleventh" (March 2002) and "Civilian Public Service Revisited" (January 1992).

Germantown Friends School for permission to reprint the following: "Pacifism: Relevant Witness or Pipe Dream?" (Germantown Friends School *Bulletin* vol. 12, no. 3 Spring 1974), "Why Quaker Meeting?" (Germantown Friends School *Studies in Education,* No. 65, Spring 1993), and "Quaker Values and Germantown Friends School" (archive material, 1996).

Philadelphia Yearly Meeting Publications Committee for permission to reprint "The Quaker Proposition" (tract, August 1979).

Contents

Part One: Roots

Part Two: The American Friends Service Committee

Part Three: Haverford College, 1955-1981

Part Four: Reflections and Conclusion

Selected Speeches and Writings

PREFACE

I had a very small part in bringing this book into being. A couple of years ago, impressed that Steve's story needed to be told, I made a threat to him. "Either you write this story yourself, or else I'm going to do it." That scared him. He started in on the book as soon as he realized that my "or else" was for real.

Now he has written the story of his lifelong mission on behalf of peace and justice, and of the joy he found in that mission. This is it.

It was difficult for him. Although I see his life lifting him into as much of sainthood as non-Catholics are permitted to get, he denied anything so distinctive in the path he chose. "Who would be interested in such a story?" he asked.

This man was my hero for 35 years. His commitment to peace took him to pulpits, to conscientious objector work camps, to jail, to foreign lands racked by war's ravages, to long talks with top political leaders at home and abroad. Lesser believers might have stopped to ask, "What's the use? Few people believe there are alternatives to war." Steve was not discouraged.

As important as his commitment was, it did not make him into a crusader with all the answers. The fate of our deepest believers in whatever their causes are is often to become self-righteous and all-knowing. Steve was an exception: he never lost the ears to hear alternative points or the eyes to read alternative approaches.

Equally important, he pursued his passion with a sense of joy. Steve laughed as much as he cried. His presence in any room, large or small, elegant or humble, enlivened that room. No one could match him as storyteller. His tales typically brought commitment, compassion, and comedy into the most delightful harmony. Love poured out from him, and love poured back to him in turn. To read what this man did with his full life is to learn what one person can do to put values to the test under even the most difficult conditions. To know his story is to become aware that you have lost the right to ask ever again, "What difference can one life make?" This man, part of a small group of peace-pursuing people, put a check on some of the worst abuses that stem from love of arms rather than arms of love. To lose even one of such people is to make the night darker, the fight bloodier.

One chapter of his book remained undone in the summer of 2002. He was unwilling to put on paper the story of his last year as chairman of the American Friends Service Committee. It was work of the deepest meaning to him—witness how faithfully he did it. But his modesty prevented him from recording what he and the Committee, the center of Quaker social action, did for peace, welfare, and human rights across the world. It remains for someone else to tell that story. We need it told.

This book also lacks a picture of some other facets of this extraordinary life. The reader won't learn here of his climbing, at the age of 60-plus, in the Himalayas and coming upon a solitary tenter on a high and lonely plateau. The tenter turned out to be a recent alumnus of the college Steve loved so much. There is no glimpse of him here as one of a crew on a small sailing ship rounding Cape Horn through furious waves. He does not tell us of his passionate love of sports, a passion so great that at a Haverford College football game he could forget his commitment to nonviolence and, red-faced, yell from the sidelines, "Kill, Quakers, kill!" Whatever he did, he did with zest .

My last visit with Steve was in late July of 2002. We met at his Cape Cod summer place, when cancer had taken away much of his physical being but none of his values. Family members left us alone for 45 minutes. Some of the time we talked about this book—its dedication, its prospects, its message. We agreed on a title for it, but others who knew him far better than I opted for a different one. No matter. What does matter for me is that I had the chance to tell him again just how much impact he has had on me. What the Quaker faith came to mean to me, what dedication to a noble cause even when few others had the courage to stick to it meant, what fun life could be even in pursuit of that cause—those were what I got from him.

When it was time for me to leave him, the family members came into the room. I hugged and kissed him in what we both knew was a farewell. I turned, tearful, to leave the room and the man. His voice called me back to him once more. His frail arms were out to me. "One more, Jack. One more." He died ten days later.

—Jack Coleman
Chester, Vermont
November 1, 2002

Acknowledgments

The Cary family is grateful to a number of people who have helped bring this book to fruition. For years friends and acquaintances had urged Steve to write a memoir, but it was Jack Coleman who finally persuaded him to begin. Jack read the chapters as they were written, made suggestions, edited, and generally acted as midwife for the book. Barbara Broomell Parry typed each chapter and then made the corrections Steve scrawled in the margins. In the end, the desire to finish the book kept Steve alive. He was determined to draft and edit his work, and he managed to outlive his doctor's predictions by a year and a half. Once the final chapter was written and corrected, however, his health deteriorated rapidly.

Others then stepped in to bring the book to publication. Norval Reece ensured the financial arrangements and worked closely with Bob McCoy, who coordinated publication for Pendle Hill. Midge Guise, Corinne Johnson, Ann Reece, Walter Emerson and family members read the manuscript and offered comments and suggestions. Alison Anderson provided her professional expertise to tweak some of the paragraphs and to soften some of the language.

Steve Cary loved to tell stories about his adventures and the adventures of others. These tales often had his audience in stitches, but they also imparted important values. His memoir and his speeches, many included in the second part of this book, reveal his deeply thoughtful and spiritual side. We are proud, and filled with gratitude, that Steve's record of his remarkable life will now reach a broader audience.

Elizabeth Summers Cary

Anne Cary Sampson

Charles Reed Cary II

Dorothy Cary

Part One

Roots

One

═►◆◄═

STIRRINGS

B Y THE TIME I WAS FOUR YEARS OLD, I could make life
miserable in the Cary household. My sister Barbara was
five, and she was allowed to go to Quaker Meeting. This
obvious sex discrimination told me I needed to bring my parents into line. Mother was a formidable lady, but even the
formidable have their breaking points. After major nagging,
she broke.

"All right, Stephen, thee can go to Meeting on one condition—that thee sit absolutely still for one hour."

"Piece of cake," I said—or its 1919 equivalent. For five
minutes I sat motionless. For five more, I squirmed. After
ten, a distinguished old gentleman rose to preach. He opened
with scripture, then paused to let the congregation reflect
on the passage. As silence settled over the worshippers, I
turned to my mother and asked in a loud voice: "Well, if
that man can talk, why can't I?"

Thus began my career as a Quaker. Abruptly aborted at
four, it wasn't actively re-launched for 20 years, despite a
Quaker education and regular, required attendance at
Quaker Meetings. In between came a joyous childhood,
marred only by failing kindergarten and taking 13 years to
achieve what others did in twelve. This misfortune pales
beside the blessing of a set of astonishing parents. The word

With Sister Barbara in the garden of house in Lehman Lane, Philadelphia. 1917

Cary Family Archives

formidable is inadequate for my mother. When the Lord finished with her, He broke the mold, thinking that one was enough. Dynamic, abrupt, colorful, generous, wildly short of temper, wildly long on enthusiasm, mother other saw the world in stark blacks and whites. Her children were always on the white side. She lavished her love on us, even if sometimes she bordered on the overpowering. Her marriage lasted more than 50 years because she had been fortunate enough to marry a saint. My father was thoughtful, gentle, patient, hard-working, ever the balance wheel, ever rescued by his abiding sense of humor, ever loving his mercurial wife through all the peaks and valleys that each day's living presented.

Our household revolved around my mother. In my early years, she was active in the Alumnae Association of Bryn Mawr College, from which she had graduated in 1908. She became the Association's president just as the country entered World War I in 1917. That war was fought in Europe, but it had its modest counterpart on Philadelphia's Main Line. M. Carey Thomas was president of Bryn Mawr, and the Main Line wasn't big enough to contain both Carey Thomas and Margaret Cary. Ms. Thomas was at least as powerful in her opinions and vigorous in their pursuit as was mother. Their meetings quickly

Germantown Friends School (top)
Classmates on the front steps of Germantown Friends School.
Stephen, as always, is front row and center.

escalated to Force Ten—full hurricane level. Time and again, my mother would return from Bryn Mawr in a towering rage, with references to "that woman," usually linked with her ulti-mate malediction of "whited sepulcher." I have no doubt that Carey Thomas, for her part, was in a similar mood, with ample justification. Indeed, Ms. Thomas and her college became so much a part of my early life that after I disappeared from home one morning, and my frantic mother had called my father home from work to join neighbors in the search for me, I was found some blocks away, lunch box in hand, explaining that I was en route "to a 'mitty meeting at Bin Mawr.'"

My early schooling was at Germantown Friends School, the natural place for a Quaker boy in that section of Philadelphia. I was shy then, which current friends find difficult to believe, but I have proof. Long after I was finished with school, I found an old report card, issued at the end of my first-grade year, on which my teacher had neatly inscribed for the benefit of my parents: "Nice little boy. Needs to be drawn out." I've often wondered whether she and others overdid their task.

Uncharacteristically serious high school yearbook picture. The caption captured Stephen more accurately: "A crowd around Stephen often collects, and when the clouds clear it then appears that they are all of the opposite sex."

The Germantown Friends high school years were among the happiest of my life. I became a big fish in a small puddle, with athletic success, the class presidency, a legion of male friends, and even a nice roster of girlfriends who saw me as a bit loud but acceptable.

Our class was close-knit and became known as a breaker of Quaker barriers. We organized a dramatic club called the Salamanders and put on plays—the first such frivolity ever permitted on the school's property. I was untalented as an actor, but was heavily into the scenery department and spent many a winter weekend building sets by day and sleeping in the teachers' lounge by night, an arrangement of which the administration was unaware. We breakfasted in the school cafeteria, which led to an effort to convert the potato masher into a vehicle for mixing wallpaper paste. When half the potato-eating upper school suffered food poisoning on the following Monday, there was a huge uproar and the Salamanders' weekend idyll was abruptly terminated. But the drama barrier was down forever.

Nor was this the only Quaker barrier that we assaulted. School dances were always held off campus, dancing having been seen by earlier generations of Quakers as "notional"—a distraction from spiritual exercises. We thought the tradition outdated. The class chose Sylvia Evans and me, as the two members with the most potent Quaker connections, to wait upon the Clerk of the local Meeting to seek permission to hold our dances on school property. The interview was intimidating. The old gentleman was stern. He didn't say much, but he conveyed such an aura of righteousness that our carefully prepared presentation was reduced to mumbling. But in the end, he said: "Well, children, I don't really see anything wrong about having your dance at the school, as long as it's over by 9 P.M." We had projected a 9 P.M. opening, but we took what we could get and fudged on the closing hour.

If school and Sunday Quaker Meeting made up one center in my early years, another was family outings and vacations. My mother was a lifelong entomologist—a collector of butterflies and moths. She pursued her hobby in the only way she knew: with passion. More often than not it was the habitat of some special winged creature that determined where we'd go on vacation. We climbed Mount Katahdin in Maine because there was a rare day-flying moth up there above 4,000 feet. We went to Tuolumne Meadows in Yosemite National Park in pursuit of a particular species of *aeneas* for her collection. Mother was on the round side, and not much given to running over rough terrain. So it was her kids and her long-suffering husband who chased down the prey. She only had to bark "There it is. Catch it!" and, aware of the consequences of failure, we took off in pursuit of the

Margaret Morris Cary, 1881-1968. Shown working on her extensive collection of moths.

prize, never mind the gullies, the brambles, the snakes, or other beasts that lurked in the area.

Most memorable was an exercise known as "sugaring," used to catch a favorite species of moth known as *catocala*. It began in late afternoon when a mixture of delicious smelling ingredients—rotten apples, rotten bananas, sugar, and near beer—were added to a bed of molasses to make a pot full of glorious glop to apply to tree trunks along a forest path.

Ideally, the mix would include real beer and real whiskey, but unfortunately there was Prohibition to contend with. Beer and whiskey were available only through bootleggers. Mother's Quakerism was flexible enough to make exceptions for her bugs' sake, and she was probably ready to traffic with these gentlemen. But my father's Quakerism was purer, and he put his foot down. Still, mother beat the system. She drove to Canada from our New Hampshire cottage, acquired a few bottles of fine Canadian whiskey, and returned home with

8

her purchase tucked under the driver's seat and a cherubic look on her Quaker face to allay any official's suspicion. My father frowned on this.

"Thee knows, Margaret, that if thee gets caught, thee's going to jail."

"Of course I won't go to jail. Don't be silly. I'll just tell the man the liquor is for my bugs." Father just shook his head.

There was no doubt that whiskey-enriched glop was much better than legal glop, and we always added a generous portion of Canadian Club to the mix before affixing it to selected trees, leaving it oozing invitingly down the trunks while we waited for moonless darkness to observe results.

By lantern light we crept through the woods. If the flickering light revealed a *catocala* enjoying a lush repast, the chosen child slipped noiselessly up and put a bottle of cyanide just under the celebrant, which, if drunk enough, tumbled into the jar. If the creature had only recently arrived, it took off into the night, with our nets swinging wildly in pursuit. Results were gratifying. Mother's collection is now housed at Yale University's Peabody Museum.

Mother taught me about moths and butterflies, but more important, she taught me to see the world around me and to appreciate the beauty of the earth, for her interests spilled over to all of nature, and her enthusiasm was infectious.

I also learned from her about obstacles. They are there for the purpose of being overcome. In the early spring of 1926, we were scheduled for a trip to Los Angeles to meet my father, returning from a business trip to Japan, when I broke my leg swinging on a rope. Six weeks of traction put us perilously close to cancellation, but Mother was, as usual, determined and undaunted. She persuaded the hospital to release me. Fitted with a brace, I was carried to a made-up Pullman berth on a train headed west, and we left on schedule.

A stopover was set for Yosemite National Park, where we were to see the Big Trees, only to be told on our arrival that the Big Tree season hadn't yet opened because the access road was still blocked by the winter's quota of downed trees. This news seriously offended mother, who produced a promotional brochure that said "year-round." "I've brought these children 3,000 miles to see those trees, they're advertised on a year-round basis, and you are going to take us to see them!"

The resident ranger was no match for Margaret Cary, and after a short session of foot-stamping he caved in. Next morning, not one but two of those huge roofless tour vehicles awaited us—the first for a park crew and a load of dynamite and the second for the Carys. We blasted our way upward. We saw the trees.

Formal schooling had a hard time competing with these adventures. For the first six grades, I coasted—working only when there was no alternative, and managing enough achievement to head off complaints from parents and teachers. This all changed in seventh grade when I encountered a great teacher. Howard Platt was still in his 20s, young enough to know exactly how to catch the interest of his students. He organized us into four touch football teams, with games scheduled at every recess and a schedule that lasted through the fall, with a beautiful felt pennant emblazoned "Champions" to go to the winner. My team won—a milestone in my career. He made the Roman Empire come to life by having us recreate its monuments in soap. I spent a week carving the Roman Forum, to the delight of both my parents and Lever Brothers. It won a prize and was exhibited in the school's Front Hall.

Mr. Platt also got us involved in debating, with an epic showdown involving another class. We were given the affirmative of the topic: "Resolved, that capital punishment

Student government committee at Haverford College.
Stephen is third from right.

should be abolished." It was my first venture into an area of social concern, and as a member of the team I prepared my arguments with unprecedented dedication. Our side won, but more important, I persuaded myself and have been opposed to capital punishment ever since.

Howard Platt jump-started my academic career. I was never a star student, but I did well enough to get into and through Haverford College. Once again, for four more years, I was into athletics and class offices and a rich social life more than I was into Quakerism, more drawn to the gym than to the library, and more active with friends than with Friends.

Even the college's "Fifth Day Meeting," which all students were required to attend, was not exempt from un-Quakerly behavior. Its pillar was philosopher Rufus Jones, who sat on the facing benches and was so regularly called by the Lord to preach that we heathen organized a weekly pool: maximum number of participants, 15; entry fee, 25 cents. Each entrant recorded a time, at 30-second intervals, when he predicted the great man would rise to preach. An official timekeeper was named, whose ruling was final in a winner-take-all contest. Rufus never knew how much rode on when the Lord called him.

Those mid-1930s years were the golden age of Haverford College's Quaker character, years when there were four distinguished Friends in our midst: William Comfort, Rufus Jones, Thomas Kelly, and Douglas Steere. Haverford alumni from those years insist that no one could meet in worship with such men, and listen to their words each week for four years, without its having an impact on their lives. It influenced us mightily in later years, despite our wagering projects.

Haverford taught me about integrity. The college's Honor Code was then—and is now—at the center of campus life, and living by it for four years brought depth and commitment to a value already nurtured at home and school. I can make fun of my mother's smuggling on behalf of her beloved bugs, but she and my father set standards of integrity in all things great and small that gave substance to the Quaker testimony that one's yea should be yea, and one's nay, nay. Thirteen years at Germantown Friends School spoke the same message, but it was Haverford's willingness to trust me to be honest in all my academic and social behavior that made the message sing. There came a will to live every day with honesty. I'd never be perfect. I've back-slid and let myself and others down, but the effort always to do better has been a joyous challenge.

These fragments of a wondrously happy childhood remind me how much I owe to my home, my Quaker Meeting, my school, and my college. They gave me the foundation on which to build a life, even though it remained for events beyond my control to bring Quakerism into its center.

Two

<hr>

First Clouds of War

It was 1941. Europe was in flames. France and the Low Countries had fallen and Hitler's armies were ravaging the Soviet Union. At home, debate between America Firsters and Interventionists was strident. A national draft squeaked past the Senate by a single vote. Millions of young men were beginning to see what lay ahead. We would soon be fighting on distant battlefields. I shared this perception, but I was a Quaker. The lessons from a Quaker childhood and Quaker schooling, up to now hidden, forced their way to the surface. What should I do? What did I have to say about Hitler's rampage, about his brutal treatment—not yet his massive slaughter—of Europe's Jews, about the threat of his fascist doctrines? I didn't know.

One evening in September my Trenton, New Jersey, telephone rang. "Come home tomorrow evening for a family council. Your father has something to discuss." It was a command performance. I appeared, along with my sisters. After dinner we retired to the living room. "I'm thinking about resigning my job. I've always said that as long as the company continued to produce its regular products, I could accept the military as a customer, but if the day came when we began to produce weaponry, I would, as a Quaker, have to resign. That day has come. Last week, we accepted a contract from the Army Air Force to produce a component of the Norden bombsight, the instrument that will increase bombing accuracy. I must decide now what is right for me to do."

The family quickly agreed that he should follow his conscience. If that meant he would take a dollar-a-year job in some Quaker enterprise, and our living standard would drop, we could accept that. The next day, he resigned. A week later he became the unpaid executive assistant to Clarence Pickett, the chief officer of the American Friends Service Committee.

That evening shook any remaining complacency. My father's work was his life. For more than 30 years he had served the same company, a manufacturer of precision instruments, rising along with it to become its executive vice president. A resignation at the height of his career had to tear him apart, but he never hesitated. Principle, keeping life consistent with profession—these were what mattered to him. Did they matter to me?

I returned in turmoil to the Trenton YMCA and my job as a building material salesman. A couple of weeks later, brooding over a cup of coffee in the snack bar, I became aware of a discussion at the next table. I was only half-listening, but references to "American Friends Service Committee" and "Air Force" startled me and I began to eavesdrop. Five minutes later, I moved over and joined in. At the time, it seemed an entertaining diversion. In retrospect, it reshaped my life.

Two of my new friends were thoughtful Cornell graduates, recently signed on with the Air Force, and waiting for their call-up. The third was a philosopher by training, a Quaker conscientious objector by conviction, and a brilliant and witty conversationalist by gift. They were talking about things that mattered: faith, integrity, duty, morality, conscience. How can pacifism be reconciled with Hitler? Christ with war? Citizenship with refusal to serve?

We met for two more evenings, searching ourselves, I mostly listening, while they engaged in vigorous debate, sharply differing but mutually respectful. On the fourth night, the Cornellians were gone; their orders had arrived. Joe Havens and I were alone. He had long known his direction. His reflections over three evenings had helped me to find mine. For the first time in months, confusion gave way to clarity. I could not kill. I could not accept military service.

What persuaded me? Certainly the things I learned as a child growing up in a Quaker household were important. It was there that I was first taught about the Religious Society of Friends, about Friends' belief in a Light within that gives every human being the capacity to know directly the will of God, and about how they see this Light as imparting a sacred dimension to human life, so that it cannot be debased, or exploited, or wantonly destroyed for any reason or under any circumstances. It was there, too, that I learned how this view of the sacredness of life had led to the Quakers' pioneering work in the care of the mentally ill, in the humane treatment of prisoners, in ending slavery, in the relief of war sufferers.

And it was in Quaker circles that I was introduced to another dimension of Friends' witness: their Peace Testimony. I read the proclamation they issued to King Charles II of England in 1661:

> We utterly deny all outward wars and strife and fightings with outward weapons, for any end or under any pretense whatsoever. And this is our testimony to the whole world. The spirit of Christ,

15

by which we are guided, is not changeable, so as once to command us from a thing as evil and again to move into it; and we do certainly know, and so testify to the world, that the spirit of Christ, which leads us into all Truth, will never move us to fight and war against any man with outward weapons, neither for the kingdom of Christ, nor for the kingdoms of this world.

This was the first public expression of a pacifism that has endured for more than three centuries, in good times and bad, in season and out, alternatively denounced and admired, depending on the ever-changing climate of popular opinion, but faithfully adhered to by the Society, if not by all members. Evil must be resisted—one cannot remain neutral between justice and injustice—but resistance must be in the ways that Jesus taught, and not by killing and destroying.

The scriptures also played a role. There was spirited discussion of them at our table. Biblical passages justifying resort to war were quoted liberally, countered by assertions that individual passages were no guide—the devil himself could quote scripture. I began to sense that it was the whole sweep of Jesus' life and, above all, his death, that mattered. Together they were an uncompromising, matchless witness to the heart of his message: that love alone overcomes evil. But he did not give us a success ethic. All he promised is that love endures—forever. The road is not easy.

Even in his own case, love appeared to fail and violence and hatred to triumph. Standing innocent before Pilate, the beauty of his lifelong teaching and witness to love's power shining before the world, his troubled Roman judge saw no evil in him, and eased his conscience by offering the multitude in the courtyard the chance to spare him. Should he free Jesus, or should he free his companion in the dock, Barabbas, the man of violence, the insurrectionist, the Rambo.

The multitude called for Barabbas, as we still do 2,000 years later in times of crisis. The world's faith then, and now, is in the fist and the sword. Barabbas was freed. Jesus was condemned, scourged, and crucified.

But we know that love didn't fail. Jesus remained steadfast and faithful to his witness, despite his agony: forgiving, accepting, loving, until death. It is this faithfulness, this bravery beyond knowing, this crowning of his life's beauty, that give power and meaning to the Cross and lifts Jesus to his Sonship. The scriptures report that the earth shook for ten miles around. And the centurion, who moments before was gambling for Jesus' garments, fell to his knees as men and women have been falling to theirs for 20 centuries.

As Joe Havens retold the story in Trenton—for him the most moving passage in all the Bible—it came alive for me as well. For him, Jesus' message was simple. It was categorical. It could not be rationalized. And so it became for me, and has remained so.

The wider world disagrees. So did our friends from Cornell. Indeed, theologians have been interpreting Jesus' message for 2,000 years with elaborate constructs that get around the Sermon on the Mount without repudiating the one who delivered it. Comforting, too, has been the ability of every generation to depict its devils and terrorists as the most malevolent in history and therefore beyond the scope of his teaching.

These rationalizations are unsatisfactory. I think Jesus meant what he said because his words are no more than a faithful reflection of the vibrant witness of his own life. He asked nothing more of us than he asked of himself. It's also been convenient for Christians to forget that he too lived in times as brutal as our own, his country under military occupation, and its terrorists differing from ours in name only. Their terrorist was named Herod, his army their al-Qaeda.

For my part, rereading the biblical record of a peerless life lived long ago, and, above all, the account of Jesus' last week, left me only two choices: to follow him in the path of peace or to abandon him in the pursuit of war. There was no middle ground. Paul writing to his friends in Ephesus put it well:

> It is the whole armor of God that we must wear, with its breastplate of righteousness, its shield of faith, and its sword of the spirit. I had no idea how far I would carry such a witness were I to be tested, but it was the armor I must wear.

All well and good. I had found in my father an inspiration, and in Trenton a satisfying spiritual and scriptural basis for a pacifist commitment. But there was still Hitler, his Wehrmacht and his fascist doctrines. And there had been Kristallnacht—the Night of Broken Glass—in November 1938. These realities left non-Quaker friends unpersuaded by my views. They found me detached from reality, sincere but irrelevant. Everywhere the judgment was the same. Gandhi's genius in translating spiritual commitment into political power was impressive, but the British weren't the Nazis.

I had no good answer to their judgments. A half-century later, after four years in alternative service as a conscientious objector, two more amid the postwar wreckage of the European continent, and 40 years in Quaker service around the world, I've found some answers. This long education began in Civilian Public Service, the first government-approved alternative program for conscientious objectors in U.S. history.

Three

<hr>

CIVILIAN PUBLIC SERVICE

IT WASN'T LONG AFTER MY EVENINGS in the Trenton snack bar that I got the letter so familiar to my generation. It began "Greetings!" and ended "Lewis B. Hershey, Director, Selective Service System." I was drafted. My draft board was no problem. I was a Quaker, and Philadelphia draft boards were used to Quakers. Mine tried feebly to persuade me to accept a noncombatant classification ("The Army needs men like you, Mr. Cary . . ."). When I told them I could not serve in any military capacity and would not consent to an assignment where I was just freeing someone else for combat, they didn't argue the point. I was classified 4-E, Conscientious Objector.

Any argument there was on this in Philadelphia was within myself. Should I agree to being conscripted and accept alternative service as provided by law, or should I reject conscription entirely because it was an integral part of the military service, and go to prison? I chose the former. Congress had for the first time provided a legal framework for the exercise of conscience in wartime. I was grateful for this advance and decided to try to live within it. I was not then ready to accept the punishment of a prison sentence in the cheerful spirit that is necessary if one's stand outside the law is to provoke thought. At the time, the decision was right for

Cary Family Archives

Stephen served in the CPS between 1942-1945.

me. A half-century and a world of experience later, it wouldn't seem right. I would need to make a more powerful witness against violence through noncooperation and prison.

But while my draft board had presented no problems, the same was not the case with my building material customers up and down the Delaware River, especially after Pearl Harbor. Almost the first topic at a construction site was "When are you joining up?" or "How about killing a Jap for me?" These confrontations were painful. The truth would hurt my company; its avoidance perjured me. The only way out was to resign. I did so. My boss gave me an office assignment where I could handle paperwork until my call-up. Decent of him, I thought.

It was a brief interlude. In mid-February 1942, I was taken by a draft board member to the North Philadelphia train station and put on a train for Petersham, Massachusetts, with orders to report to Civilian Public Service (CPS) Camp #9. I had no idea what lay ahead.

The CPS program was the offspring of an unlikely marriage between the Selective Service System and the three historic peace churches—the Society of Friends, Church of the Brethren, and Mennonite Church—who were to share in its administration. The agreement called for a network of base camps to be established in remote settings, each housing from 50 to 150 men in barracks once occupied by the Civilian Conservation Corps, the depression-era program to take unemployed young men off the streets. The camps were administered by the service agencies of the three churches. Government employees operating the work project were responsible for the assignees during work hours doing what the law described as "work of national importance." The churches were responsible for the men during nonworking hours. Selective Service in Washington maintained an eye over both and was in fact the power center. The churches anticipated that additional opportunities would be developed to provide the men with more significant and varied work than would be available at the base camp.

This structure was the result of negotiations among three peace church leaders: Clarence Pickett (AFSC) for the Friends, M. R. Ziegler (Brethren Service Committee) for the Brethren, and Orie O. Miller for the Mennonite Central Committee, and the first director of Selective Service, Clarence Dykstra, a public-spirited official who had been the distinguished head of the University of Wisconsin in the turbulent 1930s. All the negotiators assumed that the draft involved only a single year's obligation, that the conscientious objector (CO) community would reflect essentially the same religious outlook and values as the Peace Church communities, and that negotiating would continue in the same positive spirit as in that opening round. This meant that there were no formal agreements regarding ways to expand the range of opportunities, and no provision was made for pay for the men during their year of service.

These assumptions and good intentions soon evaporated. Service requirements under the draft were extended "for the duration." The men drafted proved far more culturally diverse than the church leaders had anticipated. And Clarence Dykstra was soon replaced by General Lewis

Hershey. He was a man of reasonable disposition, but ever fearful of public criticism and with a military outlook that could not adapt to the strange world of alternative service. Hershey remained in charge throughout the war. He made Selective Service administration of the CPS program rigid and bureaucratic.

With Clarence Dykstra gone, the conflicting goals of the Selective Service System and the Peace Churches surfaced and made the enterprise nearly unworkable. The church leaders were seeking service opportunities for young men of conscience, eager to use their talents in constructive ways. Selective Service was primarily interested in keeping COs out of public view, performing work so unrewarding that others would be discouraged from seeking CO status. Opening up service opportunities outside the base camps proved difficult at every turn.

The biggest problem was the pay issue. The church leaders, operating with the single year perspective, had assumed that assignees would be happy to work hard at menial tasks to demonstrate their commitment and earn the right to more rewarding assignments. They wouldn't need pay, too. Some men accepted that. But many did not and came to bitterly resent the "pay" offered by the churches, $2.50 per month for expenses, especially when the service period extended to two, three, and four years. Large numbers of COs saw themselves as slave labor. It was one thing for a well-to-do Quaker with family backing to cooperate with a government that held him in a compulsory work program and paid him nothing for four years. It was quite another for a poor boy whose family was hostile to his stand and unable to help him financially.

I became a part of this unwieldy operation when I reached Petersham, Massachusetts, in mid-February 1942 and began a four-year search to find meaning in the web of issues arising out of unpaid compulsory service in an extraordinarily diverse community.

It began routinely. I was assigned to the top bunk of a double-decker in an open barracks housing 50 men. After a fitful first night, I awoke at 5:30 to a cold and snowy dawn and climbed into my warmest gear. A short ride in an army truck dropped me and the rest of the work crew at a wooded site damaged by a recent hurricane. We were to clear slash to minimize the risk of forest fire.

Someone unwisely handed me a long double-ended saw. I slung it over my shoulder and started into the woods. Behind me came Stubby Nelson, a short, irrepressible abstract artist who lived for his painting, and whom I could hear mumbling about "the bastards" who'd sent us out to work on such a bitterly cold day. I told myself that "the bastards" were also sending out the GIs in the same weather, and we shouldn't expect better. But I kept that to myself.

Fifty yards into the woods, Nelson called my name. I turned around. So did the double-ended saw. It clipped Nelson smartly across the neckline. Blood spurted. He lay on the ground. I wrung my hands while others gave medical attention. "Oh, for God's sake, Cary, shut up! This is a big break. I'll get the day off. I'll get out my paints and go over to the Rec. Hall!" He climbed into the truck cab and it rumbled off.

For two hours we chopped at fallen trees with an industriousness that owed more to the weather than to any desire to impress the government with what fine fellows we were. Then a truck noisily labored up the hill. A figure climbed out. It was Nelson, his head and neck swathed in bandages. "The bastards sent me back out. They said I didn't need my neck to chop brush."

23

Chapter Three

Over the next weeks I got to know my campmates. We were a motley outfit. There were three farmers from New England who could cut a cord of wood three times as fast as the city-types; a Christadelphian and two Jehovah's Witnesses who carried Bibles in their parkas and spent more time in biblical splitting than in wood splitting; a follower of the charismatic black prophet Father Divine, who at meals paused in mid-flight with each forkful to converse with Father (whose replies went unheard by us pagans); a Pulitzer Prize winner of the year's best biography; a few artists and sculptors; three born-again Christians with Truth ever at the ready; half-a-dozen Quakers earnestly being the "creative pioneers" that church executives pictured in their publications; and a few others remembered more for their dissent than for their credentials.

Presiding over this collection was a 70-year-old Boston Brahmin of impeccable Quaker lineage. He lived in town, handled public relations, and reported on events to Quaker headquarters in Philadelphia. He left day-to-day administration to an assistant director whose lack of human-relations skills was obvious.

Administering a Civilian Public Service camp required skills ranging from a capacity to walk on water up to more difficult tasks. The director dealt daily with limited and sometimes ill-tempered government supervisors on the one hand, and on the other with assignees who included physicists and school dropouts, stockbrokers and ballet dancers, fundamentalists and atheists, confronters and cooperators, the sick and the healthy. He was under the eye of Big Brother in Washington, who had little use for and less understanding of any of us.

The working environment was bad. We were thrown together in open barracks with no privacy. We worked without pay six days a week on projects that were makework, tedious work, dirty work, or all three.

On one of our projects, we opened up vistas on Virginia's Skyline Drive, removing trees planted earlier by the Civilian Conservation Corps to prevent erosion. Gas rationing made forest creatures the only beneficiaries of our labor, but we were still required to dab black paint on each tiny stump to avoid jarring visitors' sensibilities with the appearance of slash. Another camp weeded endless beds of tiny seedlings. A third was engaged in draining a swamp, where men spent years wallowing in knee-deep mud.

Our performance was often less than satisfactory. There was a philosophical split among us, especially evident in Quaker camps, on how to react to the system. Some men were out to win respect by cooperating and working hard. Others took an opposite approach, doing as little as possible to demonstrate that free men could not be enslaved by Selective Service edict. Like Odysseus' Penelope, knitting by day and unraveling by night, the eager cooperators and the conscientious malingerers worked to neutralize each other. The results satisfied neither and angered the work bosses, who complained to the camp director. He in turn was both blessed and cursed by the camp factions, depending on which side of the philosophical fence he came down.

These skirmishes were troubling enough, but worse problems involved the sick and infirm. Selective Service's discharge policy was the same as its project policy: get COs out of sight, and keep them there. Draft authorities in Washington were unfeeling, cruel, and stubborn when it came to dealing with the sick and infirm.

Local draft boards did not understand the inflexibilities in the system. In their eagerness to be rid of problems, they shunted off to camps men who were emotionally unstable or physically disabled. This wasn't done to be cruel. They assumed that CO camps, like military bases, could discharge marginal draftees unable to perform their duties. It didn't work that way with us. The discharge procedure took months, during which the morale of the entire camp suffered by the presence of depressed and ill young men unable to work, unable to leave, lying on their bunks all day. Some of these men could manage on the outside, but trapped in the inflexibility of camp life, they broke down. Every camp had its quota of these idle men who could remain in the S.Q. (sick quarters) category for months, sometimes reaching such a point of despondency that we had to put a suicide watch on them.

There were bright spots. One was in the area of CO service in mental hospitals, where Selective Service and the Peace Churches found common ground. Assignments to mental hospital service were unglamorous and invisible enough to satisfy Selective Service. At the same time, help there was urgently needed. Conditions in public mental hospitals at that time were unconscionable. All were understaffed, and such staff as they had were often incompetent and sadistic. Large numbers of CPS men, working in hospitals throughout the country, brought a level of caring and competence into the system that it had not seen before. Their work led to the founding of a national mental health organization that has set new standards and brought public awareness to the care of the mentally ill. This may have been the most important and lasting contribution made by World War II COs. They also made valuable contributions to medical science by volunteering as guinea pigs in research and experimental programs in such areas as nutrition, disease control, and survival equipment.

I was tested in my early days at Petersham. For three months

I worked in the woods, coming to know and appreciate my diverse colleagues, even as they sometimes astonished and tried me.

Most difficult were the born-again Christians, whose certainty that they owned the Truth made rational discussion almost impossible. Once, when we had completed remodeling a barracks into a camp library, as a public relations gesture we had invited the citizens of Petersham to an evening reception and tour of our new facility. A corps of assignees was detailed to greet visitors and escort them around the premises. One of our born-again colleagues entered the barracks with half-a-dozen Petershamites in tow. He worked his way down the center pointing to selected double-deckers. "A Christian bunks here . . . another is up there . . . down there at the end, there's a third."

A visitor interrupted. "But I thought all you boys were Christians."

"Oh, no," our colleague said, "unfortunately not. But we have some excellent material to work on!"

By early spring, with the thaw, our project changed from clearing slash to digging "water holes," small forest reservoirs where water, diverted from adjacent streams, could be stored for use in fighting forest fires. The work was grimy but useful, as we discovered when we were called out to fight fires— exciting work that we did with enthusiasm. I was promoted to the position of nozzle man, putting me at the heart of the action.

There were many firefighting opportunities in CPS. Men were assigned to a smoke-jumping unit, parachuting into remote areas of Montana. Camps in California and Oregon sometimes spent days and even weeks on the fire lines. On one major fire in California, the authorities had to call on manpower from every available source. Soldiers and sailors on rest and recreation from the Pacific fighting, trusties from California prisons, Forest Service office staff, municipal workers, and CPS men were all recruited to contain the blaze.

One night around a campfire after a long day on the fire line, little was said by the exhausted men until a prison trusty broke the silence. "I've been thinking how we all got to this damn fire. I'm here because eight years ago I killed a Jap in a Fresno bar and they gave me 15 to 25. Bill over there is here because he killed so many Japs on Okinawa that they sent him home for a rest. Next to him is Charlie. He's here because he won't kill a Jap. I think somebody ought to make up their minds about killing Japs. It's crazy!"

But most of our time back in Massachusetts was spent building water holes, wallowing in mud, wielding picks and shovels, diverting streams. As spring warmed, the sap began to flow. We each picked out our favorite sugar maple, tapped it, affixed a tin cup, and collected deliciously cold sap, laced with just a hint of maple sugar. One lovely spring day I repaired to my tree. My cup was full. I stood watching my companions.

The scene was vintage Petersham, vintage water hole, vintage mud. The Klotsback brothers and Ben Cates, our New England farm boys, were feverishly loading their wheelbarrows. A tall, paper-thin Christadelphian, Bible in hand, leaned on his shovel and argued a text with a squat 200–pound Jehovah's Witness, armed with his Bible–both speaking from Olympus. Peaceful Brother was, as usual, conversing with Father Divine in New York, who obviously was telling him to work like a dog. Others toyed with their shovels, evincing only a modest interest in filling their wheelbarrows. Artists Nelson and Kasso sat atop the hole on one of many rest breaks, while at stage center, dead in the middle of the hole, several Ph.D.s discussed 18th-century English literature while loosening a mired boulder. The entire company was mud-caked.

Looking at this scene, I felt a belonging beyond words. These men, so difficult, so diverse, of so many faiths and abilities and backgrounds, were my family, my brothers. There was no place in the world that I would rather have been than right there, leaning against my maple tree, sipping sap in a Massachusetts forest. Tears came to my eyes. I felt a Presence in the mud, almost real enough to be loading His wheelbarrow.

It was only a moment, but it made a difference. I'd been spared from the death and dying and the agony of war, but that day in that water hole was the first time I became aware of my obligation, later reinforced by my searing experiences in postwar Europe, to work through all my life for peace.

Discussion was endless. There was little else for the isolated, the penniless, and the immobile to do but talk, and thousands did so for four years. Civilian Public Service turned out to be the finest training ground for pacifists ever devised. It's no wonder that the government has shown no interest in repeating the experiment. Some men revised their thinking and left for the military. Others decided that CPS was too much of a compromise. They walked out and went to prison. But the majority emerged in 1946 as committed, lifelong pacifists, with a deep understanding of what this meant.

Three months into this circus, I got my first break. The camp accountant was transferred and, relishing a vacation from mud, I applied for the position. Since there wasn't anyone else in camp who knew anything about bookkeeping, I was chosen by default. A few weeks later my new boss, the inept assistant director, left the scene. Once again, assignee Cary was the only man who knew much about how the place was run. Once again I got the call. Only months into my CPS career, thanks to turns of fortune's wheel, I became Petersham's head resident. My crash course in CPS administration began.

This adventure arose from the Navy Department's need for a cadre of officers who could serve in the civil administration of occupied territories once Americans captured the Pacific islands then held by the Japanese. Philip Jessup, dean of the Columbia University Graduate School of International Relations, aware of the interest of the Peace Churches in training CPS men for postwar relief work, and seeing many parallels in the problems to be faced by civil and relief administrators, thought it would be a test of democracy in wartime to train naval officers and conscientious objectors simultaneously in the same broad program. The churches jumped at the opportunity and joined Dr. Jessup in approaching Selective Service for the necessary approvals.

Surprisingly, Washington went along with the idea. Five men from each of the three church agencies were authorized to join the 30-man naval contingent for the dual-focused enterprise. I was one of those chosen, lifted out of the Massachusetts forests and deposited in New York.

My new front office contacts with the Quaker power center in Philadelphia gave me visibility. I was sent to New York City for a year's residence at International House, enrolled in Columbia University with 14 CPS colleagues and 30 officers of the United States Navy. It was a miracle, as unlikely as all miracles, one that carried a heavy work load, but that, from the perspective of the isolated, unpaid, unchallenged CPS assignee was the ultimate soft berth.

With my International House room key came a note directing me to appear the next morning at 9 o'clock in the office of Dean Jessup.

He met each of us individually in a stern, no-nonsense setting. He and his program director, Schuyler Wallace, sat behind a huge mahogany desk, eyeing me. Nobody said anything. At first the two professors measured me while I attempted unsuccessfully to appear scholarly and mature. "Mr. Cary," said Wallace. "We assume that you were not chosen for this course on the basis of your ability on the soap box, but we feel compelled to remind you that there are provisions in the Espionage Act that have to do with undermining the morale of the Armed Forces. You will be studying here at Columbia with 30 officers in the United States Navy. They are doing their duty as they see it, and you are not, repeat NOT, to attempt to convert them to your point of view or otherwise interfere with their activities. If you do, you will face immediate dismissal from the program. Do you understand that, Mr. Cary?"

"Yes, sir," I said, abashed. "I understand and I have no intention of undermining anyone's morale."

We all received the same warning and were careful to confine chats with our Naval classmates to discussion of Columbia's sports programs and New York's weather. This wasn't easy. We had classes together and twice a week we met for dinner at the Columbia Faculty Club to hear a lecture from either a distinguished relief administrator or a distinguished naval officer. The university, having read us the riot act, apparently decided to mix us up by seating us alternately, presumably so we could share academic insights on our courses.

This situation was short-lived. About three weeks into the program, one of our men was having a cup of coffee with a Navy man and told him about our encounter with the two professors, and the wraps under which we were necessarily operating. The officer was astonished. "What do you think

31

happened when we got here? It was Jessup's office for us, too, only we got a different lecture. Wallace told us we were going to be spending the year with a bunch of conchies, that you guys had a right to your opinions, and if any of us got into a hassle or questioned your patriotism, he'd be outta here. They weren't going to stand for any monkey business. We've been walking on eggs ever since."

By dinner time at the Faculty Club, everyone in the program knew of this turn of events. Caution evaporated, conversation flourished. No topics were barred. It was a great year. We worked hard, we learned much, and we received wise counsel about how to organize and administer relief operations in difficult settings. It was a unique opportunity for me. This could happen in few places in the world.

I never finished the course. It was so successful that the American Friends Service Committee prevailed upon Selective Service to permit the creation of similar year-long training units at four Quaker colleges—Haverford, Swarthmore, Earlham, and Guilford. Each was to enroll 20 men from Civilian Public Service units who would form a leadership nucleus for the postwar relief program that the Friends anticipated would be undertaken. Because of my experience in New York I was asked to be the director of the Swarthmore program. I reluctantly withdrew from Columbia in June 1943, six weeks before my "class" was to finish its work.

Swarthmore College in the summer of 1943 was a lively and exciting place, academically challenging and warmly welcoming, but for a pacifist a center of contradictions. As a Quaker institution, Swarthmore was eager to be part of a CO training program and made all its resources available to us. But we were heavily outnumbered by a massive campus military presence. A naval V-12 unit, the "90-day wonder" wartime program that turned out commissioned officers in three months, was on campus. So were a large contingent of uniformed Chinese, enrolled in the first Chinese naval training unit of its kind in the United States. Delicious moments emerged from this mix.

An early event was Commencement. The campus almost sank under the weight of bemedaled admirals, there to honor the day's speaker, newly appointed Secretary of the Navy Frank Knox. A military band offered John Philip Sousa's finest martial airs. At the appointed hour, the college's Board of Managers, led by its weighty Quaker chairman, marched in to a rousing rendition of "Johnny, get your gun, get your gun"—a marvelous blend of Quakerism and militarism.

The captains and the kings soon departed, and we were immersed in our studies. Alas, the program was barely airborne when it crashed. U.S. Representative Joe Starnes of Alabama, angered that Europeans and Asians might discover that there were U.S. pacifists, attached a rider to the 1943 military appropriations bill specifying that no funds appropriated under it could be used for any training of COs for relief work. The AFSC was meeting all the costs of the program with private funds, but the Selective Service official authorizing unit members to come to their new posts was an Army colonel. His pay while signing his name came from the appropriation in question. This made the transfer order illegal under the Starnes rider. The units had to be closed down, and the men returned to the camps from which they had come.

I went back to the woods, this time to West Campton in New Hampshire. I was there for five months, working as a rank and filer, clearing hurricane slash. Late in the fall Selective Service decided to close the camp and I was dispatched to a Mennonite camp near Luray, Virginia. Heading south from New Hampshire, I naively thought it would be comfortably warm. It wasn't. The camp was high on the Skyline Drive, where in December it felt like Mount Washington. All 20 of us importees from West Campton were in for a shock. One dark, frigid morning, I climbed aboard our truck en route to the project, and asked a shivering Quaker colleague whether he oughtn't to go back to his bunk and get another sweater. "No point," said he. "I've got on everything I own now, including my pajamas."

The project at Luray was as bad as the weather. It was the camp where assignees were opening up vistas for sightseers who couldn't get to them. But there was one attractive feature. We were reasonably close to Washington, D.C., now the residence of Janet McCloskey, a Swarthmorian I had met earlier in the year. On Saturday noon, when our work week ended, I had the truck let me off at a pass over our mountain. With any hitchhiking luck, I would make Washington by late afternoon.

Janet's father Mark was head of the Office of Community War Services and presided over a warm and welcoming Irish household. Dinners were lavish. Franklin Roosevelt and Democratic Party politics were richly, regularly, and approvingly discussed, and the house shook with Irish laughter. The McCloskey house was overloaded, so I was put up at the nearby home of their friends, the Jonathan Danielses. Daniels was Franklin Roosevelt's press secretary, intimately involved with the nation's and the world's war leaders, and in daily consultation with the president on how the war story should be reported to the American people. I was touched by the spirit of the Danielses who could welcome a conscientious objector into their home at such a time and make him part of their family over many weekends. I loved them.

I spent Christmas 1943, at Luray. It was the worst—and the best—of Christmases. Like our GI brethren, we had two rec- ognized holidays, Christmas and July Fourth. We planned a party and trimmed a tree in the recreation barracks. We even had bacon for breakfast—and gathered for the festivities. Then . . . the siren! Forest fire! All hands to the trucks. Ten minutes changing into heavy gear, five minutes throwing brooms, machetes, and water tanks into the trucks, then off.

The fire was burning up a steep hillside, its long, jagged line inching toward a ridge 1000 feet farther up. Some grabbed tanks, strapped them on their backs, and clambered up the mountain toward the fire. Others grabbed brooms and machetes. All day long we beat back the flames, refilling tanks, smothering outbreaks with brooms, chopping fire lines with machetes. The ground was too hard for trenching. It was bitter cold and we had nothing to eat, not even a cup of hot coffee. There was no rest. The terrain was exhausting, steep, and laced with gullies and icy streams, from which the tankmen refilled their tanks.

Ten hours later, well after darkness had made matters more treacherous, it warmed and began to sleet. The mountainside became a skating rink over which we slipped and slithered, shivering and wet to the skin. But there was an up side: the sleet put out the fire.

By 9 P.M. it was finished and so were we. Down by the road someone had built a fire, and we sat around it waiting for the trucks to pick us up. The mood was ugly. Bitching flourished. "Some holiday! I'm freezing! They'll never give us compensatory time! Not even a sandwich! My ankle hurts! I'm soaking wet! Where are the trucks? Nobody gives a damn!"

I was a lead singer in this choir, lying on my back with a wet wool cap as a pillow, making clear my view of the world's unfairness. Only one man sat still, staring silently into the fire. It was Charlie, a Georgia farm boy whose illiteracy should have exempted him from the draft, but in Georgia it had not. When the words of outrage momentarily subsided, he spoke. "I don't understand what all you guys are complaining about. I think this is the best Christmas I've ever had!"

Stunned silence. "What the hell are you talking about?"

"Well, guys, when again in my whole life will I ever have another chance to spend Christmas Day giving a hillside back to God?"

I soon got transfer orders to Big Flats, a new orientation camp near Elmira, New York, where I had been appointed assistant director. I was at Big Flats for 21 months, until September 1945. It was there that I learned how to be a CPS administrator, how to deal with Selective Service far away and with difficult personalities close at hand.

Most of the camp community came and went every three months, but the handpicked permanent crew was a fine group of men. Rich in talent, in humor, and in commitment, they made a difficult job and a stressful life a happy experience. We had a lot of problems, but we had a lot of laughs.

One of the problems was the work project, weeding endless seedbeds that stretched for acres in every direction. Crews had to squat for nine hours a day, bending over to pull tiny weeds away from tiny seedlings in a never-ending circuit around the nursery. The monotony was depressing and the back strain shortened tempers.

A second problem was our resident government superintendent, Milton Johnson. His supervisory experience had been limited to Civilian Conservation Corps high schoolers, and the independence and candor of our CO community often pushed his blood pressure to explosive levels and led to visits by Selective Service troubleshooters from Washington.

These visits in turn raised my blood pressure—I feared hostile demonstrations by CO firebrands—and on one occasion it led me to the camp director's office to ask what we should do to get ready to greet General Hershey's emissary. Tom Potts was leaning back in his chair, with his feet on his desk. "Cary," he said, "I don't know what you're going to do, but I'll tell you what I'm going to do. I'm going to follow my standard policy of drifting and dreaming." It was good advice. I came to take such crises in my stride, which was a good thing because there were plenty of them.

The American Legion in a nearby town was a recurring source of difficulty. These warriors from World War I had decided that their contribution to the nation's war effort could best be made by safeguarding western New York from the grave dangers posed by "that camp." We were always under the eye of vigilantes, ever ready to inform the media of our iniquities. Happily, we had good friends in town and they helped us to refute baseless claims.

This Big Flats experience with surrounding communities wasn't unusual. The thousands of COs scattered around the country had few problems with men currently in uniform. It was the aging veterans of earlier wars, some of whom had gotten no closer to the front than Fort Leavenworth, who were the super-patriots of World War II. The current crop of GIs were more tolerant than intolerant, more curious than critical. The first Quaker CPS camp was in Patapsco, Maryland, immediately adjacent to Fort Meade. COs were a great curiosity to its draftees-in-training, who used to wander over to get a look at the conchies. One hot summer afternoon, three soldiers entered the camp grounds as an assignee was digging a latrine. He was a big, strapping young man, a former football star at an Ivy League university, and as he shoveled the muscles rippled across his bare back and his arms, bronzed by the sun. The GIs paused. "See, there's one! There's one, right there, that's him, digging that hole!" Another pause . . . a quick whistle. "Man, oh man, I'd sure hate to have him hit me with a fist full of love."

Life at the Flats wasn't easy. But at least the pressures on me were stretching pressures, pressures that challenged me in new ways, teaching me patience, teaching me to relate to difficult people, teaching me how to sort through difficult problems. Compared to others who were fighting the boredom of the seed beds and the physical discomfort of squatting, with little to challenge them intellectually, my assignment was easy and I had no reason to complain.

Early in September 1944 Tom Potts received an induction notice, and shortly after he resigned as the Big Flats camp director and returned to Philadelphia. An election was held to name a new director, following a primary in which Bill Huntington and I emerged as the two candidates in a run-off. Because we were the closest of friends, we were reluctant campaigners. But events conspired to give a different impression to the voters. It was Thanksgiving, and five days before the election Bill's wife sent him a huge smoked turkey which Bill felt obliged to share with the electorate. His party was instantly labeled a campaign event, and speculation flourished as to how Cary would counter the Huntington move.

Cary was embarrassed. Weeks before, and long before there was any thought of elections, he had invited Janet McCloskey of Swarthmore fame to visit for the weekend. It was too late to head her off, and 24 hours after the Huntington turkey party there arrived at the camp a stunning blonde, at once identified as Cary's response to smoked turkey. Janet was a hit. She carried me to victory by two votes.

This turn of events meant that I was now, and remained for the next year, the director of the Friends induction camp at Big Flats, New York. My leadership got mixed reviews. The resident government boss thought I was a wimp. Camp factions blew hot and cold depending on my stand in crises. Residents with medical problems were angry—they wanted discharge. Here I did beat the system. A Binghamton psychiatrist, angry at Selective Service's regular disregard of his recommendations, suggested I rewrite his report in language that would satisfy Washington. He examined my redraft to assure that it in no way compromised his diagnosis, and we promptly secured ten releases. Semantics was more important in Washington than medical findings.

By September 1945, the war was over. Japan had surrendered in August, and both the U.S. military and the tiny CPS corps were talking about demobilization and discharge. With my three years and seven months, I figured to be out by the end of the year. Instead, to my chagrin, I was sent out to Oregon to direct a camp that was in major disarray. Elkton had been the jewel in the Friends' CPS crown: good leadership, hardworking assignees, useful projects, high morale. But over time, with every Friends' camp sending their problems westward to Oregon ("they should have a few"), Elkton had drifted from the top of the heap to the bottom. Morale was bad, many men were refusing to work, Selective Service was angry, and the Quakers in Philadelphia were at their wits' end.

The solution: Send Cary out there. Send him with orders to either salvage the camp or close it. I went west. Janet went east to the United Nations Relief and Rehabilitation Administration (UNRRA) in Germany. We remained friends. At Elkton, my reception was cool. I was Philadelphia's man, and "Philadelphia" at Elkton had the same ring as "smallpox." Assignees willing to work had all been sent to a side camp at Bear Creek, leaving behind three groups: those who were willing to work but only for the Friends and were assigned to the kitchen; those who were designated unfit to work and were sullenly awaiting discharge; and those who were refusing to work and were awaiting arrest.

I quickly saw that the situation was beyond repair and recommended to Philadelphia that the camp be closed. My recommendation was accepted, probably more because of the accelerating pace of discharges than for any other reason. Some men were discharged for seniority and some for ill-health. Some were arrested and some were transferred. By mid-January 1946, all were gone but a handful left behind to close up. It was then that I had a phone call from Philadelphia asking if I would accept appointment as one of two Quaker commissioners to oversee all American Quaker relief work in Europe for the next two years. I accepted on the spot, thrilled with the prospect that at last I could contribute actively to healing the pain of war. At last I could be part of the drama in which so many of my friends had played parts at the risk of their lives. It meant that I would have not four but six years of war-related service, but what service it might turn out to be!

My discharge came through and my CPS career ended while I was en route home. For many, the grave flaws of the system had made these years painful, for a few, embittering. For the three Peace Churches complicity in administering conscription and putting men in jeopardy of prison compromised their integrity in ways that shouldn't be repeated. For me, there were trials, but the experiences were good to me. In CPS I found a mission for myself.

AFSC Archives

"Their homes were burned at the time of German retreat and now they live in caves, cellars, and even abandoned cars." (Finland 1946)

Four

━━━◆━━━

EUROPE IN RUINS

THE NEXT YEARS, spent amid the suffering of Europe's millions, shaped my life. The bombs of World War II no longer fell, armies no longer fought, but in their wake, from Norway's North Cape to Italy's Abruzzi, from the English Channel to deep within the Soviet Union, there was wreckage and human misery on a numbing scale.

Europe, except for the Soviet Union, was my field of operations. I was charged with an assignment awesome for

41

one so young: overseeing, with another colleague, all of the scattered outposts of relief and compassion established by American Quakers to ease the suffering of the war's homeless and hungry, its sick, its bereaved, its cold, its naked. In those years I saw and felt the magnitude of the price paid by the human family for war's wickedness.

The spectacle of a continent in ruins—its cities rubble, its treasures destroyed, its monuments lost forever—was overwhelming. Destruction was massive, ugly, universal. Yet, over time, one becomes inured to physical wreckage. What years of air raids, shellings, firebombs, and scorched earth leave behind has a numbing sameness that deadens shock.

But there is no way to become inured to human wreckage, the suffering of millions—populations displaced, living in cellars or broken buildings or crowded camps, their lives in ruin, often lacking shoes or blankets or soap, malnourished, families separated, lonely, homes and possessions gone. And, in country after country, government too in shambles, the fabric of society torn apart, services disrupted, men, women, and children left to fend for themselves. Grief, despair, anger were all in the air one breathed.

Of course there were brighter moments, heroic moments, even joyous moments when the human spirit, indomitable and unbroken, burst through the gloom of tragedy. Those moments sustained me. So did the companionship of our relief teams, who, though stressed and exhausted from their efforts to help, still found time to enjoy each other and to laugh.

Laughter amid tears? Yes, and a mix that needs no apology, for both are the possessions of caring human beings. Living in the midst of tragedy persuaded me that our human capacity to cry measures also our capacity to feel joy. Together they lift life from the flat and the two-dimensional to the rich and the three-dimensional. My years in Europe

*Betty Summers in 1946 when Steve first met her.
Legend has it he jumped over a meetinghouse
bench in his eagerness to meet her—
a story he flatly denied.*

helped me in my capacity to care, to cry, and to laugh. And I count each to be a gift. Those years gave my life new direction. To see what I saw, to experience what I experienced led me to a commitment to spend the rest of my life laboring in the vineyard of peace.

It began inauspiciously. In January 1946, scores of young pacifists—men just released from Civilian Public Service and women eager to serve—came for training at Pendle Hill, the Quaker center near Philadelphia. Preparing for their relief assignments overseas, they shuttled between area studies and language studies at Pendle Hill and reading field reports in Philadelphia from their assigned stations.

Everyone sympathized with poor Steve, who, carrying the overblown title of European Relief Commissioner, had to study every area, every language, and every field report to prepare him for his roving assignment. Truth be known, however, "poor Steve" probably wasn't either at Pendle Hill

43

or in Philadelphia. He was out in the suburb of Germantown visiting Betty Summers, who had stumbled into his life at a moment singularly inconvenient for both him and the American Friends Service Committee, and doubtless for Betty as well. Every waking moment was supposed to be spent reassuring the committee that it had made no mistake in appointing him its European relief chief, but this became translated into too much time trying unsuccessfully to persuade Betty to marry him and move to Paris.

I was supposed to leave for France in mid-February. Not entirely to my distress, dental problems forced a delay. Seven teeth, damaged in a long-ago auto accident, had finally given up the ghost. And it was decided that all must be removed before I could be medically cleared for the rigors of postwar Europe. Accordingly, on a miserable day early in March, all seven were extracted and, my mouth stuffed with gauze, I was dispatched across town, where what the trade calls "partials"—appliances miraculously created in advance— were inserted, not without painful adjustments. Twenty-four hours later, I took off for Paris, accompanied by hot irons in an angry mouth, but leaving behind seven teeth and my beloved Betty Summers.

The plane broke down in Newfoundland—fortunately on the ground—and we had to spend three days in a Gander Nissen hut waiting for replacement parts to arrive. Then it was on to Paris. The city in the early months of 1946 was not glamorous. Heat was scarce. Overcoats were the dress of choice inside as well as out, and support staff typed with gloves. Food was adequate but bore little resemblance to fabled French cuisine: coarse bread, sugarless oatmeal with powdered milk, canned goods from the States. Rabbit was the meat staple in restaurants, except for black market es- tablishments, where Châteaubriand and wild strawberries

Delivery of light rails. (France 1945 or 46)

were available at prices that made it easy to observe Quaker scruples against under-the-table dealing.

In those early days, the Service Committee had relief teams in France, Italy, Austria, Poland, Finland, and Norway. Germany was a special case, involving entry negotiations with occupation authorities in the American zone, and Quaker work there was just beginning. In addition, a European Transport Unit (ETU) was being assembled, equipped with 6 x 6 trucks acquired from the U.S. Army and headquartered in Paris. Young drivers were trained to service their vehicles and were then dispatched to provide transport for Quaker relief teams scattered across Europe. Chaotic conditions at national borders and years of highway neglect made projected arrival dates meaningless. One caravan of ten vehicles laboring slowly eastward across France, Germany, and Czechoslovakia to Poland required two weeks, including one memorable day with 30 flat tires. Once on site, vehicles hauled

"This sign is a magic symbol for the school feeding station located on the streetless route it marks." (Poland, 1946)

relief supplies to distribution sites, stones and lumber to construction projects, and sometimes family possessions to new quarters. Most of the members of the ETU were in their 20s. Relief was predominantly a young people's business because the young had the best mix of energy, enthusiasm, and fresh idealism to endure under isolated and stressful conditions.

My assignment called for constant travel, interrupted only by periods in Paris headquarters to write reports to Philadelphia, consult on the purchase and shipment of supplies, deploy trucks and personnel, and discuss future plans. Unless one had diplomatic or military credentials, moving around Europe in 1945–47 was a challenge that could be met only by the willingness and stamina to get aboard anything that moved. Occasionally, through some connection, I obtained priority status for military flights, but this was frowned upon by Quaker superiors who wished to keep our relief operations free from association with the military.

Trains were available in some settings, with comfort levels that varied inversely with the distance from former war zones.

46

The Paris-Rome run, for example, required 24 crowded hours, but at least there was heat in the cars and glass in the windows, to say nothing of breakfast in Switzerland with fresh cold milk and white rolls with real butter. The Warsaw-Gdansk run was another story. Here I sat on my backpack, jammed into a grossly overcrowded corridor, in a car with glassless windows, seemingly square wheels, and a maximum speed of 25 miles an hour.

I remember one all-night run over that route in bitter cold, sitting uncomfortably in front of a restroom with an out-of-order sign dangling from its door. Hour after hour, passengers stepped on me and over me en route to the toilet, only to stumble away with what I assumed were choice Polish expletives. Eventually we rolled into Warsaw. I stirred aching limbs and was about to throw my pack out the window and jump out after it when a round-faced little peasant woman opened the restroom door, removed the sign, and prepared to unload several crates of cabbages and a supply of plucked chickens that she was bringing to market in space she had creatively requisitioned.

On another occasion, rolling slowly southward along the Vistula River toward a rendezvous with a Quaker relief team in Kozienici, I fell in with three Poles capable of fractured English. As the train fell behind schedule it was clear that darkness would overtake us. This presented a problem. My station was on the wrong side of the river, and to reach Kozienici I had to cross a bridge that featured a checkpoint manned by a squad of Soviet soldiers. The behavior of Russians in Poland in 1946 being unpredictable, especially at night, I found this scenario an unattractive one.

My new friends saved me. They miraculously located a troika during our stopover, and impressed on its driver the singular importance of getting a distinguished American relief worker across the bridge to his headquarters that night. They were persuasive. By the time we rolled out onto the bridge, the troika men regarded me with awe. Toward midstream, the clip-clop of our horse roused the Russians, who tumbled out of their guardhouse, weapons pointed menacingly in our direction, and ordered us to halt at once—an invitation that needed no repetition. My driver launched into his speech and I presented my documents, attempting to appear alternately disdainful and irritated at an unwarranted intrusion. Both performances were marginal, but Russian weaponry gradually assumed a more benign angle and, to my astonishment, their owners bowed, saluted, and let us pass. I was soon safely delivered into the arms of my startled Kozienici colleagues.

Of course trains—with or without amenities—often didn't go where I wanted to go, and more often than not I bounced along Europe's war-scarred and pitted roads in any vehicle with wheels, my belongings tossed in the back. Sometimes we crawled. Sometimes we tinkered with balky engines. Sometimes we careened wildly. I always made it, though often in need of a night's sleep.

Officially, my role was to assess programs, discuss problems, and weigh future directions. Unit leaders often delayed meetings with local officials until "a Quaker visitor from our headquarters" could be present to lend weight to requests for assistance or complaints about the lack of promised cooperation.

Unofficially, however, I found that my more important role was lending an ear and offering understanding and support to young workers, isolated and exhausted, depressed by the limits of their ability to help, and overwhelmed by the suffering around them. I soon discovered that in such a setting a word of gratitude, an arm around the shoulder, and a few laughs could make a difference. I learned to exploit a modest talent to lighten an evening with tales of some of my adventures, drawing on an ever-expanding repertoire based on dumb behavior. One of my favorites was about the fashionable New York matron who stopped at Bonwit's en route to volunteering at the AFSC clothing room. She bought a beautiful winter coat, which she draped casually over a clothing room chair. From there it was snatched up, thrown into the last bale of a shipment to Poland, and on its way down the East River before the distressed lady found it missing. In Poland at the time, I was ordered up to Gdynia, found the bale, retrieved the coat, tied it to my backpack, and carried it back to Paris via Warsaw and Vienna, where it was sent back to New York. The matron got her coat, blocked and cleaned, the staff member who took it received a certificate of merit, and I had a cable of commendation from AFSC's chairman.

One unexpected involvement in my travels was the occasional encounter with U.S. intelligence agents. There weren't many American civilians roaming around Europe in those years, and those who were were apparently deemed sources of useful information. On several occasions, I was waited upon by CIA operatives or other sleuths flashing badges and asked if I had seen anything that might be of interest to U.S. authorities. I always politely declined to comment, explaining that one reason Quakers were able to work in sensitive areas was because we were trusted to be there for no other reason than to help. I appreciated the fact that in these situations my explanation was accepted. I was never pressed.

This is an issue about which I have strong feelings. Humanitarian undertakings of all kinds and intelligence activities must, at all costs, be wholly divorced from each other. This has not always been the case, and those who mix the two do a serious disservice to all who seek to meet human suffering. The greatest need is often in sensitive areas, and any intelligence role played by one agency raises questions about the motivation of all agencies.

A case in point: in 1946 I visited an AFSC relief team in Czerwonka, Poland, a war-devastated area under Soviet control where the only accommodation available was on the second floor of a railroad station on the main rail line be-tween Germany and the Soviet Union. From these quarters, our team had daily exposure to what the Soviets were taking from eastern Germany—a matter of high interest to Wash-ington. The Russian authorities trusted Quaker motives, and we never betrayed the trust. Relations were cordial, and because the relief team included a registered nurse, loaded trains heading east stopped at our station when medical help was needed. Friends have been criticized for this policy, but in the long run we believe it serves the cause of international comity and stability.

Against this general background of stressful but adventur-ous service, a report on three distinctive relief programs, based in Italy, Germany, and Finland, makes clearer what we were trying to do.

ITALY

The recovery program mounted by the AFSC early in 1945 in Italy's Abruzzi region, a poor mountainous area bordering the Adriatic Sea, shows how a private agency undertaking a small pilot program can open the way for a more massive recovery operation. The Abruzzi, its ancient villages perched on mountain tops or nestled in rugged valleys, had the misfortune of being at the eastern end of the Gustav Line, the scene of the heaviest fighting of World War II's Italian

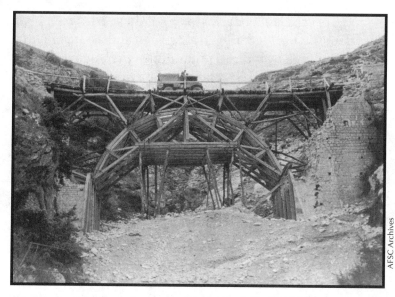

AFSC Archives

"A hazardous temporary bridge." (Italy 1945)

campaign. Between Allied bombs and German scorched earth, the area was devastated, its people scattered and eking out a miserable existence in remote refugee camps.

British and American Quakers, already active in Rome to help the emigration of Jews and others who had reached Italy from the north, learned of conditions in the Abruzzi, and late in 1944 sent a small team to investigate. They found conditions as bad as reported, with little evidence of recovery a full year after the cessation of fighting. Two problems created paralysis. First was a lack of transport: resources for rebuilding—kilns, forest reserves, and limestone—were available, but without wheels were inaccessible. Second was the legacy of years of Fascist deceit and lies: mistrust was so pervasive that no cooperation, no barter agreements, no advances of government funds were possible between village leaders or homeowners drifting back from refugee camps.

Nobody trusted anybody. On top of these barriers, there were depressed spirits, universal fatigue, and an inability of villagers to understand the terms under which government rebuilding subsidies were available. The result was paralysis.

The Service Committee decided to undertake a small pilot project involving two Abruzzi communes. We would provide five 6 x 6 trucks with drivers and support staff, all of transparent integrity, all young, strong of back, and eager to make at last a constructive contribution to peacemaking after their years as pacifists in Civilian Public Service or in U.S. prisons. It was the AFSC's hope that these young people could become poles of trust around which barter agreements, fair labor prices, and a loosening of government funds could take place.

The acute observations of the investigating team led to a recommendation that became the key to the project's success. They noted that, although the devastation was catastrophic, most of the houses' foundations were relatively sound. This made rebuilding individual houses a practical option, and with AFSC always favoring a one-on-one approach, house by house reconstruction became part of the project plan.

In the poverty-stricken Abruzzi, with villagers drifting back from refugee camps, the opportunity for a homeowner to contribute his own labor so reduced the out-of-pocket cost of rebuilding that the government subsidy of 60% of the estimated charges was sufficient to meet all costs. This left only the barrier of mistrust as the remaining problem.

Initially, in our two communes, suspicious, untrusting householders insisted on riding with our drivers to protect their interests as barter terms were hammered out and kiln prices negotiated. Slowly confidence in our integrity grew, the enthusiasm of drivers became infectious, and owners only went along to help load and unload the trucks. The new mood spread to village building committees with their access to government subsidy funds, and they began to advance government funds to householders with Quaker drivers as co-signers. These loans paid for the skilled stone masons needed for instruction and to assure the soundness of foundations, with repayment coming from the 60% subsidy paid on completion of the rebuilding. These advances became a kind of revolving fund.

"Many houses can be repaired with comparatively small effort."
(Italy 1945-47)

"Stream is crossed on small ferry. Fee for crossing—3 cigarettes."
(Italy 1945)

The dam was broken, new life began to stir, and within a year the five trucks became 75. In less than three years there were 3,000, now under the auspices of UNRRA-CASAS, an Italian government agency. With each expansion, the governing agency continued the house-by-house approach because it was working. The Abruzzi was rebuilt.

I visited the project more than a year after it had been launched. It was already in transition, with AFSC drivers dividing their time between their original role and training Italian drivers in a larger program. In Rome, I participated with the program director in negotiations with the Italian government agency responsible for coal allocations. We had promised kiln owners in the Abruzzi that, if they adhered to price agreements and treated villagers fairly, they would be assured of quality coal. This promise had to be kept if emerging trust was to survive.

From Rome, I traveled to Scauri on the Adriatic coast and spent three days accompanying 18-year-old Arthur Emlen in his truck, meeting with building committees and owners ready to rebuild, and loading and unloading the truck. Emlen was a good example of what we sought in our drivers: reaching easily across the cultural chasm, mastering the patois that passed for Italian in the Abruzzi, and reflecting the enthusiasm and integrity that were of such importance in the depressed and suspicious environment.

He had been on the job for six months, and everywhere we went the affection of villagers and building committees was palpable. Haggard faces lit up, the ragged pitched in, and committee members made themselves available. One day we were walking through a village and passed a make-shift barbershop with a customer getting a shave. He saw Arthur, ran into the street, and threw his arms around him, with lather flying in all directions. No wonder life was stirring, and a few houses were beginning to brighten the desolate landscape!

From Scauri, I moved westward into the Aventino Valley for a tour with another driver. We were returning one evening when his truck had a second flat tire. With no spare, we had to leave the truck and walk to his cellar. While preparing supper, my host told me that he had to walk to Colledemacini that evening to see the mayor, to whom he'd promised a load of wood in the morning. I knew the village was high up on a ridge, and asked whether we could fix our flat tire in the morning and deliver the wood by early afternoon.

"No," he said, "that's not good enough. These people have been lied to and deceived for years. All I've got going for me around here is my word. I either keep it or explain why I can't. Otherwise, I might just as well pack up and go home."

Chapter Four

After supper, we set out. It was a beautiful night. For an hour we climbed up a rough road with endless switchbacks lit by a full moon. Eventually, Colledemacini appeared. A single church spire, miraculously spared, reached into the sky, around it only jagged walls, still and dark and lifeless. No creature stirred, no one walked streets piled with rubble, as we made our way to the mayor's house. But along the way, bits of light flickered here and there at ground level, marking cellars where families had come back to reclaim what was left of their homes.

An astonished mayor, responding to our knock, asked what we were doing in his village at this hour of the night. The explanation was too much for the fellow, and he burst into tears. Once inside, and after a few moments, he whispered to his ten-year-old son, who ran off. Soon a few of the villagers joined us—all those expecting wood from our truck. One brought a jug of wine, another sausages, a third coarse bread, and a fourth a battered accordion.

A party erupted, one of those spontaneous, joyous occasions where barriers fall away, cultural gaps disappear, and the world is brightened with laughter. For an hour we sang and danced, made speeches, toasted America and Italy, sipped wine, munched on sausage sandwiches, and pledged eternal friendship. The welkin rang!

Finally, we said we'd better be getting back. The mayor, tracing his fractured English to a Pittsburgh steel mill, announced that everyone would go down together. They knew shortcuts across the switchbacks. They could get back to the valley in half the time it would take us. So down we all plunged with the party still in full cry until we reached the place where the road went straight. Here we parted. The two of us started silently and alone down the road. Then: "Steve, maybe you can understand now why I love these people."

56

Several months later, I returned. Trucks were everywhere. Many of the ancient villages had more roofs, and here and there shops were appearing. AFSC programs were now focused on community enterprises—work camps to repair simple water systems or build a playing field. We started day care centers or helped in orphanages, all the while keeping in close touch with UNRRA-CASAS, where we had enough influence to assure their continuing the house-to-house focus instead of reverting to the usual approach of large public construction of new housing. The Abruzzi was reborn.

Team members who shared in this enterprise have kept in touch, and 50 years later, under the leadership of a distinguished Italian historian, and with the help of a substantial Italian government grant they were invited to revisit the Abruzzi. They participated in celebratory events in three cities, featuring photographic and material exhibits and speeches by dignitaries, including the U.S. ambassador. I attended the event in Chieti, being driven around by an Italian warmly remembered by team members. As a young man he had been a driver hired by the Quakers. He had continued in the construction business and prospered. Now he drove a Mercedes.

Germany

Ever since its large-scale child-feeding program in 1920–21, the American Friends Service Committee had been active in Germany, staffing a Berlin peace center and supporting the struggling Weimar Republic. With the rise of Hitler, the AFSC and German Yearly Meeting worked to aid persecuted Jews and, through the Berlin Center, to facilitate emigration for those trying to leave.

This between-the-wars activity culminated in the spring of 1939 in the visit to Germany of three distinguished American Quakers hoping to meet with high-ranking Nazi leaders for permission to set up exit stations at the French border through which larger numbers of Jews could be processed for emigration. The trio got as high as Heinrich Heydrich, the deputy chief of the Gestapo, widely known in the west for his role in the Lidice massacre. Midway through negotiations, the Germans left the room "to consult." In their absence the Quaker delegation settled into a quiet meeting for worship and only later discovered a hidden microphone placed by the hosts to monitor Quaker conversation. Hearing nothing, they returned, baffled but satisfied, and permission was given in writing. Unfortunately, the border stations never opened because the war broke out five months later. The tiny German Yearly Meeting continued, heroically and often at personal risk, to help the Jewish community. They tried unsuccessfully to rally mainstream German Christian churches to do the same— 80 letters were sent to church leaders throughout the country. Only eight responses were received, seven of them refusals. A single response, from the Catholic Bishop of Cologne, was supportive.

As soon as the war was over, the AFSC was ready to send in relief teams to help meet urgent needs. It wasn't possible. The four allied powers divided the country into four sectors, with each establishing its own military government and its own entry regulations. Approvals to enter were slow in coming.

The AFSC focused on entry to the American sector, which proved particularly difficult because of the number of agencies making application. The need to avoid duplication of effort, to sort through aid proposals, and to identify sites all resulted in red tape. The American military eventually insisted that an umbrella agency be established to serve as a clearing house. The AFSC played a major role in creating the Council of Relief Agencies Licensed to Operate in Germany (CRALOG). Defining CRALOG's relationship to military governance delayed action. Finally, in the fall of 1946, the necessary structure was in place and Eastburn Thompson, lent to CRALOG by the AFSC, took off for Berlin to assume office as CRALOG's president. Tragically, the plane crashed in Newfoundland and Thompson was killed. I lost a close friend.

By that time I had been in Europe for almost eight months, and there had been scattered openings to enter Germany. My first visit was in late March, to Ludwigshafen in the French sector, where I arrived in the midst of a late winter storm with snow softening the landscape of war's wreckage. Ludwigshafen, as an industrial city, had been heavily bombed for years—its buildings shattered, rubble still piled in the streets, bridges grotesquely sunk in waterways, surviving trees with branches stripped for firewood. Its citizens were exhausted, sad-faced, and listless, wrapped in whatever they could find for warmth, scavenging for food and firewood on a cold, gray day. I could look forward to a dry, heated barracks, they only to a damp, cold cellar, the wretched remnants of a gifted but deluded people. Watching them on their rounds, I couldn't help wondering how many had once enthusiastically displayed the swastika and given the Nazi salute as Hitler's Wehrmacht marched toward the front. How many had just been swept along, helpless, naive victims, on the tide of arrogance and propaganda that war makers have always generated?

I sought out city officials to learn more about conditions. Most were not to be found, so I continued my own explorations, only to be accosted by the burgermeister himself, who had heard there was an American Quaker in town and had set out to find me. I asked him what was most needed. He said blankets, warm clothing, shoes, and food supplements. Could the Quakers help as they had done before? I couldn't promise, but I could certainly report the city's urgent need to my superiors in Philadelphia. We did send a team to Ludwigshafen, where we mounted clothing distributions and shared in child-feeding programs with the Mennonites.

Fortunately, in contrast to 1920, the victors called on the newly-established United Nations to mount major international efforts to meet Europe's staggering needs, and throughout the postwar years UNRRA carried the major relief and resettlement burden. The AFSC and other private agencies met special needs and reached out to groups and communities that fell through the cracks.

Needs always exceeded resources, making decisions painful. It was necessary to check lists provided by local officials to be sure that politics or other personal considerations hadn't influenced the selections. More painful were choices as to which distinctive constituent groups should be helped. Tubercular patients in a hospital who would likely die without a richer diet? Factory workers unable to do essential work? Badly undernourished schoolchildren? No one should ever have to make these kinds of choices. Sometimes I was angry, wishing that the captains and the kings had to live face-to-face with the victims of their handiwork. Sometimes, more worthily, I sought guidance. Either way, sleep was hard to come by.

Clothing distributions were easier, especially those involving children. The quality of the clothing bales shipped in from Quaker collection centers in the United States made distributions a rare source of happiness. Too often, clothing coming to disaster areas was mass-collected, thrown into bales, and shipped unpatched, even unwashed. AFSC clothing was widely regarded in the finest condition, clean, folded, and in good repair. To help a child select an item, to see the sparkle in the eyes of a little girl with a new dress or a boy rubbing his hands over the wool of a new coat, reduced me to tears.

Particularly distressing during these early occupation years was the so-called "cigarette economy." In the absence of money, cigarettes became the medium of exchange. A carton, which any G.I. could purchase in the post PX for 75¢, would easily fetch a fur coat, expensive jewelry, or other valuable possessions, with the cigarettes then going to buy food or other necessities. This black market, universal in Germany, was a bonanza for the occupiers but a humiliation for the occupied. Our relief teams were encouraged to stay away from PXs, and all our money dealings had to be at official rates, even though such honesty made life expensive. I tried to be faithful to these guidelines, but I'm afraid I occasionally back-slid when the appeal of a 15¢ milkshake won out.

All of the emerging German relief proposed during my first year in Europe met urgent needs—especially because the winter of 1946–47 was unusually cold, but it was in the next year that Friends made their most important contribution to German recovery. A Bryn Mawr College professor of anthropology, German-born Hertha Kraus, was an AFSC consultant for whom I arranged a tour of our relief centers in mid-1946. She went home convinced that the greatest need for German recovery was facilities where community life could be reborn, where citizens could participate in planning the restoration of services, find a place for rest or recreation, leave their children, or just meet over a cup of coffee.

Her Neighborhood Center proposal was accepted, but acting on it became a headache for our relief teams and for the committee's hard-pressed commissioner in Paris. Sites had to be found and approvals sought from local authorities, military government, and CRALOG. Construction schedules, involving prefabricated material from Sweden, furnishings from Switzerland, and supplies from the U.S., all had to be coordinated, and the supplies shipped over malfunctioning German railroads. Key items were lost on obscure sidings, leaving operations stalled. Over it all loomed the imposing and imperious figure of Hertha herself, doggedly German in the certainty that there were only two ways to solve a problem, her way and the wrong way. Her field visits were always a source of friction and a cross to carry, but Hertha Kraus knew German culture and knew what she was talking about. She was the engine that carried the program to fruition.

Every center—and there were six—had its special construction problems. One particularly difficult one was planned for Brunswick in the British zone, where a different military structure added its own complications. Red tape and lost supplies caused increasing delays, to the point that it seemed the center would never materialize. But through it all the relief team remained patient and determined, regularly reassuring skeptical city fathers that there soon would be a center. Finally, construction was ready to start. The burgermeister asked if the city could provide the cornerstone.

Permission was granted, and on the appointed day he and three members of his council appeared with a cart carrying a block of granite covered by cloth. The mayor made a little speech thanking the Quakers for their persistence and patience, and removed the cloth. "You'll notice," he said, "that we've had three letters, AMA, carved in the corner-stone. That's the Latin word for love, and if ever there was a building that only love could have produced, it's this one. Of course, it's only the sheerest coincidence that these same letters are also the initials of A. Margaret Atkinson, your team leader. On behalf of the city of Brunswick, we thank her." It was a healing moment, when a sometimes bitter past gave way to the rebirth of warmth and friendship.

The centers proved to be all that Hertha Kraus had predicted. Quaker workers staffed them during the first years of German reconstruction. Management gradually devolved to German staff. The centers became affiliated with German cultural and educational institutions—as impressive a Quaker contribution to German recovery as the child-feeding operation.

Fifty years later I was among those invited to attend a massive exhibit in Berlin's Historical Museum to commemorate British and American Quaker contributions to German recovery after both great wars. The honorary sponsor was Roman Herzog, president of the Republic of Germany. He was to address the opening ceremony.

Unfortunately, the date coincided with François Mitterand's funeral in Paris, which the president was obligated to attend. We thought we had lost our lead speaker, but to everyone's surprise he managed to leave Paris moments after the service. With the help of the presidential jet and a motorcycle escort, he made it to the Historical Museum with 15 minutes to spare. His speech was stunning—the frankest public apology for the terrible atrocities of Nazi rule, combined with gratitude for Quakers having twice come to Germany "with no axe to grind, no evangelical motives, concerned only to succor a defeated enemy." He said he had hurried back from Paris because "I wanted to tell you all that when I was a high school student, the head of my school called me into his office and asked me to leave the class 15 minutes early every day to help unload the 'Quaker Speisung' and carry the food containers into the elementary school for the daily food supplements provided for our young students. Of course, I accepted, and today I have hurried back from Paris to open the exhibit because any organization that could get me excused 15 minutes early from my classes deserves my full support!"

Afterward, those of us from England and the United States who had been invited to attend as former relief workers were given a bus tour including a rebuilt Berlin, sites of destroyed Jewish synagogues, and notable centers of German Quakerism. It was a tour that showed us a thriving country, blessed this time with the statesmanship of George Marshall instead of the vindictiveness of Georges Clemenceau and Lloyd George.

Finland

Finland was unique as a setting for World War II relief work. Technically it was an enemy country, allied with Germany and twice at war with the Soviet Union. It was the only country on the continent with kindly feelings toward Germans, even though the scorched earth retreat northward through Lapland left that the worst destroyed area of all Europe.

This disaster came to Finland in 1944 in the wake of the Winter War, when part of the harsh truce terms laid down by the USSR called for the Finns to drive the Germans out of Finland. Reluctant to turn on their ally, the Finns made a secret deal that called for heavy but innocuous ground fire and a daily five-mile German retreat. Unfortunately, the Soviets caught on to this scheme and told the Finns to get down to business or they would come in and do it for them. Faced with this unacceptable option, the Finns were forced to attack the Germans. The result was that the Germans, thinking their ally had turned against them, scorched the earth as they retreated northward through Lapland. Villages were burned, bridges blown up, telephone poles cut down, snow fences burned, fields mined, broken glass strewn on the roads. Lapland, when the AFSC arrived to help, was a disaster, its people scattered, its land desecrated.

The Quaker relief team was based in Rovaniemi, on the edge of the Arctic Circle, itself badly destroyed with little but stark chimneys poking toward the sky from burned-out buildings. Primary relief during the cold winter of 1945–46 was the focus—blankets, warm clothing, shoes distributed to Lapps drifting back to their villages to live in cellars or make-shift shelters.

AFSC Archives

"A typical street in Rovaniemi. Only the ghostly chimneys are left. Large numbers [of people] have only their cellars to get them through the winter." (Finland 1946)

65

AFSC Archives

"War orphan in Lapland." (Finland 1946)

Suffering was intense, but the returning villagers could at least reclaim their own land. That was all the incentive they needed to start over again. A spirit of mutual cooperation and helpfulness, unique in my experience in all of postwar Europe, prevailed. In Finland there was little of the hatred and mistrust that paralyzed recovery elsewhere. All parties worked together —the government, the Finnish churches, the Red Cross, international agencies, returning Lapps—to clean up and rebuild. Sawmills, with limitless resources of wood available, worked day and night.

The pace of recovery was a miracle. By the time I visited the area in June 1946, new buildings—well-constructed, permanent structures—were evident in Rovaniemi, and Lapp villages were beginning to be reborn. AFSC supplemented its relief operations by organizing work camps, staffed by American and Scandinavian young people, to rebuild the homes of war widows. In these camps, enthusiasm was infectious, and courage and cheerfulness triumphed over tragedy. In the village of Autti I was present at the camp's farewell party, and wrote in my report to Philadelphia:

The entire community walked in from their scattered farms for miles around. There was hymn singing and a sermon, preached by team leader Bill Fredrickson on the subject of a house builded upon a rock. Speeches were short but heartfelt. One old lady had carefully written out her words ahead of time . . . telling what the campers had done for her family and how much it had meant to their getting started again, concluding with Jesus' words to his disciples: "inasmuch as ye have done it unto the least of these, ye have done it unto me."

I found the same spirit at a second camp, where I spent two days mixing and pouring cement. One American camper was determined to learn Finnish and seized every opportunity to practice it. On my last evening, when we broke the handle from a frying pan, she volunteered to ride the camp bicycle into a recently opened village shop to acquire another. Twenty minutes later, the little hand-cranked wall phone at the camp rang and the alarmed voice of the shopkeeper asked if "everything was all right out there at your camp."

"Yes," we said, "why do you ask?"

"Because there's a young woman in here asking for a midwife."

Finnish is not an easy language to master.

On my way north to visit that camp, I encountered further evidence of the harsh truce terms exacted by the Soviets: miles and miles of cordwood neatly stacked beside the railroad track, awaiting shipment to the USSR. On top of their own recovery problems, the Finns were saddled with this additional burden, which they were determined to meet ahead of schedule to demonstrate that, this time, there would be no renewal of hostilities.

67

Even more powerful evidence of peaceful intent was a cabinet appointment in Helsinki, unique in the annals of international relations, when the Finns named the nation's best-known pacifist, Yrjö Kallinen, its minister of war. I was so intrigued by this move that I decided to visit the minister in the hope that I could learn enough to persuade Harry Truman to name A. J. Muste or Clarence Pickett secretary of defense.

We had a charming interview. He told me that, when approached, he thought the idea preposterous, but had to admit its logic and eventually accepted on a one-year-only basis. I asked him what he was doing with the army and air force now under his command. He said he was deploying army units to Lapland to clear mine fields and equipping his air force with pontoon planes, based on Lapland's endless lakes, to serve in medical evacuation of Lapps wounded in land mine explosions. Another of his initiatives was to accept recruits into the military services, but only as volunteers. No one would be drafted during his term of office. It appeared to me a great way to run a War Department.

Most of my time on this Finnish visit was spent in discussing AFSC's future role in the country. With UNRRA now active, and Lapp rebuilding well advanced, the need for help in the north could be limited to organizing more of the work camps that had been so successful in the previous year. The greatest need now was in central Finland, where many thousands of refugees from the southern province of Karelia were now living on the edge of survival. They were devastated by the loss of this province—their beloved homeland, the ancient seat of Finnish culture, seized by the Russians as a war prize to protect Leningrad from future invasion.

The loss of Karelia was the most deeply felt cost of Finland's two wars with the Soviets. Two years afterward, Finns often

AFS-C Archives

"Shipments of clothing from America have inspired great joy."
(Finland 1946)

broke into tears at the mention of Karelia. I observed the wretched conditions under which Karelians in the Jyvaskyla-Suolahti area were living—sometimes eight or ten to a room in barns and sheds, poorly clothed, and without hope of immediate change in their circumstances. All dreamed of returning, with no roots where they were. "It is a challenging area for a Quaker undertaking," I wrote in my report, "and will require the best we have."

We decided that in the year ahead AFSC would focus on the Karelians, helping to meet urgent need for shoes and warm clothing and undertaking a craft program to counter idleness and provide at least a meager source of income. Even more important was an intangible: the provision of loving, comforting support, the shoulders of young Finns and Americans to lean upon, to counter despair.

"Transport of timber up the river Kemijoki." (Finland 1946)

We made plans for the visit of two prominent Americans: Arthur Morgan, the creative dynamo in the development of the Tennessee Valley Authority, who, it was thought, might have valuable suggestions for revival of the Finnish economy, and David Hinshaw, a Friend who planned to produce a film on conditions in Finland, to be used in raising funds among Finnish Americans in the U.S. to support AFSC work. Both came and rendered valuable service, though neither possessed a temperament compatible with the leisurely, coffee-drinking culture of Finnish life. Quaker follow-up visits were required in their wake to repair wounded feelings.

My next stop was to be Finnmark, Norway's northernmost province, where we had a team helping in the rebuilding of Hammerfest. There were two ways to get there—the long way around by Helsinki and Oslo and up the Norwegian coast, or directly from Rovaniemi through Lapland. The latter was shorter, but maps showed no roads leading to Finnmark. There was a work camp in Inari in Lapland's far north where I could visit, and I thought I could find a way to cross the uncharted area from Inari to a Norwegian outpost at Kvalsund.

A Red Cross truck could take me 250 kilometers north to Ivalo, from where a bus was said to be available to take me 50 kilometers west to Inari. Armed with some appropriate translations for needed services, I appeared at Rovaniemi's Red Cross headquarters. The only space available was among a pile of crates on a trailer, where, joined by a colorful Lapp who generously kept slicing off chunks of raw fish for me to share, I tried to make myself comfortable. It was June and we were above the Arctic Circle, so all night we bounced along gravel roads as Lapland forests and lakes slipped by with the midnight sun casting its long shadows across endless pines and birches.

By four in the morning we reached Ivalo, still reduced to rubble, where a crew of lumbermen, well nourished with alcohol, were resting from their labors. Seeing no other sign of life—or any bus—I produced my list of Rovaniemi translations. Pointing to one that read: "Where is the bus for Inari?" I showed it to a friendly lumberman. The reaction was raucous laughter, repeated by his brethren as my note passed among them. But there was no useful response. Discouraged, and feeling alone and lost in a strange and desolate place, I climbed to the top of a pile of rubble and surveyed the scene. Something that might be a vehicle roof loomed in the distance and proved to be a decrepit bus. I was soon the only passenger on my way west.

It was a wild ride with little evidence of a road, and from time to time we threaded our way through herds of reindeer, shepherded by frantic Lapps and their dogs. With each herd, my driver delighted in singling out one unfortunate beast and giving chase. I hung on for dear life, asking the Lord to postpone other chores to spare me and, if possible, the beast as well. He graciously did so, and eventually the sight of a familiar Quaker face appeared in Inari, coming to check on possible mail but finding only a frazzled representative from Philadelphia. I quickly learned that my problem with the lumbermen was not too much liquor in Ivalo but too much deviltry in Rovaniemi. The note about the bus read: "What time do the movies start in Inari?"

Quaker colleagues up there in the north proved less treacherous than those in the south, and after two days as a work camper pouring cement I was handed over to a sturdy young Lapp who was prepared to take me down the Tana River 25 miles to Kvalsund, where a Norwegian army garrison was located and might be able to get me to Hammerfest.

My Lapp guide seemed at home in his canoe and aware of my projected destination when I took a seat on the bottom of his bark-covered craft and we headed downstream. It was a silent day-long journey, with no means of communication, no real idea of where I was going, my life in the hands of a total stranger from a wildly different culture in an area as remote from my world as any on the planet. But the weather was beautiful and the rhythmic gurgle of his paddle hour after hour was reassuring. Still, I found it a relief when Kvalsund appeared and with it an English-speaking sergeant who booked me on a convoy to Hammerfest.

Nearly 40 years later, in 1983, I was invited by the provincial governor to return to participate in ceremonies marking the 35th anniversary of the rebuilding of the province. The government wanted a new generation of Laplanders to be aware of the courage and resolution with which their parents and grandparents had faced disaster. Schoolchildren all over Lapland collected stories of the miracles wrought by everyone working together, with prizes for the best essays.

Veterans of the effort joined with the representatives of Finnish organizations and foreign agencies for two days of celebration in Rovaniemi.

Two events highlighted the celebration. The first was in the city's new opera house, where 600 Lapps from all over the province gathered for songs and dancing and speechmaking. I had found in AFSC's archives the original dog-eared copy of my 1946 report. Its first four paragraphs were devoted to the exhilaration I felt at the spirit of helpfulness that prevailed on all sides—a spirit unique in all of Europe. In my speech before a packed house I read my comments verbatim. This brought authenticity to the occasion and was warmly received.

I turned to the present, reminding the audience that American Quakers had come to Finland's aid when it was needed, and suggested that now it was time for Finns to come to the aid of America. Their country, I said, living in the shadow of the Soviet colossus with whom they had fought two bitter wars, had found a way to live with it in peace. Without fear, they enjoyed a free press and a parliamentary democracy that included an active communist party holding minority seats at various levels of its government. My country, on the other hand, though 5,000 miles away, was living on the edge of a precipice, consumed by fear, bristling with nuclear arms in a bitter climate of cold war, and regarding the Soviets as an evil empire.

In this situation, I noted that Americans were fortunate that, at the moment of our Rovaniemi celebration, their President Koivisto was paying an official visit to the United States. Wasn't it time to make a deal? Let us keep your president and send you Mr. Reagan. He can help us and you can help our president. Six hundred Lapps cheered with delight at this proposal, and while I couldn't read the

Lapland press during a subsequent tour of the province, I noted in village weeklies the English words "Cary," "Koivisto," and "Reagan," and gathered that my idea received wide circulation. I never found out what the American Embassy in Helsinki thought of it.

The other noteworthy event was the final banquet, hosted by Lapland's governor, featuring cloudberry liqueur, reindeer steak, and a parade of speeches. When it was over, the governor rose to thank us for coming and to bid us goodbye. He was, however, interrupted by the official representative from West Germany, who said he couldn't leave without a final word. He said he'd been ordered to come to Finland for the occasion, but had dreaded doing so because he was too aware that it was his country that was responsible for the destruction of Lapland 40 years earlier. He'd been part of the celebration for two days, and not once had there been even a passing reference to who had wrecked the province. The focus was on the heroic recovery. No one in the room, he said, could appreciate what this meant to him as a German. His voice broke, and with tears coming down his cheeks he thanked the Finns for their spirit of forgiveness. It was a beautiful moment, and for me powerful, compelling, confirmation of the triumph of generosity over vindictiveness, a lesson above all others that a hateful world needs to learn.

On December 20, 1947, my European service ended and I flew home to take up new duties as assistant director of AFSC's Youth Services Division. It was the beginning of 23 years as an AFSC staff member, in a variety of assignments including assistant to Clarence Pickett, the committee's renowned executive secretary, director of U.S. programs, director of information services, and associate executive secretary.

Ten days after my return, on January 1, 1948, I married Betty Summers, the wisest decision of my life.

Part Two

THE AMERICAN FRIENDS SERVICE COMMITTEE

Five

━━►◆◄━━

What is the AFSC?

The American Friends Service Committee, though tiny internationally, is the largest Quaker agency in the world. Founded in 1917 with the dual mission of ministering to war victims in Europe and providing a channel of service for young Friends and others whose conscience would not let them serve in the military, the AFSC has carried forward three centuries of Quaker witness for peace and justice in the wider world.

Its field of operations is not the classroom nor the library nor the pulpit, important as those venues are. It is in those places where violence and oppression, hatred and poverty, tear apart the fabric of human society, trying, in William Penn's words, "to see what love can do."

I was drawn to it because the years in Europe in the wake of war changed my life. I was no longer interested in pursuing the business career of earlier years. Living amid suffering made me want to devote my life to doing what I could to strengthen peace and broaden justice in a nation where wealth and power made it at once the world's greatest threat and its greatest source of hope.

I entered its service in 1948, and for more than half a century it has played a major role in my life, as sometime administrator of its U.S. programs, counselor to its regional offices, editor of various of its publications, traveler through-out the world on its behalf, chairman of its Board of Directors, and its servant in troubled places.

From the perspective of these endeavors, AFSC's distinc-tiveness rests on its unwavering commitment to nonviolence and the faith that love overcomes. Its response to gospel imperatives has never been *"yes, but."* It has been *"yes, therefore."* There may be no other agency that has followed this ideology in so many ways, in so many places, and under so many conditions.

The AFSC's work is global. In Asia, Africa, the Middle East, and Central and South America, it has worked at the grass roots in development programs to lift the quality of life. It offers material aid and comfort to refugees and war victims. It has brought together moderates on both sides in

"Taking food supplies from the truck to the school." (Italy, 1946)

78

In St. Petersburg (then called Leningrad) standing in the square in front of the Hermitage. In 1955 Stephen was one of the first American civilians to enter the Soviet Union after World War II. He traveled with an AFSC delegation that sought to promote peace at the height of the cold war.

areas of conflict to find avenues of conciliation. It has promoted exchanges and conferences across battle lines. In the United States, the AFSC has been a leader in the peace movement. It has opposed military adventures in Korea, Southeast Asia, and Central America, called for greatly expanded humanitarian aid to poor nations, supported the United Nations, opposed nuclear testing, and burgeoning military budgets. It has reached out to Native Americans, migrants, and illegals, pushed for fair treatment of prisoners, campaigned against capital punishment, and joined civil rights leaders on ending discrimination in employment, education, and housing.

During my years with it, as the demands of power politics have led to ever changing alliances, the AFSC has found itself with a variety of transient bedfellows as it has gone about its manifold enterprises. It has been called unpatriotic, charged with undermining law and consorting with fascists, communists, socialists, and isolationists. During one week in 1962, when I was its acting head, we came under simultaneous attack in Richmond, Indiana, for the alleged pro-communist character of a high school work camp and in Leningrad, USSR, for being fascist lackeys in the conduct of a student seminar. In both we were pursuing our standard course, refusing to make devils out of enemies, and exploring approaches to conflict that neither surrendered in the face of evil nor compelled us to do evil in the name of doing good.

AFSC Archives

"A member of the Quaker transport unit built these children a dollhouse." (St. Nazaire, France, 1948)

The AFSC, like every human enterprise, sometimes disappoints, but I honor it still for being out in the world year after year, grubbing around amid the ugly realities of violence and hatred, seeking to feed the hungry, reconcile the estranged, and restore faith to the despairing. In so doing it has helped to breathe new life and meaning into Jesus' message for our time. Love, persistent and enduring, does overcome.

An experience I had with the AFSC in El Salvador tells me why I have loved and served it for so long. I had gone there to evaluate a wartime refugee project. While there I had a phone call from Charlie Clements, an ex-Air Force pilot in Vietnam who had had opportunities to visit province hospitals and had been so shocked by the suffering his bombing raids had caused that he refused to fly anymore. Charlie eventually obtained his release, returned to the U.S., went to medical school, and ended up a Quaker doctor ministering to several thousand villagers in the hills of El Salvador. He had heard I was in San Salvador. "Steve," he said, "I've learned that some of my former patients have fled and they're in a refugee camp on the edge of the city. I'm going to go visit them later this afternoon. Would you like to come along?" I said I would.

On the way to meet him I passed the American Embassy. It was an imposing structure, a great stone pile, virtually windowless, surrounded then by double walls 12 or 15 feet high, with pillboxes on all four corners manned by armed marines. The only entrance was by a serpentine path through steel posts embedded in concrete. Between the posts were 55-gallon barrels filled with cement. Embassy cars were equipped with one-way glass—passengers could see out, but no one could see in—and vehicles leaving the embassy were followed by a station wagon filled with soldiers riding shotgun. This was a country which was our ally, and to which we had given hundreds of millions of dollars in aid, and yet we had to make of our embassy an impregnable fortress.

I met Charlie. He had a couple of young men with him, one of whom was carrying a folded wheelchair. We entered the dusty, ramshackle, rundown camp, teeming with men, women, and children in rags. We were barely in the gate when someone spotted Charlie and called his name. There was an instant rush of people to his side. They shouted and laughed. Everyone was trying to hug him at the same time. Women were handing him their children. Sometimes he had three in his arms at the same time. It was pandemonium. When things calmed down a bit, Charlie asked for a little boy he'd cared for when the child was a baby and a polio victim. He'd heard he was there, and sure enough his mother carried in the little fellow, now five, and gave him to Charlie. Charlie put him down in the wheelchair and told him to "put [your] hands on the wheels and push." The child did and moved forward a few feet. Charlie said, "Do it again," and he moved forward another three or four feet. The little kid was laughing, but when he turned around a look of wonder came over his face and he burst into tears. It was the first time in his life he had ever propelled himself. Charlie cried; I cried; everybody cried; and the little boy wheeled around the camp with about 100 children running after him. I asked myself—my God, my God—what is the path to peace? Is it in those cars with their one-way glass and their shotgun escort, or is it in Charlie's wheelchair? The American Friends Service Committee bets its life on Charlie's wheelchair.

Six

━━►◆◄━━

DISSENT: UPSTREAM IN TROUBLED WATERS

FOR SWIMMING UPSTREAM, one of my role models has been Fred Libby, who headed the National Council for the Prevention of War, a Washington-based organization between the two World Wars. Fred was indefatigable, ever hopeful, ever buoyant, ever certain that Friends' views would one day prevail. The council regularly beat the drums in support of peaceful initiatives around the world and against all expression of U.S. militarism.

After one particularly bruising campaign against a military appropriations bill in the House of Representatives, the Libby position went down to crushing defeat. Next morning his office was a morgue, its exhausted staff dispirited and discouraged. Not Fred. He bounced in with all his customary enthusiasm.

"How can you be so cheerful? We were buried!"

"What's the matter with you people?" said Fred. "We got 16 votes! Last year, we only got 12!"

I like doggedness. I like buoyancy. And minority voices, even small ones, can be harbingers of change. Historically, it has been the quiet rebels, the men and women of conscience, standing alone and peacefully affirming, at whatever cost, the truth as they saw it, who have lifted humanity out of barbarism. So it was with Socrates and with Martin Luther

King. These spirits, far more than the warriors, the captains, and the kings, are the ones who have purchased human freedom and human dignity, with their own blood, not the blood of their enemies. In the 17th century, 40,000 Quakers burnished the tradition by lying in English dungeons for witnessing to religious freedom. In more recent times, Friends, with their reputation for integrity, their testimony to the sacredness of human life and to human perfectibility, have both the credentials and the spiritual basis for carrying forward pioneering witness, but haven't often enough had the fire of conviction to do so. Convenience too easily takes precedence over principle.

In a speech at Haverford College, at the height of the shameful Joseph McCarthy era, the great president and chancellor of the University of Chicago, Robert Maynard Hutchins, chided Friends: "You Quakers are the last licensed radicals left in America, and you're not using your license!"

The American Friends Service Committee has tried to use its license. It has done pacifist battle with the voices of political correctness on many fronts over many years: challenging the view that peace depends on military power; that our lion's share of the world's wealth carries with it little responsibility to lift the burdens of poverty elsewhere; that tougher sentences and more prisons are the answer to crime; that billions must be spent on drug interdiction but little on treatment and prevention; that capital punishment is appropriate and just; that corporate welfare is acceptable but human welfare is not—to name a few of the AFSC's concerns.

All these expressions of accepted wisdom are backed with enormous resources. The army can pay millions for 30-second Super Bowl commercials urging young Americans to join "to be all you can be." The media, the Congress, the administration, corporate lobbies, labor unions, and other private institutions bombard us daily with the mantras of conventional wisdom.

How one carries on an encounter with these juggernauts is crucial. Clarity and volume are important in getting attention, but impact depends even more on the way minority views are put forward. Traditionally, Quakers have been advocates challenging the status quo or reconcilers mediating conflicts. Both have long and honorable traditions; both carry risks. The passion of the advocate can appear as self-righteousness and closed minds. The gentleness of the reconciler can weaken needed challenge.

These problems have provoked friction among Friends, but the conflict need not exist. John Woolman's labors among slaveholding Quakers in the early years of the 19th century so combined passion with a loving spirit that he was at the same time both an advocate and a reconciler—a welcome guest even when he insisted on sleeping in the barn rather than accepting the service of family slaves.

I found these same qualities in Margarethe Lachmund, the brave German Friend who had dared to speak truth to Nazi power. Her daily sense of the immanence of God's love gave her the courage to challenge evil, but with such a gentle spirit that she was spared. Her example, together with the witness of Friends of my father's generation, showed me the road I wanted to travel when I came home from my years in Europe.

There was soon an opportunity to walk it. An emerging cold war and the mindless anti-communism evoked by Senator Joseph McCarthy were creating such a climate of fear that the foundations of our society were threatened. There may never have been a time in our country when voices of dissent were more needed.

For most Americans the price of dissent was high: loss of livelihood, ostracism, charges of disloyalty, even persecution. For me the price was much lower. I had a supporting family, a supporting community of Friends, and a secure livelihood. I also had personal qualities that needed tempering: too much volatility in debate, and too little discipline in remembering that my goal was to persuade, not to score points or to "win."

I did try in those years to use my Quaker license, denouncing the indiscriminate blackening of reputations and the outrageous tactics of the House Un-American Activities Committee. I refused to sign loyalty oaths or cooperate in FBI investigations of others' loyalty, limiting my response to expressions of confidence in the individuals' integrity.

I tested my license in a tour of the U.S. after I had been a member of a small delegation of Quakers that traveled 12,000 miles through the Soviet Union in 1955, making 153 speeches in 50 days, trying to report fairly on conditions and put a human face on the enemy. Many of my sponsors were nervous that I might be a leftist and asked me to be sure to wave the flag. I managed to escape overt outrage except in Texas, where a well-organized women's group calling themselves the Minute Women attacked me as a communist. I tried to respond in good spirit, but was tempted to call them the Mi-nute Women.

Even these relatively modest dissents made me a target for J. Edgar Hoover's anti-communist sleuths, as I discovered when I responded to an invitation to apply for the position of the New York representative of the High Commissioner for Refugees, based in Geneva. I thought the opportunity to become an international civil servant in the United Nations would be valuable enough to warrant taking a leave of absence from the Friends Service Committee.

Five weeks later I received a formal interrogatory from the International Loyalty Review Board, advising me that my application could not be processed pending satisfactory answers to six allegations that raised questions about my loyalty to the United States. The questions:

1. In 1948, I had been a member of a committee to oppose the Mundt-Nixon Anti-Communist Bill (later the McCarran Internal Security Act) sponsored by the Civil Rights Congress, an organization designated by the attorney general as subversive.

2. I had been a member of a committee to welcome the dean of the Canterbury Cathedral to Philadelphia (Hewlett Johnson, the so-called Red Dean, who had been denied a visa to enter the United States).

3. I was known to have had contacts in 1953 with Jack Zucker, a Philadelphia leader of the Civil Rights Congress.

4. In 1954, I had been among those who had signed a letter to the attorney general protesting the use of notorious liars and informers as prosecution witnesses in trials of alleged leftists under the Smith Act.

5. I was known to have expressed pleasure over the Supreme Court's reversal of the conviction of Steve Nelson, a Communist Party leader, accused of seeking the overthrow of the U.S. Government.

6. I was known to have been the speaker at a forum of the Yonkers (New York) Committee for Peace, a communist-affiliated organization.

These allegations were true, as I would have been glad to report if asked, along with the context in which they took place, and saved the taxpayers' money used to ferret them out. As it was, I had no difficulty explaining why I had acted as charged, and in five more weeks I received word that I was no longer viewed as a threat to the country. The only trouble was that by this time the New York post had been filled, and I never got to serve as a UN staff member.

This episode illustrates the privileged position that permitted me to pursue my concerns without the burden of fear that others faced, but more important, it shows the depth of McCarthyism's invasion into people's lives. The fact that thousands of investigators were snooping around to dig up such violations of political correctness as those they hung on me illumines the climate that gripped the nation. I was inconvenienced and lost an opportunity to serve the United Nations, but any one of those six charges could have cost another person a job or a reputation.

Fortunately, McCarthy was brought down and some sanity returned to American life, but there have still been occasions when conscience compelled costly dissent. One such followed the passage of the 1986 Immigration Reform and Control Act, which, among its provisions, required employers to extract from every employee proof of legal residence in the United States, a device designed to drive "illegals" out of the country by excluding them from a job. I acknowledged the right of the government to control immigration, but thought that the criminalization of work was a cruel approach to the problem. Far better would be to review U.S. war-making and economic policies that were driving desperate people across borders to feed their families. Signing an I-9 form would make me an agent of the Immigration and Naturalization Service, a role I refused to play. When Haverford College presented me with one as a necessary condition for my employment to teach a course on

International Mediation, I declined to sign it. Without my doing so, the College could not pay me. This left me with two choices: cancel my course or teach as a volunteer. I chose the latter—a small sacrifice for me, an impossible one for many.

A form of dissent open to us in our free society is through participation in demonstrations—marches and vigils— calling for enactment of legislation to widen the parameters of justice or to protest government policies one believes to be wrong. Public witness is a powerful way to draw attention to minority concerns that so often are ignored by the media or buried on back pages. The civil rights movement, under Dr. King's leadership, used massive demonstrations in Washington and disciplined nonviolent marches by black Americans to have an impact on our nation's awareness of the injustices inflicted on our African American citizens.

I was a foot soldier in many of these demonstrations and was among the thousands who marched across the bridge at Selma, Alabama, in the wake of a brutal assault by local and state police on King's peaceful legions a few days earlier.

Selma had a tragic dimension for me. An AFSC colleague, James Reeb, was brutally attacked by white hoodlums and the tires shot out from the ambulance taking him, mortally wounded, to a Birmingham hospital. When I heard on the radio what had happened, I drove immediately to Birmingham and was with his parents when they decided that life support should be withdrawn.

The Vietnam War was another cause that provoked protest demonstrations. Fresh from Vietnam myself, I was an organizer of an early Quaker march that brought enough Friends to Washington to circle the Pentagon in a silent two-hour vigil asking for complete U.S. withdrawal from its ill-conceived adventures in Southeast Asia. Most

Cary Family Archives (photo: Paul S. Buck)

Stephen frequently picketed the White House during the Vietnam War.

moving was a massive candlelight march in the early 1970s that lasted well into the night, with 50,000 marchers stopping one-by-one in front of the White House to call out the name of an American soldier who had been killed.

In the spring of 1969, I joined five religious leaders in fasting for a week in silent vigil at the White House fence to protest President Nixon's escalation of the war with heavy bombing attacks on Hanoi. The group included the Moderator of the Presbyterian Church, U.S.A., the Episcopal Bishop of the Diocese of Pennsylvania, the Methodist Bishop of Wisconsin, the Chief Rabbi of Washington, and the Catholic President of La Salle College. We dined on V-8 juice, slept in the Florida Avenue Friends Meeting House, and stood silently in front of the White House from 8 in the morning until 6 at night. It was a wonderful week, with joyous and distinguished company sharing in humor and worship. We responded when passersby asked questions, which many hundreds did. One such was Carl McIntire, the prominent fundamentalist preacher and anti-communist, who strode up to Robert DeWitt one morning and, towering over the slight Episcopal bishop, looked sternly down at him and said: "Bishop, I hope you realize that what you are doing is playing right into the hands of the communists!"

"Carl," said the bishop, "our aim is to play into the hands of God."

Over the course of the war, I became familiar with the White House fence and with Lafayette Park across the street, where I made several speeches. Some years later, when Betty and I were invited to the swearing-in of our friend William T. Coleman as President Ford's secretary of transportation, we were enjoying the reception in the White House when Bill introduced us to the president. "Gee, Bill, you've invited a lot of Quakers down here today."

"Yes, Mr. President, I invited them all to come on one condition."

"What was that?"

"That they all agree not to picket the White House for two weeks!"

"Yes, Mr. President," said Betty, "my husband has spent a lot of time on the other side of your fence."

The president laughed and replied: "Mrs. Cary, if you want to protest, that's a good place to do it!"

Visiting AFSC programs around the world, exploring new opportunities to ease suffering, opening avenues of reconciliation in troubled places, and meeting with moderate leaders on both sides of a conflict gave me insights into the grievances and aspirations of the grass roots and what might be done to make lives easier. Many of these experiences I reported on to officials and policy makers, both on

Cary Family Archives

Stephen shares a front row seat at a peace rally with
Representative Paul McCloskey and Senator Eugene McCarthy

site and back in the United States. Results varied widely, from thoughtful exchanges to empty reception.

In the first category were visits with John Whitehead, undersecretary of state during Ronald Reagan's presidency. John is a distinguished Haverford College alumnus who saw me on my return from visits to Central America, where the United States was heavily involved in the civil wars raging in El Salvador and Nicaragua and in the fragile situations in Guatemala and Honduras. On those visits, I knew that he had access to important information that I didn't have, in-cluding diplomatic and military intelligence and corporate evaluations important in shaping policy. At the same time, I suggested there was one area that was seriously undervalued in U.S. thinking: the mood of the campesinos and the little people who make up the majority of the population of all the countries in the region. I thought that the misreading of the rice paddy loyalties and grievances in Vietnam had contributed to our failed policies there, and that we were making the same mistake in Central America. There it was groups like the Jesuits, Franciscans, Maryknolls, Mennonites, and Quakers who best understood this dimension of the Central American scene, a dimension that in the end could prove decisive in the outcome. I told him of some of my visits with these groups to places where no American officials had been for two years for security reasons. John Whitehead was in no position to comment substantively on these reports and judgments, but he always listened and raised thoughtful questions—all that a minority voice can ask for.

I had similar encounters in the Middle East, where the AFSC had contacts with moderate voices on both sides of the Palestinian-Israeli conflict. On one of my visits to the region with a small delegation of Christian and Jewish religious leaders, we were able, with their help, to meet with

Yasser Arafat, the Palestinian leader. Picked up at midnight by two black limousines with submachine guns on their back seats, and driven around Amman, Jordan, for 40 minutes to disguise our destination, we passed a heavily-armed check-point and at 1 a.m. entered a house. We had an hour's conversation with Arafat. The weight of our message was to urge him to remove the inflammatory language in the Palestine Liberation Organization protocol that called for driving the Israelis into the sea, arguing that, as long as those words remained in the PLO's basic document, there could be no peace settlement. Arafat agreed that it had to go, but insisted it be retained as a bargaining chip in negotiations. He had no American-equipped army to bring to the table as a power base, and he had to have something to give in return for concessions he would demand. It was a valuable exchange, remarkably candid, especially considering that we had two rabbis on our side of the table.

On another visit, I had sharply contrasting meetings that challenged accepted wisdom. The first was an evening spent with Abu Jihad Khalil al-Wajir, the PLO war minister, a man at the very least complicit in planning bombing attacks against Israel. The other was a meeting with Israel Harel, the president of the Israeli Council of Jewish Settlements and architect of the principal barrier to any peaceful settlement of the bitter conflict between Jews and Arabs. I looked forward to neither one, knowing how sharply I disagreed with the commitments of both.

My interview with Abu Jihad took place in his home. With him were his two sons, one of whom was wearing a T-shirt with "Coca Cola" emblazoned on it and playing with a toy truck. The other son sat on his father's lap. His wife served us tea and cookies, listening silently to our conversation. Abu Jihad spoke of the terrible suffering his family had endured when he was a boy and they had to flee their home in Jaffa. He hoped the day would come when Jew and Arab could again live peacefully together as they had for centuries. As strife eased, he thought the need for an Israeli state would wither. I shared his hope, but said it would never be facilitated or accompanied by the withering away of Israel. He and those in the Arab world would have to realize that the dream of Jews for 2,000 years to return from the Diaspora was deep in the heart of every Jew and would never be abandoned. We didn't carry that point any further, but conversation flowed easily as each of us tried to listen to the other. Abu Jihad was a hard-line, violent man, but he had a soft side that could have been lifted up had conditions permitted it. I saw that side of him, and I was saddened when a few months later he was assassi-nated by an Israeli commando team that stole ashore in the middle of the night and in a daring and widely celebrated raid broke into his Tunis home and killed him.

A week after my meeting with Abu Jihad I drove out to Jericho to meet with Israel Harel. I had long regarded the Israeli settlement program as ill-advised and the biggest barrier to a peace settlement. Harel at first declined to see me. I was a Quaker, and he didn't like Quakers. When I told him that was just why I wanted to meet him, he relented and the appointment was made.

To my astonishment, and to his as well, we had a good talk. There was no wavering from his belief that the Jewish state rightfully should extend all the way to the Jordan River—at a minimum—but he was willing at least to listen to my plea for Palestinian rights, and pressed me for information about Quakers. He found our beliefs personally appealing, but only possible in secure America and not in beleaguered Israel surrounded by enemies. After 90 minutes, he said he had to leave for another appointment, but could we continue our discussion the next morning at breakfast in the Jerusalem Hilton? I said I'd be delighted, but where in the city was the Hilton? He exploded. "Who are you Quakers? You're supposed to be a prominent representative of your faith, but you drive out here in a broken-down old car that I doubt will make it back to Jerusalem, and now you tell me you don't know where the Hilton is. Everybody knows where that is. You seem to know what you're talking about, and obviously you don't squander your money on yourselves, but I can't figure you out."

We did meet for breakfast. How I wished I could have found a setting where these two men, so ready to kill each other, could instead sit down together and talk! Even hard-line enemies have a human side. I've met a number of alleged devils, and sometimes I haven't found that side, but I believe that no devil is beyond redemption, and that there is always a possibility of reaching across mounds of hatred.

I've had my failures. One was during the same period when I was in touch with John Whitehead. I had returned from a visit to Pinochet's Chile, badly shaken by the palpable fear that gripped the poblaciones of Santiago, by the submachine guns and water cannons on its street corners, and by the suffering of the Mapuche Indians, whose way of life was being cruelly destroyed. I had been stunned by AFSC colleagues on the way in from the airport who cautioned me not to intercede if I saw someone being beaten up in the street. "You won't be killed, because you're an American. You'll just be deported. And if you do get into trouble, don't call us, call the U.S. Embassy. They can help you. We can't, and we'll be deported."

I had gone from Chile directly to Nicaragua, then governed by Daniel Ortega, the Sandinista leader. There, too, were some of the trappings of authoritarian regimes: press censorship, one-party elections, and ubiquitous propaganda. But Managua was not Santiago. There was none of the fear I had found in Santiago. Visitors could walk its streets day or night. Meetings protesting government policies were held openly in city hotels or other venues. I visited many rural communities where schools and health clinics were opening, many of them in "intentional communities" governed by the "other Catholic Church," dissidents from the official church with its ties to Rome.

Eager to share these experiences with a Washington so strongly allied with General Pinochet in Chile and with the Contra forces in Nicaragua, I sought appointments in Washington at the State Department, the Congress, and the National Security Council. At the Council it turned out to be with a Marine colonel named Oliver North. I didn't know the colonel but I soon would, when his connections with the Contras became public a few weeks later. North was an impressive figure in his smart uniform, flanked by U.S. and Marine flags. He was welcoming and articulate. I looked forward to an interesting exchange; it wasn't. I tried to be balanced in my observations, but he saw me from the outset as a bumpkin, well-intentioned but naive, an easy victim of communist propaganda. These shortcomings had prevented me from seeing the real Managua with its thousands of political prisoners and its ruthless repression. I asked him if he had recently been in Chile or Nicaragua. He said he was fully briefed by authoritative sources. The interview was a waste of time for both of us. There was no communication either way. What could have changed that?

From these and other public expressions of dissent and minority views, my quarter-century with the Service Committee was filled with writing and speaking about concerns on the Quaker agenda. I wrote AFSC position papers,

97

copy for newspaper statements, and articles for the religious press. I participated in more extensive studies with prominent Friends called together to draft Quaker proposals for easing the cold war or conflicts in the Middle East and Southeast Asia.

The most useful and well regarded of these efforts was as the staff representative on a committee of distinguished pacifist leaders who came together in a serious attempt to design a pacifist approach to the U.S.-USSR conflict, and to examine its relevance in an atomic age. We spent a summer week together at Haverford College in intense, and, at times, brilliant debate, with discussion spilling over into college washrooms at 2 a.m. Most difficult was how harshly we should picture the USSR, a conflict we might not have resolved without the presence of Bayard Rustin, the great civil rights leader, who combined brilliant intellect with a reconciling spirit that made him a key figure in our deliberations.

Bayard had to leave a day early, and on his last afternoon asked that his name be left off the list of authors. He was gay, at a time when homosexuality was grounds for imprisonment, and he felt his name would hurt sales of our study. We refused. The next morning, we met together in a Quaker meeting for worship, and out of the gathered silence Bayard rose and sang two beautiful spirituals: "Nobody knows the trouble I've seen, nobody knows but Jesus," and "There is a balm in Gilead that makes the whole world free." Then he said simply: "I am at peace. Please leave my name off." We wept, but we did.

From that day on, Bayard Rustin was my brother—a whole, beautiful human being. From that day on, I have never been able to assign a moral dimension to sexual orientation, and I can never demean the integrity of my brothers and sisters who are homosexual by referring to them as following a "chosen lifestyle." Bayard gave me a meaning of diversity and community that I treasure.

Our study was published under the title *Speak Truth to Power* and became the largest selling piece in AFSC history. The La Follette-founded *Progressive* magazine devoted a whole issue to it under the heading "Is There Another Way?" assembling five prominent Americans: George Kennan, Karl Menninger, Norman Thomas, Reinhold Niebuhr, and Dwight MacDonald, to submit critiques. Robert Pickus, the driving force behind the project, and I were given space for a rejoinder, which we drafted over three 15-hour days in a Boston hotel room.

Speaking was just as important an avenue of dissent as writing in voicing Quaker concerns over the years. I've endured endless potluck suppers and frequented more

Cary Family Archives

Stephen fasted for peace outside the White House during the Vietnam War with other religious leaders.

church basements, classrooms, lecture halls, and radio and TV outlets than I can count, covering more topics than I possibly could have been competent to speak to.

Through all these channels, I've made a career of swimming upstream. It's been hectic and hard on my family, but it's been a happy adventure. I'm grateful to have lived in a land where dissent is possible and where no one lacks daily opportunities to offer it.

And not every dissent called for long faces and weighty problems. Take the case of a gentle lady of 90 who served as a welcoming receptionist at the old Twelfth Street Meeting House in central Philadelphia at a time when the American Legion had its national convention in town. The Women's Auxiliary had asked for and been granted the use of the Meeting House for a midday meeting. The ladies duly arrived, and as proceedings were about to start, two of the bemedaled organizers hurried out to the receptionist and asked for the American flag.

"We don't have an American flag."

"You must have an American flag. Why don't you have an American flag?"

"I don't really know, but maybe it's because we don't think God is an American."

Seven

═══➤◆⬅═══

DISSENT: CIVIL DISOBEDIENCE

BEYOND CONVENTIONAL AVENUES OF DISSENT, there is civil disobedience, at once the most powerful and most dangerous instrument of social change. It is dissent outside the law, dramatically challenging the status quo, to be undertaken only when an issue becomes so compelling that conscience demands a visible and public response.

Civil disobedience has a long and illustrious history in the millennia of human struggle for dignity and freedom. As early as the 5th century B.C. it was the centerpiece of one of the world's great literary masterpieces, Sophocles' *Antigone*. It was practiced by the Hebrew prophets and by leaders of other faiths, including Jesus in his day. The history of the Christian era is replete with acts of brave dissenters who stood against repression or bigotry or dogma, often at the price of martyrdom. In more modern times, the names Thoreau and Gandhi and King are among those whose deliberate violation of unjust laws has proved a blessing to the human family.

But civil disobedience improperly exercised can have dangerous consequences. Society, if it is to be ordered and just, must function within a framework of law, and when one deliberately breaks laws, one risks undermining the foundations of social order. This happened in our country during the Prohibition era, when the sale, purchase, or possession of alcoholic beverages was illegal. Millions of Americans defied the law, buying liquor from bootleggers and patronizing secret "speakeasies" where it was served behind locked doors. Law was sneered at. Lawlessness and corruption flourished.

What safeguards civil disobedience against such an outcome? Because there have been times in my life when conscience has driven me to stand outside the law, I have tried to answer that question for myself, and established six guidelines that I must observe. Three are immutable and must be observed under all circumstances, and three must be weighed, but are not absolute. The first three:

1. Civil disobedience must be directed at a goal that will contribute to a more just society, and not to personal gratification. A selfish motive merits contempt and destroys the witness.

2. Civil disobedience must, under all circumstances, be carried out nonviolently. No matter the provocation, the civilly disobedient must avoid violence. With it, the cause is lost. The issue becomes law and order. Authorities know how to deal with violence. What baffles them, and provokes thought, is nonviolence. This was the great strength of the civil rights revolution of the 1960s. Who can forget the electrifying impact on the nation of black Americans' response to Bull Connor's attack dogs in Birmingham? Am I prepared to accept this hard discipline?

3. The civilly disobedient must understand and expect punishment. The duty of authorities is to uphold the law and to punish lawbreakers. Am I aware that

cheerful acceptance of that outcome is part of the persuasive process? Am I strong enough to reflect it?

All of these are "musts." The violation of any destroys the witness. There are three others to weigh:

4. Civil disobedience should be a last resort, not the first. Have I made an effort to seek my goal within the law? Circumstances and the compulsion of conscience can sometimes override this requirement.

5. Civil disobedience should be carried out openly, not in secret. Openness gives integrity to the action. It adds to persuasiveness. But openness may not be possible. I spent an evening in 1946 with André Trocmé, the brave French pastor of the village of Le Chambon-sur-Lignon, who had led his community in hiding more than 2,500 Jews during the Nazi occupation of France. He told me of his anguish at having to abandon a lifelong commitment to openness and truth-telling, and to re-sort daily to secrecy, lies, and deception in order to save lives. There are priorities among values.

6. Civil disobedience should not be carried on in ways that block others from doing what they believe is right. Con-science can also overrule this consideration, but only with recognition of the added and heavy responsibility assumed in doing so.

The first time I tested these guidelines was in 1968. Two concerns came together to compel my conscience. The first was my involvement in plans for the Poor People's March on Washington, when I had my only opportunity to work personally with Martin Luther King and his immediate asso-ciates. The American Friends Service Committee had the responsibility of assuring the participation of the Appalachian and Native American communities on the march. In working with Dr. King's Southern Christian Leadership Conference, I became personally committed to the project, which took place in June 1968—alas, without the leadership of King, who fell in April to an assassin's bullet.

During this same time span, I was active in pressing for federal legislation to provide food stamps to all who were too poor to feed their families but unable to qualify for them under restrictive state laws. A colleague had returned from a trip South and told me of seeing children in a Memphis hospital with stomachs distended from hunger—American children literally starving because residency requirements in their home states prevented their parents from receiving food stamps. I was outraged. No child in affluent America should be left hungry.

I was caught up in this issue when the Poor People's March descended on Washington, with thousands camped on the Mall. One of the demands of the march organizers was for food stamp legislation. On June 23, Andrew Young of the Leadership Conference called me to say there would be a food stamp demonstration the next day, and did I want to join the march? I did.

He met me at Union Station, and we joined some 400 marchers on Pennsylvania Avenue already en route to the Capitol. It was surely the most ragtag army ever to try to carry a message to the U.S. Congress, but we never reached our goal. Two hundred police blocked our path at the edge of the Capitol grounds. Their commander announced through a bullhorn that we could go no further. Our leader, Ralph Abernathy, said we were entirely peaceful and wanted only to exercise our constitutional right to petition the Congress for the redress of grievances. The officer was not impressed.

He gave us a choice—either go back across the street or face immediate arrest.

I knew I wasn't going back. I hadn't planned on civil disobedience, but I stood where I was. So did Abernathy and Young and about 200 of their troops. The bullhorn announced our arrest. For 20 minutes there was silent confrontation in the hot sun. Then police vans appeared and we were carted off, 20 to 25 at a time, to precinct stations across Washington. There we were relieved of belts, watches, and wallets, booked, and locked up.

The cells in my precinct were small, about 5x7 feet, and each had to accommodate seven of us marchers. Four sat on a metal bench, two sat on the floor, and one on the only furnishing, a toilet. It was the Poor People's encampment in miniature: two mountain men from Tennessee, one of whom was blind, two Hispanics, one African American, one Native American—and one aging Caucasian agency executive.

Our little company remained in these quarters for nine hours, nourished only by a baloney sandwich and an occasional cup of water provided by a sympathetic sergeant. It was wretchedly hot. Finally, at nine in the evening, we were loaded into a van and taken to a courthouse, where 64 of us were locked in a large, brilliantly-lit basement room with a marble floor. Space on the hard floor was at a premium, becoming available only when someone abandoned his spot to use the toilet. About midnight, I inherited a space next to a young man with a huge crown of black hair and an enormous beard to match. I was marveling at this bear-like creature when he pulled himself up on one elbow and said: "Aren't you Steve Cary? I had a date with your daughter last week!" I didn't sleep well, astonished at Anne's taste in men and stiffened by unyielding marble.

At three the next afternoon, after a short interview with a court-appointed attorney, I stood before a judge, entered a plea of *nolo contendere*, and, with his permission, made a statement. I wrote it down afterward:

Your Honor, I want to say first of all that I respect the law, and do not take casually a decision to violate it. This is in fact the first time I have done so. There are two reasons that compel my conscience in this case. First, I consider it intolerable that in this rich country of ours any child anywhere under any circumstances should have to go to bed hungry. The Secretary of Agriculture can advance his legalisms, and the Congress can talk righteously about refusing to be coerced, but the fact remains that it is wicked and wrong that food stamps are not made available without charge to those who have no funds to pay for them. The rich are subsidized with crop payments; the rich can coerce Congress with their lobbies; our nation can pour 30 billion dollars a year into destroying a poor peasant culture 10,000 miles away; but the poor in America must continue to starve. This is wrong, your Honor, absolutely wrong. I have tried to protest through legal channels; now I must make my protest more visible by making it more costly. It seems to me a responsible citizen can do no less.

Second, I believe that the options are running out for our country. There is not much time left for us to redeem the American promise to our poor and dispossessed, for they are not disposed to wait longer. We who are white and affluent must therefore stand behind responsible leadership who crusade for change in peaceful, nonviolent ways, or we shall shortly be confronted with irresponsible leadership who crusade for change with revolutionary violence. When this happens—and if we fail now, I deeply believe that it will—our choice will be between repression and insurrection, and neither of these is to me a viable option for a free society. Therefore, your Honor, I feel compelled to identify myself wholly and without reservation with the Southern Christian Leadership Conference. The nation honors Dr. King in death. I must honor what he stood for in life.

The judge responded, "I respect your views, Mr. Cary, but my duty is to uphold the law which you willfully broke in disobeying orders. Fifteen days." I thanked him.

A number of judges were called into service that day, and sentences varied widely. Mine was in the middle range. One young Catholic priest I met in jail was given three months. He explained that his judge was Catholic and disapproved of his actions, underlining his disapproval with scripture. "We had a little contest in biblical exegesis. I won, but he had the last word."

It took five tedious hours to process me and my van partners into the Washington City jail. First, we spent an hour and a half in a stifling windowless room, just sitting. Then we were ordered to strip and were lodged, naked, in another windowless room, this one heavily air-conditioned. Here we shivered for 45 minutes, taken out one by one for fingerprinting and checking our orifices for smuggled contraband. Then supper, and more waiting.

Finally, we were escorted to cell block four. It was under

the roof, a sort of dormitory that 25 of us marchers shared with a number of others already in residence as guests of the city for more standard offenses. The only furnishings were double-deck bunks and a TV that blared ceaselessly all day long, with programming tightly controlled by the earlier arrivals. We could exercise for an hour each day on an outside court. We could play cards. We could lie on our bunks and read, drawing on a bizarre literature shelf with titles ranging from the Hornblower adventure stories to an illustrated study of Byzantine silver coins. We were roused daily at 6 a.m. for the first of several prisoner counts, and the lights dimmed at 11 p.m.

For meals we lined up in an adjacent area, passing en route through another large dorm-like room with 70 double-deck bunks. The occupants were 140 black men locked up in April on looting charges in the riots following Dr. King's assassination. They had been there for three months. None had seen a lawyer or had a day in court. There was no chance to talk to them.

The worst problem was the heat. An exhaust fan didn't work. Temperatures were well into the 90s even at night. Once I was taken to meet my only visitor, a lawyer friend, in the visitors' area. Here the inmate is locked into a narrow space with glass on one side through which I could see my friend as we talked by phone. When he left, I lined up with two other occupants waiting for release from our special oven. Nobody came. A prison chaplain explained that there had been a miscount of the prisoners and everyone was frozen where he was pending a recount. It made no difference that our release into the larger visitor area would not have affected the count, since it was all a single counting unit, but the book said stay where you are, and in the criminal justice system the book governs.

For a long, painful 90 minutes, we lay on the floor in our stifling little prison. My head screamed. I felt faint, soaked in perspiration. The temperature climbed to over a 100°. When we were finally rescued, I managed to keep quiet, but John Woolman and Margarethe Lachmund would have given me a failing grade for attitude.

Another vexing problem was the misspelling of my name. This had occurred on entry, where I was booked as Corey, not Cary. Despite heroic efforts at correction, I remained Corey and was discharged as Corey. The first result was that no one could find me. There was no Stephen Cary on jail records. For 48 hours all the American Friends Service Committee could tell my ever-patient but worried wife was that "we think he's in jail, but we're not sure." Finally, a U.S. senator was called in to help, and I was in the superintendent's office in ten minutes.

While my identity was still under study, most of my marching colleagues were sent south to a minimum-security facility in Lorton, Virginia. Corey's name was removed from the transfer list because of senatorial inquiries, but Corey's money, clothes, and possessions went as planned. Corey was now without funds. He badly needed them for credit at the prison canteen, where a toothbrush, stamps, and writing paper were available. To meet this crisis, I signed a document declaring myself a pauper, which made me eligible for welfare assistance. One acquisition: a small box of Pebeco tooth powder, dated 1943, a brand long since ordered off the market by the FDA as too abrasive. The D.C. Department of Corrections had probably gotten a special price on the company's remainders.

I did eventually get down to Lorton, thanks to the unexpected arrival in my cellblock of 20 young men from a Quaker conference in New Jersey. They had kept vigil on the food stamp issue on the Capitol steps, and when ordered to leave had declined. This cost them a five-day sentence. This added number of Quaker-related protesters led to the transfer decision, and we were all dispatched 18 miles south, in handcuffs, tailed by a station wagon riding shotgun. It seemed unlikely that a van load of pacifists with only three days left on their sentences would make a break for it, but the book said handcuffs and armed escort.

We looked forward to the more relaxed atmosphere of a minimum-security jail. But not for long. A battery of armed guards awaited us, and as each descended he was seized by two guards, and escorted—still handcuffed—to solitary confinement. No explanation. In due course a mattress, blankets, soap, and supper were handed through the bars.

A few hours later, the superintendent appeared. He let us out of our cells for a meeting in the corridor, informing us that our colleagues were on a work strike and had suffered the loss of all privileges. We were to decide whether we would work. In the meantime, we were permitted to move to a dormitory. The show of toughness on our arrival was designed to make us more cooperative.

Our decision on work baffled the high command. The cause of the strike was perceived discrimination in work assignments. Without evidence ourselves, we decided we should work at least until evidence appeared, but only if we were reunited with our brethren and could share their loss of privileges. The superintendent said okay, but complained that the Quakers were "the most uncooperative cooperative inmates" he had ever had.

Our decision did not please the strikers and produced a three-hour dorm meeting. Unity was never reached, but something else was: an image among the administration of "good" Quakers and "bad" strikers. This was intolerable.

We quit work and joined the strikers. My final days were passed in idleness, punctuated by workshops, religious services, and singing.

What was the impact of this witness? The widespread publicity given to the Poor People's encampment and to our mass act of civil disobedience probably added to the rising tide of indignation over hungry children. Federal legislation mandating free food stamps came a few months later.

As for its impact on me, prison was difficult. Time passed slowly. Processes seemed deliberately dehumanizing. An inmate is a number, especially if he's named Corey and is a pauper. And if he's black and friendless, like those forgotten 140 alleged looters, forget justice. The system seemed mindless. And the oppressive heat of a Washington summer in an old, uninsulated, badly ventilated building didn't help. Looking back, jail time is a rich experience for an affluent Quaker. He gets a new perspective on criminal justice.

And there were exhilarating moments. Food stamp protesters were in all parts of the jail, and more kept coming as encampment leaders organized still more peaceful assaults on the Capitol. As new van loads of marchers entered the jail courtyard, they were always singing the freedom songs that electrified the civil rights movement in those exciting days. Their voices were the signal for the whole jail to erupt in song, with fists shaking from barred windows in an outpouring of solidarity. In those moments I felt wondrously free. My body was locked up, but my spirits soared.

Then there was the companionship of the poor, the only setting where, as a pauper, I could hope to meet them on a level playing field. I remember Charlie especially. Charlie was a drifter—homeless, uneducated, and alcoholic. His language was unprintable—a pity, really, because without it some of the man's character is lost. His age was hard to determine.

Life had treated him harshly. He had few teeth left. He told me he'd only come to the Washington encampment because he'd heard there was cheap liquor and women, and he'd agreed to drive a truck down with supplies. He'd gotten caught up in the food stamp march and ended up in jail.

In that bleak setting, Charlie took center stage. He had a jagged smile, contagious laughter, and a raucous sense of humor. His assessments of our jailing, our guards, and the D.C. justice system, couched in his unique syntax and vocabulary, were pungent and, we thought, accurate. Whenever there were negotiations to be carried on with the authorities, in Washington or in Lorton, Charlie was a member of our team.

His greatest gift was musical. Charlie would wrap toilet paper around a comb, empty the sand from a can for cigarette butts, blow through his comb, and beat the can and his hips in a frenzy. He produced the sound of a full rock band. His laugh and his music filled the tedious hours.

Charlie and I became friends. On our last evening he came to me and said: "Steve, let's have a party. I'll play my comb."

"Not me, Charlie, I'm beat. We get out of this dump tomorrow. I need some sleep."

"Okay, but I never had two weeks like here in this jail, and I'm going to have a party. When I got locked up here, a guy tried to bum a cigarette. I said 'Go to Hell, Honkey, get your own.' You know what I did this morning, Steve?"

"No, Charlie."

"Well, you know those lousy little bags of tobacco they hand out, with the paper you can use to wrap tobacco in to make cigarettes? I took some of those bags, and I must have spent an hour rolling cigarettes. And when I got done, I laid 'em out on my bunk for everybody to take. You know why I did that, Steve?"

"No, Charlie."

"Because I found out in this jail that us niggers and you honkies can get along together and I never thought that. And I want to play my comb."

I could hear Charlie playing his comb as I went to sleep. I tried to find him, but I never saw him again. A wasted mind. A wasted life. A beautiful human being who never had a chance.

I've been civilly disobedient on behalf of other causes. I undertook one such action in Leonardo, New Jersey, in 1972, where bombs destined for U.S. warships and planes were being loaded onto Navy vessels for transport to Vietnam.

I had expected only to join in a demonstration against the escalation of the war that President Nixon had just ordered. The antiwar crowd stood on a beach beside a long pier, down which a locomotive was pushing cars loaded with 500-pound bombs in open crates. I watched this operation with mounting anguish. I knew the bombs that I was looking at would soon be lobbed onto Vietnam's rice paddies and hamlets from the battleship *New Jersey*, lying in sanctuary in the China Sea.

I thought the operation was obscene, too obscene to let pass without protest. I had to intervene. I left the demonstrators and joined a small band of young men and women who were about to climb up the pilings to the quay to stand between the bombs and the ship.

As a train approached on the quay 20 feet above us, we scrambled over the pilings until we were within three feet of the top. A squad of Marines was stationed along the track. They prevented us from climbing further by stepping on our fingers. The bomb-laden cars, pushing a tank car equipped with a water cannon, were now approaching.

When they came near, the Marines had to step back to let

the cars pass. At that moment our leader vaulted to the quay and lay down across the tracks. We followed him. The water cannon was turned on in an attempt to flush us from the tracks, but we hid our heads between railroad ties and hung on against the torrent.

The train stopped. The water cannon ceased fire. The Navy wasn't any more anxious to create martyrs than we were to be martyrs. The Marines leaped forward. One strapping young man who looked as scared as I was grabbed me by the scruff of my neck and lifted me up until my feet were dangling. He screamed at me. "I guess you think you're pretty smart, you son-of-a-bitch."

"No," I said. "I'm sorry I've taken you away from your family on a Sunday afternoon."

He was so startled, he dropped me like a sack of potatoes, and I landed in a heap. Quickly he picked me up, bedraggled and muddy. He shook some mud off my trousers. "Just stand over there, sir. I'm sure someone will tell you what to do next."

We were arrested for trespassing, turned over to the police, and transported to a handsome new jail in Hightstown. I was allowed to phone my wife, Betty, who was surprised, but, as always, supportive, sharing vicariously in a witness we both were drawn to. Her loving cheerfulness reduced me to tears.

It was a clean, new jail, but a bad jail. The youngest member of our little band was separated from us and lodged with other more violent prisoners. When a lawyer told us the next morning that he had been sexually assaulted, we went on a hunger strike demanding his return. The jail authorities obliged.

Meanwhile, I was trying to decide how to plead when we were taken to court, scheduled in three days. In earlier lockups, I had been in the employ of the American Friends Service Committee, which is in the business of social change, and it didn't bother me that I was on its payroll while languishing in jail. Now, I was an officer of Haverford College, whose business is education. I was uneasy about being paid while I was on such distinctively noncollege business as living in jail, AWOL for goodness knows how long. I decided to plead guilty and was fined.

I had no opportunity in court to make a statement, but had thought about what I would say to the judge if I'd been given the chance, and as soon as I returned to Haverford, I wrote it:

ON TACTICS OF OBSTRUCTION

On Sunday, I was among a group that tried to prevent bombs from being loaded on the USS *Nitro*, bound for Vietnam from Leonardo, New Jersey. This is the first time I have been part of a witness that employed tactics of obstruction. Up to now, it has always seemed to me that my protests should stop short of trying to block others from doing what they felt they should do, however much I disagreed. Two factors in the present situation compelled me to violate this long-standing conviction.

First, it seems to me that as this endless war drags on—and now once again escalates—it carries with it an ever-increasing measure of mindlessness. More and more, the men and women who are caught up in fighting it, in supporting it, and in supplying it do so not because they believe it is right, but because it is there. It's a job. It's orders. It's policy. The government is responsible. I just do what I'm told. This is the attitude that chilled us in Adolph

Eichmann. To oppose it—even to blocking the actions that flow from it—does not seem to me to be preventing others from doing what they feel is right. It prevents them only from doing what they are told to do.

Italy 1947

Second, there comes a time when one perceives an evil to be so monstrous that conscience compels new commitment. Presumably, if the freight cars I sought to block had been loaded with Jews on their way to the crematoria, my government would have stood with me on the causeway instead of turning on the water cannon and throwing me in jail for illegal trespass. As it was, the cars were not filled with Jews. They were filled with bombs for our carriers and shells for our destroyers. But how much less obscene than the crematoria is the spectacle of American technology raining endless death from its sanctuaries in sea and air on a nation of bamboo huts and rice paddies? And for no other reason than to repel an invasion of Vietnam by Vietnamese, across a line that was explicitly stated by international agreement not to be a boundary, and which only became one because the United States government and its Vietnamese clients refused to hold an election that would have obliterated it forever?

The death that flows from this tragic history is more impersonal and antiseptic than the deaths of the crematoria, but the result is the same: a people driven from their homes, a culture destroyed, millions slaughtered, and for my part, I doubt that God makes His judgments on the basis of the niceties.

Where, then, does one draw the line in this situation between good citizenship and irresponsible trespass? I drew it at the point of trying to halt the export of death in a war I believe to be wholly wicked, and wholly unjustified. I think every American should decide, now, how far he will go toward the crematoria before he draws it for himself.

The statement got some local circulation, but the major press ignored it.

Did my witness at Leonardo serve a purpose? We stopped no bombs. Few people learned of it. But, as with food stamps, it was one more contribution to the public indignation that stopped the war.

Public outrage, whether in support of a cause or against an injustice, begins with individual outcry. It is easy to feel powerless in an age of mass communication, wealthy lobbies and bought politicians, but no one is powerless. It is still possible here, as in few countries of the world, for an individual to stand up and say No or Yes.

Eight

━━━━►◆◄━━━━

MEETING THE DOUKHOBORS

DURING MY YEARS WITH THE AMERICAN FRIENDS SERVICE COMMITTEE my most unusual assignment was one involving the Doukhobors, a small Christian community in British Columbia with which the Society of Friends has had a fraternal relationship since the 19th century. Doukhobors (or Spirit Wrestlers) originated in Russia in the 17th century. They were industrious farmers, living communally, with pacifist teachings. They had hereditary leadership. For two centuries members of the Verigin family held all the community income and managed its affairs.

Periodically, the Doukhobors suffered czarist persecution for refusing to serve in the imperial armies. When this persecution was renewed in the 1890s, it was deeply troubling to Leo Tolstoy, the Russian novelist who was himself a pacifist, and in 1898 he issued a public appeal for help in England. Friends there responded by petitioning the czar to permit the Doukhobors to leave Russia. Permission was granted, and Friends in England and America undertook to arrange resettlement. After exploring various sites, they selected Canada, which at the time was eager to encourage migration to its sparsely settled western provinces.

Two vessels chartered by the Canadian government made two trips to the Crimea early in 1899 and brought 5,000

Doukhobors to Halifax, where the ships were met by Joseph Elkinton, a Philadelphia Friend, and Prince Dmitry Hilikoff, a Russian pacifist nobleman who had assisted in making arrangements for the migration. From Halifax the settlers were transported to Saskatchewan, where they received land.

For a number of years they prospered. They retained the communal lifestyle and resisted integration into Canadian society. Their leader, Peter (Lordly) Verigin, managed their affairs well. But in 1923 he was mysteriously killed in a train explosion and was succeeded by his son, who squandered community funds on his own pleasure. Foreclosure resulted, forcing the Doukhobors to move farther west into British Columbia. There was a second foreclosure, after which most Doukhobors abandoned communal living and became integrated into Canadian society. Some called themselves Independents; others became members of the Christian Community of Universal Brotherhood under a new generation of Verigin leadership.

There was, however, a remnant, numbering about 2,000, who were embittered by events. They split from their brethren, calling themselves the Sons of Freedom, and blamed all their troubles on Canada, which they regarded as a materialistic, war-making society. They rejected every intrusion of Canadian values into their lives, refusing to send their children to school or to observe other requirements of citizenship.

Their anger first expressed itself against their own brethren, whom they accused of succumbing to materialism, and whose homes they burned when their owners painted or upgraded them. The authorities paid minimal attention to these attacks on the grounds that they were an internal Doukhobor problem. This encouraged the Sons to escalate their protests by dynamiting or burning more public targets—railroad tracks, electric pylons, even churches—always, in deference to their pacifism, accompanying their attacks with prayers that no one would be hurt in the action.

The women, transferring to a secular setting a Doukhobor religious ritual of disrobing as a sign of purity, began to march naked through British Columbian towns as a form of protest, knowing that Canadians weren't drawn to women walking about without their clothes. To curb this practice, the provincial legislature mandated a one-year prison sentence for nudism.

The American Friends Service Committee was unaware of this growing crisis in western Canada, though its leaders knew of the long Quaker-Doukhobor relationship and of the fraternal visits paid to Doukhobors over the years by individual Friends. A surprise visit to AFSC headquarters in early 1950 by the deputy commander of the Royal Canadian Mounted Police brought the committee up to date on what was happening. On the day he appeared, Clarence Pickett, AFSC's chief, was out of town. I was his assistant at the time, and was told that a gentleman from Canada wished to see me.

Enter Colonel Frank Mead, resplendent in full RCMP uniform. He remarked on the recent history of the Sons' behavior and said he had come to ask the Quakers for help. He said:

> The RCMP has concluded that the problem in British Columbia is not one of criminality, but of religious fanaticism. The Sons won't listen to anyone, but maybe you Quakers can reach them. They remember that you rescued them from Russia, and they still speak kindly of you.
>
> The worst problem at the moment isn't violence, which continues sporadically, but nudity. The

legislature's mandatory year in prison isn't effective. Martyrdom is a badge of honor.

Let me illustrate our problem. Last week, a fresh group of 50 women were convicted of nudity, but all our women's prisons in the west are full. This made it necessary for us to contract with the Canadian Pacific Railroad to attach a special car to one of their transcontinental passenger trains to transport our prisoners to the east where prison space was available.

When the women were put on the car, the first thing they did was to take off all their clothes. Word quickly spread of this development, and as the train made its way east, crowds gathering along the route got bigger and bigger with each stop. Regular passengers couldn't get to the platform. At this point the railroad had had enough. They deposited our car on a remote prairie siding in Saskatchewan and told us the women were again our responsibility. We located the car, boarded up all the windows, cut a slot in the door for the passage of food, and persuaded the railroad that the car was now sufficiently secure to continue its journey east.

The women reached Toronto, but we now had the problem of transferring 50 naked women to another train headed east. To meet this difficulty, we arranged for a large detail of Toronto police to line both sides of a walkway, and at 3 a.m., with only a few vagrants in the station, we marched the women to their new car. A few of these fellows did wake up, Mr. Cary. They thought they'd died and gone to heaven. . . . I don't know what we're going to do with the next 50.

The colonel continued with a report on the current lawless behavior of the male members of the group. Here again, punishment wasn't effective. Religious fervor was a stronger force than fear of imprisonment.

I reported this visit to Clarence Pickett, including the saga of the 50 women. This tale brought laughter, but we both recognized that beyond the humor lay a painful human problem. Serious discussion of Friends' responsibility went forward in committees and with the Elkinton family, and at the next meeting the Board of Directors authorized the AFSC, jointly with the Canadian Friends Service Committee, to send a team to British Columbia to explore what might be done to help.

Emmett Gulley, the chief of the AFSC's Portland, Oregon, regional office, was asked to undertake this service. He was so challenged by what he found in British Columbia that he resigned his Oregon post, moved with his wife to Grand Forks, and for the next five years committed his life to working on a range of Doukhobor problems. In the course of these years, Emmett made many contributions. He increased Canadian awareness that the Sons of Freedom were a small minority of the Doukhobor community whose behavior should not reflect on their law-abiding brethren. He and Colonel Mead created a National Commission headed by the president of the University of British Columbia, with a mandate to examine Doukhobor history and the roots of the Sons of Freedom movement, and to bring forward recommendations for resolving the problems they raised. He helped secure release of Doukhobor prisoners, restoration of voting rights, and recognition of Doukhobor marriages. He pressed for legislation to recover Doukhobor land.

But he failed in his primary mission. He never won the confidence of the Sons of Freedom or succeeded in changing their behavior. Perhaps no one could have done so. In dealing with fanatics, there is a fine line between maintaining one's own integrity and reaching out to the dissidents. The Sons took the position that either you were with them 100% or you were against them.

Beyond this obstacle, hereditary leadership, which had always drawn absolute obedience, was missing. The Verigin holding the leadership title was living in the Soviet Union, his whereabouts unknown. In his absence, the Sons fell under the influence of an itinerant Baptist preacher named Soroken, who claimed to be the reborn Christ and who became the accepted leader, reinforcing their off-key views and doing nothing to change their behavior.

These problems were made worse by mistakes in Emmett's approaches to the Sons. He made too much of nudity, walking out of any meeting where it occurred, and allowed himself to be too visibly identified with law enforcement authorities, fueling Sons' suspicions of a Quaker neutrality already compromised by the Service Committee's willingness to have British Columbia assume financial responsibility for Emmett's work.

These problems allowed a crisis to develop, destroying Emmett's effectiveness, propelling me into the center of the controversy, and casting both the Canadian and American Service Committees in a bad light. It had its origin in a government decision to enforce school attendance. Emmett supported this decision despite the misgivings of a number of British Columbian Friends, who questioned Quaker identification with coercion. Events soon took a dramatic turn. The government lost patience. All curricular and teaching concessions had been rejected, and efforts to put the children in schools failed because their parents hid them in the forest when officials appeared. This led to police being sent to the Sons' mountain hamlets, and in the dead of night taking about 100 children from their beds and transporting them many miles north to an abandoned tuberculosis sanitarium in New Denver, which had been converted to a school. Here, the children were locked up and put in school.

This action produced an uproar. The Sons were outraged and blamed Gulley and the Quakers for instituting it. Friends, both Canadian and American, were divided on the action, but those in British Columbia with the widest knowledge of the overall problem opposed it.

At this point, the committees in Philadelphia and Toronto decided to send a small delegation to British Columbia to investigate the situation. I represented Philadelphia and was joined by two prominent Canadian Friends, Fred Haslam and Dorothy Starr, and together we spent two weeks in April 1955, traveling widely in British Columbia. We met with the attorney general of the province and other government officials, with Friends, and with Doukhobor leaders. We traveled to New Denver, saw the school in operation, and visited the Quaker communities in remote Argenta, where a number of Friends were well informed on Doukhobor issues. This community was strongly opposed to the province's coercive educational policy, and the visit confirmed our emerging view that Friends should break with the New Denver program. This came as a shock to Emmett Gulley, who felt we had been misled by people who didn't have an in-depth understanding of the situation.

After my colleagues went home, I made one more visit in the area. At the suggestion of John Verigin, leader of the Universal Brotherhood, I traveled to Krestova to meet with William Moojelsky, the resident leader of the Sons of Freedom. Moojelsky, calling himself Michael the Archangel, was the stand-in for Soroken, who by now had gone to Uruguay, ostensibly to find a new home for the Sons, but who was reported to be living handsomely in Montevideo. I hoped to discuss the school attendance problem with Moojelsky, alias the Archangel, to see if there was any chance of breaking the impasse and returning the children to their parents.

Krestova was an isolated community on a mountain ridge far above the main road. I was driven to the base of a trail leading upward, and left alone. Knowing how angry the Sons were, and fearful of my reception, I became more tense with each upward step. I recalled my response to Betty when she asked me on my departure what I would do when my hostesses began to disrobe. "I'll just look bored," I'd said—a response she doubted I could manage. She was right, I thought, but my mood was closer to panic than boredom.

On arrival on that bare plateau, the little hamlet looked sadder than I had imagined. My plan was to avoid any sighting by women, and ask directions only from males—a plan that required abrupt changes of direction. Eventually, I reached my destination, frazzled, and introduced myself to Moojelsky, alias the Archangel. He turned cordial, no doubt thinking I could get the children released, and invited me into his little shack to share a bowl of borscht.

Our conference was barely underway, however, when angry shouting erupted outside. I looked out the window and saw 20 naked amazons bearing down on our shack in pursuit of the Quaker kidnapper of their children. It was not a moment for boredom, nor one to remind me of Peter Paul Rubens. It was a moment for fright. How was I to meet this attack nonviolently? What would it be like to be surrounded three deep by screaming women six feet tall and nude? I never found out. Michael, anticipating the possibility of attack, had prepared for it. He whistled through his teeth, and a number of young men, armed with staves, quickly appeared. They took off after the ladies, flailing wildly, and scattering them screaming in all directions. It was mayhem, viewed with a mixture of horror and—honesty compels me to admit— relief.

Fearing that these friends would return—with reinforcements—and wondering already how I would report this event at the AFSC staff meetings in Philadelphia, I decided on a shorter stay in Krestova. I assured Michael that I was opposed to the removal of the children and that I would do what I could to have them returned. I told him that return would be more likely if the Sons could show some flexibility on the matter of school attendance, reminding him that the authorities had been open to negotiation and might still be. I was not optimistic. He offered no response beyond demanding the immediate return of the children.

I made an escape to the exit path, expecting to be confronted by angry women, robed or unrobed, at every corner. None appeared, and I returned to more normal Canadian society, shaken but unscathed, my mission a failure.

As promised, I conveyed my concern to local authorities, but, contrary to the Sons' impression of Quaker influence, there was little impact. For their part, the Sons quickly assumed that, because the children weren't returned at once, I wasn't sincere and had only pretended to care.

After three weeks, the last word was theirs, in the form of a seven-page telegram that left no doubt about their views. "You are like unto Judas Iscariot who sold his soul for 30 pieces of silver," it ended, "but remember, Cary, shortly thereafter he went out and hanged himself."

That was the end of any formal Quaker relationship with the Doukhobor community, but individual Friends have continued to visit from time to time. The Sons' violence gradually subsided, at least partly as a result of kind treat-

127

ment given by Canadians to a large-scale march to Vancouver by Doukhobor women seeking the release from prisons of their husbands and brothers. After three years in New Denver the children were returned. Peace came, although the Sons' alienation from Canadian society continued, expressed now in debate rather than in violence.

Nine

———❖———

Association with the Nobel Community

Life with the American Friends Service Committee was full of the unexpected, ranging from Washington's jail to Washington's White House, from a general's jet in Vietnam to a Lapp's canoe in Finnmark, from fried termites in Zambia to pot-lucks in Kansas. It has also included meetings with Nobel laureates, winners of the world's most prestigious prizes. The Service Committee and its British counterpart were the recipients, on behalf of the Society of Friends, of the Nobel Peace Prize in 1947. That has brought me invitations to their meetings as the representative of an organizational winner.

My connection began in the fall of 1947, when I was overseeing Quaker relief programs in Europe after the Second World War. I had called a meeting in Amsterdam of representatives from our relief units scattered across the continent. We met, as we had every six months, to discuss our problems, share experiences, shape our future plans, and, most important, reinforce our connectedness with one another.

It was not a happy occasion. There was low morale in the scattered units, isolated and lonely and stressed, struggling imperfectly to succor the needy. Too many trucks were grounded by flat tires and lack of spare parts. Essential supplies were lost on the disrupted railway systems of Central Europe. Exhausted local authorities were unhelpful. By the last afternoon of our four-day meeting, we were a discouraged company. Our contribution was so small and imperfect and the need so great. Suddenly a Dutch Friend burst in, holding aloft a newspaper with a banner headline: "Quakers win Nobel Peace Prize . . . honored for relief service . . ." Stunned silence . . . silence that quickly became a Quaker meeting for worship . . . the living silence of a gathered community.

I thanked God for the gift of commitment. He had given us a chance to make a difference. We had tried, and someone had noticed. Our sense of fellowship, our love for each other, needed no words. There was only a single message, from a young worker in devastated Poland: "All I can say is—a little love goes a long way." I've remembered her words for more than 50 years.

Friends in Britain and the United States were naturally pleased that their society,

AFSC Archives

"One of the ailments that Helen is called upon most often to treat is dermatitis—the prolonged cold, the lack of fuel to heat water for washing, and the limited diet all contribute to skin disturbances. Here Helen is bandaging a hand whch its young owner has been unable to use (hence he has been unable to work) for almost six weeks." (Poland 1948) through the effort of their service agencies, had won such a signal honor. It was hard for us to hold on to the quiet modesty that is supposed to be a Quaker characteristic. Henry Cadbury, the chairperson of the AFSC board, reported the Monday after the award that "Friends at my Meeting were bursting their buttons with humility." So was I.

On December 12, Henry joined his counterpart, Margaret A. Backhouse of the Friends Relief Service of London, to receive the prize in Oslo. He did so in the obligatory dress suit. He had none of his own, but had borrowed one from the Service Committee's clothing workroom, which was in the midst of a drive to outfit members of the Budapest Symphony Orchestra who had lost their dress suits during the war. Henry returned the suit after the Oslo ceremonies, and perhaps it was then worn by a Budapest cellist.

The money that came with the prize was used a few years later at a dangerous point in the Cold War, where it financed seminars and exchanges between the United States and the USSR to try to reduce mutual distrust and ignorance. This disposition was not as warmly received by the American public as the award had been. Everyone cheers when you give a cup of cold water to the suffering, but enthusiasm may wane when you ask why the cup was necessary, and what might be done to lessen the possibility that it might again be needed. Anti-communism was the prevailing American mood, and bridge-building was seen as evidence that the committee was soft on communism. There were rumblings, but the committee's decision resonated with its efforts over the years to steer a steady course, faithful to the dictates of its Quaker roots.

With the Nobel money spent and the medal stowed in the AFSC archives, that chapter appeared closed. But another encounter came in 1973, after the Nobel Committee awarded the Peace Prize jointly to Henry Kissinger and Le Duc Tho, of North Vietnam, for their negotiations in Paris ending the fighting in Southeast Asia. (Le declined the prize on the grounds that peace was not yet established.) Quakers in Britain and America found this award to geo-politicians inappropriate and considered returning our medal in protest. It was decided instead to send a small delegation to Norway to voice their concern.

The purpose was not to challenge the Nobel Committee's decision, which was by then a *fait accompli*, but to share with the Norwegian community and the Nobel Committee our perception that the Peace Prize had gained worldwide prestige and moral authority over more than half a century because it had been awarded to individuals and organizations that had labored over decades to build the foundations of peace, reducing hatred and reconciling enemies. This great tradition had, we felt, been broken, and the prize demeaned, by an award to persons committed to the politics of power, for whom peace negotiations were no more than a tactic dictated by the needs of the moment, and who were ready to turn again to the business of slaughter whenever they deemed it necessary.

To carry that message, I was asked to go to Norway with two Friends from England, Roger Wilson, former chief of Friends Relief Service, and Myrtle Wright, a British Friend who had been trapped in Norway by the Nazi invasion. She had stayed there throughout the war and had been decorated by the Norwegian king for her role in the underground.

This small delegation reached Oslo ten days before Christmas and found a city ablaze with lights in the long winter darkness, its stores filled with Christmas goods and its streets with happy shoppers. The king's palace, sitting atop a hill in the center of town, its grounds floodlit, had hundreds of Oslo's children hauling their sleds up to the king's front door and plunging with happy shouts down his front lawn. How His Majesty slept in such a hubbub was a mystery. For an American all too familiar with the fortress-like character of the White House, the King's House was a reminder of the blessings of smallness, powerlessness, and stability, and of the leadership these characteristics made possible for peaceful, enlightened Norway.

The Quaker delegation found evidence that we were not alone in our distress over the Nobel Committee's award. Norway was in an uproar. Two members of the Committee had resigned in protest, the chairman was in seclusion, and Norwegians had organized a movement to raise $250,000 for a People's Peace Prize to be awarded to Archbishop Dom Helder Camara of Recife, Brazil, in recognition of his work on behalf of Brazil's landless. This national climate and the Norwegians' affection and esteem for Myrtle Wright assured us a warm welcome. We met with the prime minister, the secretary of the Nobel Committee, and the two committee dissidents. We were on national television. Our mission added a bit to the national movement to reexamine the purpose and value of the Prize, and met Friends concern to give public expression to their views.

Fifteen years later, in January 1988, there was another Nobel-related event. I was asked to represent the American Friends Service Committee at a four-day meeting of Nobelists in Paris. It was the first and only time that living Nobel winners from every field had been invited to come together to share insights and discuss major world issues. The sponsors were François Mitterrand, the French president, and his friend Elie Wiesel, the world's leading authority on the Holocaust and himself a Nobel peace laureate.

The purpose of the gathering was "to confront the urgent ethical, moral, and practical problems" facing the human family on the eve of the 21st century, with the hope that the creative minds of the Nobel community might "identify fresh principles, policies, and strategies to meet these challenges." Discussion was to be on five topics: disarmament and peace, human rights, development, science and technology, and culture and society. Because of the shortness of time and the complexity of the issues considered, no formal findings were anticipated and no press coverage was to be permitted.

There was clearly a second goal: to provide an opportunity for the diverse Nobel community to get to know each other. The sponsors envisioned that such familiarity might prove useful in times of dangerous international crises, when a moral voice is most needed but is seldom heard. Could Nobelists, whose moral stature is admired, develop a loose structure enabling them to join together to play this role?

In Paris, plenary sessions were held to a minimum. Small groups assigned to the five specific topics were the main focus of conference business. Other events were designed to afford opportunity for laureates to meet each other. Most lunches and dinners were leisurely, with elaborate menus served in the gracious setting of the Palais d'Élysée, the French president's residence. We sat at each meal with a different table of six. Conversation flourished. Each of the five small discussion groups had 15 to 20 participants. We gathered around large oval tables for eight hours over two days. I was with the Disarmament and Peace group. On the first morning I arrived early and took my seat in front of a large wooden marker reading "S. Cary." Unused to moving in such rarefied circles, I looked nervously at the marker to my right. It read "H. Kissinger." That spelled to me: Geopolitics. Cambodia. Secret bombing. Secret coups. Now even more nervous, I looked at other markers. These were more reassuring: W. Brandt, G. Wald, M. Maguire, D. Hodgkin. The panelists drifted in, 16 in all, split between activist laureates and science laureates versed in analytical thinking.

Discussion was far-ranging. Henry Kissinger, present only on the first day, contributed constructively with his concern over the burden of Third World debt and its potential as a source of violence. Others were preoccupied with reducing the nuclear threat, which became the central focus of our deliberations. Surprisingly, in view of the diversity of viewpoints and philosophies among our members, we were, after eight hours, able to unite on a statement for presentation to the conference. It was signed by 12 participants, including me on behalf of the AFSC (two left early and two didn't sign for organizational reasons). The statement welcomed the proposed 50% reduction in nuclear arsenals, opposed extending the arms race into space, called for a comprehensive test ban treaty and progress toward abolishing all weapons of mass destruction, and demanded reduction of arms budgets to provide funds to control malnourishment and disease in developing countries. I thought it a strong and useful document.

It was read in full at the final plenary. But Wiesel did not cover it in his summary of conference findings at our closing session in the Palais, where the press was present. This offended some members of our working group, who complained sharply to him both in Paris and afterward in New York. We never knew why he left it out. Was he reluctant to embarrass President Mitterrand publicly? French policy at the time was at odds with our consensus document.

The closing event was a banquet at the Cité des Sciences et de l'Industrie, hosted by Madame Mitterrand and Elie

Wiesel. Each conference member had the opportunity to invite two guests, so that nearly 300 persons were present. I had few connections in Paris and was at a loss to know who might be my guests. I finally settled on Magda Trocmé, the widow of André Trocmé, the French pastor from Le Chambon, noted worldwide for his aid to Jews in World War II, and Madelaine Barot, the retired chief of Protestant Social Services in France. I'd never met Mme Barot, and I hadn't seen Mme Trocmé for 40 years, but both ladies, astonished at my phone calls from Philadelphia, accepted my invitation.

I realized that both were well into their 80s, and when I was told the Cité was very large, I decided to equip them with wheelchairs. This was easily arranged, and when I arrived at the Cité I was pleased to spot my wheelchaired guests. Their rolling stock was motorized, and it was soon clear that neither of my ladies was a licensed operator with even minimal mechanical capabilities. They were gunning their vehicles forward or backward at random, laughing de-lightedly as world-famous Nobelists leaped in all directions to escape. The scene called for instant action. A French gentleman accosted me and asked if these "were Monsieur Cary's guests." Indeed they were. "I am your guide, Monsieur, for the museum tour, and I think it would be better if we went on our own separate tour. I will chase that one, you chase the other one." With this formula, we avoided crash-ing into scientific exhibits designed for hands-on use but not head-on collisions, and safely reached the banquet area. We had just enjoyed the opening appetizer when we were joined by a visitor. Mme Mitterrand, our hostess, had left her table on the dais, threaded her way through the tightly packed tables until she reached ours, and sat down between my two ladies. They were overwhelmed, but the charming First Lady put them quickly at ease, and they chatted together for several minutes. It was a gracious gesture, and it made the occasion an unforgettable one for Magda and Madelaine.

I had wondered what an assembly of laureates would be like. Would their brilliance in one field lead them into illusions of equal brilliance in other fields? Would they appear arrogant? My fears were unfounded. A few seemed infected with the virus, but the vast majority were fun—and inspiring—to be with. Brilliant, of course, but warm and compassionate, eager to exchange ideas, listening as well as advocating. The threat in Paris was to my ego, not theirs. Life with pot-lucks in church basements and years spent in Quaker committee rooms, doesn't prepare one for life in the top tier of French society with caviar and vintage wines and giant intellects. It was dangerously appealing.

Those days in Paris have had no follow-up. The whole Nobel community has never met again together, nor has any loose structure developed, probably because of the cost of doing so. But one subset of Nobelists, the Peace Prize winners, with common interests and more manageable numbers, have continued to meet, and I have twice represented the American Friends Service Committee at these meetings. One was in October 1989, when the Indian government invited Peace Prize laureates to New Delhi to join with leading Indian scholars and diplomats in a three-day seminar commemorating the 100th anniversary of the birth of Jawaharlal Nehru. The discussion theme was to be "Humanism, International Politics, and Nehru's Thought." The occasion was as glittering as the Paris event. But in New Delhi there were political overtones. Prime Minister Rajiv Gandhi was in a reelection campaign. His opponents charged him and the Congress Party with arranging a high visibility event to capitalize on the prime minister's close ties to his renowned grandfather, the architect of India's rebirth as an independent state.

Gandhi hosted a luncheon for seminar members and joined us for tea between sessions, moving informally among the delegates and chatting with small groups scattered around the room. He and his minister of state for external affairs, Kanwar Natwar Singh, were guests at our final banquet, which was hosted by the president of India at his residence in the former Raj's palace, built along the lines of Versailles, large and imposing, reflecting grandeur, dominance, and permanency—just what its British architects wanted. Inside, a marble staircase swept up to a large reception hall. At the foot of the stairs, it was easy to imagine the British Raj looking down on his humble subjects. In our case there was no Raj, but on every third step on both sides of the staircase stood a tall turbaned Sikh, in full uniform and motionless. Properly awed, and silently climbing the stairs beside a Russian scholar from the Soviet Academy of Science, I had trouble suppressing a laugh when my austere companion whispered: "I think they're statues!"

Once in the chandeliered and carpeted reception hall, and through the line to be received by the president, we gathered in smaller groups in informal conversation. I was with a Quaker colleague from Britain, Andrew Clark, head of Quaker Peace and Service in London. English Friends had played an important role in the struggle for Indian independence, so Quakers were well known to Indian leaders, and the prime minister made a special effort to engage Andrew and his junior colleague from the American colonies in extended conversation. I found Rajiv Gandhi to be a modest and charming man with a keen sense of humor. It was a tragedy for India and the world that he was assassinated so soon afterward.

The seminar was more formal than the sessions in Paris. There was less opportunity for informal exchanges and forging friendships. All sessions were plenaries, with scheduled speakers and a follow-up question period. But with featured speakers wordy, discussion was limited.

There were two attendees from the United States, myself and Dr. Selig H. Harrison of the Carnegie Endowment for International Peace. Both of us spoke at the final business session on the broad topic of "Disarmament, Peace, and World Order." Our perspectives were sharply different. Harrison gave a scholarly, structured, and documented analysis of what U.S. naval power was needed in the Indian Ocean to meet any Soviet challenge and assure the integrity of the Indian subcontinent. He discussed how ships in our fleet should be deployed and where they should be based.

My perspective was different. I suggested that the unlocking of the atom compelled us to think in new ways about security. Nuclear weaponry with its power to destroy the world could never provide security, offering only the prospect of living permanently on the edge of a precipice. The only practical alternative was nonviolence, which the genius of Gandhi and Nehru had lifted from a philosophical concept to an effective instrument of political power, and one that now needed further exploration.

There was no time for follow-up discussion of our two presentations. Everyone was left to draw his or her own conclusions.

Four years after New Delhi came Vienna and my final entry into the Nobel world. Austria was playing host in June 1993 to the World Conference on Human Rights called by the United Nations. Austrian leaders, capitalizing on the siting of the conference in their country, convened a meeting of Peace Prize laureates to coincide with the opening. The charge to the laureates was to produce their own statement on human rights, which would be presented to the conference with the hope that the moral stature of the Nobel community would assure consideration by the delegations from UN member nations.

The laureates were invited to attend the opening plenary in reserved seating, but this gesture created an uproar that erupted some days before the scheduled conference opening. One of those planning to come to Vienna was His Holiness, the Dalai Lama, and the prospect of his presence so angered the Chinese that they announced that their delegation would refuse to attend the conference if the Dalai Lama appeared. When negotiations failed to break the impasse, the UN gave in to Chinese demands and barred His Holiness from joining in the opening session, on the grounds that Chinese participation in the conference was essential.

This was the situation when I reached Vienna on Sunday, June 13, and met Brenda Bailey, the representative of London's Quaker Peace and Service, who was to be my Quaker colleague at this Nobelist meeting. Brenda told me that Betty Williams, the Peace laureate from Ireland, had held a press conference on her arrival at the Vienna airport and called for all Nobelists to boycott the opening session to protest the Dalai Lama's exclusion.

We were both troubled by this proposal. We understood Betty Williams' outrage, but felt that a group identified around the world with peacemaking and reconciliation should not unilaterally mount a protest action without at least exploring other approaches. Changing Chinese minds was unlikely, but wasn't it appropriate to seek out their delegation and urge them to make a distinction between His Holiness as a distinguished Nobelist and world citizen and His Holiness as a Tibetan? We could point out that by accepting him in the first capacity they would be recognizing that the issue of human rights rises above the web of politics. Such a gesture would be welcomed around the world.

The more we talked about this idea, the more we were persuaded to act on it. But Brenda thought it would be wise to find out what the Dalai Lama himself thought of it. I agreed, but said it seemed impractical. She reminded me that His Holiness' suite was seven floors above us in the Intercontinental Hotel. Why not phone and ask if we could come up and see him?

She picked up the phone and reached His Holiness' secretary. She told him that we were two Quakers attending the laureates meeting with an urgent concern to discuss with His Holiness. Could we see him? "Probably not," said the secretary, "because he has a press conference in 15 minutes, but I'll ask him." Two minutes later, he returned to say that if we came at once, His Holiness would see us.

On the 11th floor, we emerged into a sea of saffron robes, security officers, Asian dignitaries, and UN personnel. The secretary met us and took us to a small reception room. A moment later His Holiness, a big, robust, jovial man in a saffron robe, burst in, offered us his hand, and invited us to sit down, a warm and welcoming figure.

What could he do for us? We spoke of our concern and raised two questions. What was his feeling about the proposed boycott, and did he think our suggestion of contacting the Chinese was a useful idea? The first he declined to answer, saying that it was up to his Nobel colleagues to decide what they wanted to do, but he warmed to the second. "It is always better to talk than to confront. I don't think you will be successful, but success isn't necessary. What is necessary is to keep trying to communicate, with faith that someday a breakthrough will come. I encourage you to contact the Chinese and make your plea."

Brenda and I spent the next hour and a half drafting a letter to the Chinese and attempting to locate their delegation, holed up somewhere in Vienna. Unfortunately, it was Sunday and most diplomatic phones went unanswered. The parties we did reach gave conflicting information. Every lead led nowhere. We had to admit defeat, but we were buoyed by two phone calls from His Holiness' secretary asking about progress. That told us that the Dalai Lama was truly interested in our enterprise.

We learned that the laureates were to meet early the next morning to decide whether to boycott the opening conference session. I continued to be troubled, and decided I should make a direct plea to the laureates to postpone boycott plans until we had made an effort to bring to the Chinese delegation the message that Brenda and I had drawn up the day before. If we failed, as was likely, we could boycott on Tuesday, but at least we would have tried.

Next morning at eight o'clock, I made my case—rehearsed many times in the small hours of the night—emphasizing that it seemed to us as Quakers that it represented a better sequence of events for a peacemaking community. Betty Williams immediately opposed our proposal on the grounds that the key moment to bear witness was at the opening session when all the press would be there. Adolfo Pérez Esquivel, the Argentinean Nobelist, joined her for the same reason. Norman Borlaug, 1973 winner, supported our position. A spirited discussion ensued. It was clear that the Williams-Pérez Esquivel argument would carry the day, and the group agreed to boycott that morning. We did so.

We needed a statement for the press. I was asked to draft it for presentation to the group before our scheduled luncheon with the Austrian minister of justice. The minister permitted me to read it between courses, but it was quickly apparent that Nobelists, like Quakers, are an independent lot. Agreement on the wording eluded us. We tried again at our first business session, where I thought I was back clerking the AFSC Board. As suggestions came forward, I retired to redraft, and was met each time at the door by eager reporters asking if our statement was ready. The end product, like most group productions, read as if it had been patched together by a committee. But it covered the bases and was signed by all present who weren't barred by organizational restrictions.

We then began the substantive work of the week: drafting a human rights message to the conference. These meetings were ably chaired by a ranking officer of the Austrian foreign ministry who was about to assume an important role in the new European Union. Only the invited Nobelists were permitted in the room, with the exception of two advisors to the Dalai Lama, who sat behind him, whispering in his ear from time to time and occasionally passing him notes. From the vigor and frequency of His Holiness' participation, however, I thought he needed little advice. He was his own man.

The chair presented an outline of topics we might want to cover, kept the discussion focused, and encouraged broad participation. What emerged after two days of discussion was a useful, though not electrifying, document. It painted human rights with a broad brush, involving economic, social, and cultural dimensions as well as civil and political rights. It asserted that respect for all these rights was the key to peace. The international community could no longer tolerate the terrible violations of human rights still occurring around the world. We called for steps to bring to justice those committing such crimes.

Beyond these broad sentiments, there was one unexpected and vigorous recommendation: a powerful denunciation of the death penalty. We said it "constitutes a cruel and inhumane punishment and should be abolished throughout the world. Once abolished by a state it should never be reintroduced."

We had a press conference to present our message, with well over 100 journalists present. Questions were directed at us for over an hour, with Rigoberta Menchu, as the most recent Nobel winner and a prominent spokesperson for the world's indigenous—and often most exploited—peoples, as the star performer. All of us had a chance to comment. I spoke of the importance of listening to the voices of the marginalized, voices that the power brokers tend to undervalue, but which ultimately have a major impact on outcomes. It is private, nongovernmental agencies working at the grass roots who have the best understanding of those voices, and the conference was making a major mistake in excluding these bodies from any significant role in its deliberations.

The final event was a roundtable with an invited audience of Austria's notables, where each of the 15 individual and organizational Nobelists was given three minutes to say whatever she or he wanted to about human rights. I focused my remarks on militarism. Quakers see it as one of the greatest threats to human rights, subject to no civil authority and fed by an international arms trade now flourishing at an unprecedented level.

The result of this dangerous combination of ungoverned militarism and easy availability of arms—from Rigoberta Menchu's Guatemala to Aung San Suu Khi's Burma—is the exercise of authority in the most brutal and inhuman ways. I felt then, and I feel now, that the trade in arms must be controlled. The UN should establish an arms registry that publicly lists all international arms transactions and call on all nations to provide advance notice of plans to provide arms. Once the full dimension of the arms trade and the slaughter that flows from it is given the light of day, the need for control will be clear and the way paved for the enactment of a total ban on all international arms transfers.

With the Dalai Lama, 1993

The Vienna meeting was notable for the easy informality that marked our deliberations, but best for me was the privilege of spending three days with Tibet's Dalai Lama. His life is a miracle. Here is a man, identified at the age of two as the reincarnated Buddha, taken from his family in a tiny village in northeast Tibet and secreted for 12 years in remote monasteries to prepare him for his role as the leader of millions of the faithful. From that background has emerged a man of renaissance learning, joyous, robust, witty, committed to nonviolence. He is a tireless champion of Tibetan independence, but is free of bitterness over the rape of his country. To reflect with such a man, to laugh with him, to drink tea with him, to be embraced by him, was a priceless gift.

A small incident on the last day sums up the Vienna experience. I was in the dining room of the Intercontinental Hotel enjoying a breakfast bowl of cornflakes when the hostess said I would have to move because I was sitting in an area reserved for the Tibetan delegation. I started to move. Two tables away were two Buddhists, the Dalai Lama's private secretary and his Geneva representative. Hearing the eviction order, the private secretary interrupted. "No, no, Mr. Cary is more than welcome to eat with us!" I finished my breakfast, but when I got up to leave I walked to the Tibetans' table. "Unlike the Chinese, I want to apologize for invading Tibetan territory."

They laughed. "Don't worry, you Quakers are welcome to invade Tibetan territory any time you want." It was a fitting end to the privilege of meeting and working with some of the greatest and most courageous peacemakers of our time. I am grateful for the opportunity.

Ten

———⟫•◈•⟪———

The Vietnam Quagmire

A FSC involvement in Southeast Asia did not begin until 1954, when the defeat of the French in Indochina was imminent. In Washington's anti-communist climate at the time, many voices were being raised calling for U.S. intervention to do what the French had failed to do: crush the Viet Minh forces of Ho Chi Minh and liberate Indochina.

The history of the region since the end of World War II had been a sorry one. A once-promising prospect for membership in the French Union of the Associated States of Indochina, as negotiated in Paris by Ho, was destroyed by the treason of the commander of France's Far Eastern Fleet, who refused to accept the agreement and ordered his ships to attack Haiphong to reassert French colonial power. The war this launched lasted for eight years, during which the United States, intent on courting French support for NATO, gave its tacit support to French-Asian policy.

In June 1954, with disaster looming and U.S. policy drifting toward intervention, the Service Committee issued the first of many public statements on the crisis:

> The American Friends Service Committee is profoundly disturbed with the pressures for United States military intervention in Indo-China . . .We

are convinced that nothing but disaster lies down this road . . . We urge our fellow citizens to remember that a real victory for freedom in Indo-China . . . requires that America understand the legitimate yearnings of Asian people for independence and a better standard of life. These are the fundamental issues of the . . . Indo-Chinese revolution and they are not issues that can be met with military threats.

Shortly after this statement appeared, the French suffered their final defeat at Dien Bien Phu and surrendered. A conference was convened in Geneva to establish settlement terms and a plan for Indochina's future. As these deliberations went forward, Catholics and other anti-communist elements were fleeing south across the 17th parallel, the temporary truce line established to separate the armies. A refugee crisis loomed, and the AFSC sent its foreign service secretary, Louis Schneider, to Saigon to see whether there was a role for the committee in easing suffering.

It was a difficult assignment. Physical needs were modest, but major social and political problems paralyzed resettlement efforts, and there was urgent need for training Vietnamese in public administration and social responsibility after a century of colonial rule. But Schneider found no way to explore these possible avenues of service because the government in Saigon was in disarray. President Diem controlled neither the army nor the police, both in the hands of independent generals. His financial support came from the French, requiring him to be conciliatory at a time when the rural population, whose support was essential, not only hated the French but were in fact dominated by the Viet Minh.

Washington's response in this crisis, instead of supporting and strengthening the U.S. Operations Mission (USOM), which Schneider found to be the one positive force in the country, sent yet another military figure to assess the situation, whose report called only for additional military advisers. Louis Schneider returned home without a recommendation for an AFSC program.

For a decade, 1954–1964, Washington's preoccupation with the cold war and anti-communism shaped U.S. policies both at home and abroad. For Southeast Asia it dictated a hard line. Communism had to be stopped. It was a monolith, and if it were given a foothold anywhere, surrounding countries would be swept into its orbit like falling dominoes.

To preempt this possibility, the United States declared the formerly French-dominated southern region of the country an independent state of South Vietnam. The new nation, Secretary of State John Foster Dulles announced, would be transformed into a "showcase of Western democracy" and a bulwark against Chinese communist aggression southward. Countrywide elections scheduled for 1956 were canceled, and the temporary 17th parallel truce line was converted into a national boundary, both in direct violation of the 1954 Geneva Accords by which the United States had promised to abide.

The Dulles policy ignored reality. It ignored Ho's popularity throughout Vietnam. It ignored 1,000 years of Vietnamese-Chinese enmity, which would have made Ho an ally against any Chinese southward expansion. It ignored the artificial character of the new state, the historic loyalties of its people, their aspirations, their war weariness, and the corrupt and dispirited military government.

The "showcase" proved an illusion. South Vietnam drifted, its government a hollow shell. Alienation of the countryside deepened under repressive Saigon policies. The U.S. response under Presidents Eisenhower, Kennedy, and Johnson continued to be a military one: sending ever-increasing numbers of "military advisors" to train the Army of the Republic of Vietnam (ARVN).

By 1964, U.S. public opinion, shaped by Washington's confidence that our military, highly trained and equipped, would make short work of the ragtag communist forces, was ready to support direct intervention to save its new state. The only problem was to find a credible excuse for doing so, and an alleged North Vietnamese attack on a U.S. naval vessel in the Gulf of Tonkin in August provided it. An outraged Congress overwhelmingly passed the Gulf of Tonkin Resolution, authorizing the president to "take all necessary measures to repel any armed attack against the forces of the United States and to prevent aggression."

Throughout this period, the American Friends Service Committee had been a voice of protest, calling for U.S. adherence to its commitments at Geneva, and opposing military responses to social, political, and economic problems. When intervention finally came, the AFSC sent its board chairman, Gilbert White, and Russell Johnson, a staff member widely acquainted in Southeast Asia, on a visit to Saigon early in 1965. They recommended that it be followed promptly by a longer visit of at least three months, with three objectives: to provide first-hand reports on the situation in Vietnam, Cambodia, and Laos; to identify local Vietnamese groups with whom the Committee might work in easing suffering and lessening city-rural alienation; and to explore priorities for direct AFSC service.

Would I undertake this assignment? It was an appealing challenge, sited in a region and a culture entirely new to me. But it would be in a war zone. It would be stressful for my family. It would mean months of separation. But Betty shared the challenge; she urged me to go. That tipped the scales. I accepted.

There followed weeks of preparation. I talked with colleagues who knew the region, reread their reports, and listed their contacts. I met with State Department personnel with Southeast Asian responsibilities. I read David Halberstam's *The Making of a Quagmire* and Bernard Fall's *Street Without Joy*. Two other Friends would join me in Vietnam for at least part of the time: Woodruff Emlen, a Philadelphia banker, and Kenneth Morgan, a Buddhism scholar from Colgate University.

On May 9, 1965, I left for Saigon, with planned stops in London, Geneva, Delhi, and Bangkok. I reached my destination on May 18, was met by the ever-gracious Mennonites—there ahead of Friends—and was temporarily housed with the Everett Metzler missionary family, whose four small children welcomed me warmly. They soon invited me to live with them "permanently," and I ended up doing so. Everett spoke fluent Vietnamese and was a big help in making contacts. Their home was a quiet refuge from stress.

Initially, I wondered if a useful visit would be possible. Everything seemed so disorganized. Promised appointments were postponed. Even to discuss peace was at the time regarded as treason. I made contact with the Asia Foundation, the U.S. Operations Mission, the U.S. Embassy, and two groups that shared AFSC concerns: the International Voluntary Service, a U.S.-based program sending young people to improve the agricultural skills of villagers, and the Vietnamese Youth Association, made up of young university students repairing war damage that inflicted hardship on villagers.

I also had a talk with the South Vietnamese minister of social welfare, whom I met at a meeting of voluntary agency

representatives. When he learned I was a Quaker, he took
me back to his office. It turned out he'd been to two AFSC
Seminars for Young Leaders and had great admiration for
Friends. When I mentioned my interest in meeting Buddhist
leaders, he picked up the phone and called the president of
the Buddhist University and the president of the Buddhist
Institute, the Venerable Thich Tam Chau, the ranking monk
in Vietnam, and made dates for me to see them. It was my
initial contact with a major force in Vietnam, with outreach
to every hamlet.

During those first weeks, I moved around Saigon by taxi—
little blue and tan Renaults, all decrepit, all dating from the
French period, most without mufflers, and all belching forth
clouds of blue exhaust smoke blanketing the already hot and
humid atmosphere of the city. Riding in them was an adventure, darting among scooters and bicycles, bullock carts,
pedicabs, and swarms of pedestrians, in disregard of white
lines and right of way. The rule of the road: if you think you
can make it, go for it!

I abandoned cabs in favor of a Mobylette, a two-seater
motor bike, on which I was at least master of my own fate,
and was personally challenged to cope with the traffic maelstrom, now increasingly worsened by massive U.S. Army
convoys rumbling through the city and adding to the din of
normal traffic.

I was making the Saigon rounds in my new vehicle when
students at the New School of Youth for Social Services at
Buddhist University invited me to join them on an "outing."
It turned out to be a visit to a large military hospital where
these young people went each weekend to comfort the
wounded.

Our first stop was beside a concrete apron where helicopters brought in wounded from the battlefields. Two big U.S.

helicopters had just arrived and were unloading their pitiful cargoes, their stretchers shoved into racks on waiting ambulances. No one moved, no one cried out, but the agony on their faces was numbing. We spent the next hour and a half in the orthopedic wards. Some patients were recent arrivals, with fresh casts, fresh bandages showing red, fresh amputations, lying still and unsmiling, drugged against pain. Others, veterans of a dozen operations, were hobbling around with misshapen legs that the doctors were trying to rebuild. One patient, unable to speak, stared silently at the ceiling, and the man in the next bed said that every night he just cried. Another, with both hands amputated, prayed that he could kill himself.

The young people were wonderful. The girls in their graceful Vietnamese gowns sang and laughed and helped write letters. The boys took names and promised to get in touch with relatives. They, too, joked and played games. Watching them brought tears, as I was overwhelmed by the pain and suffering around me, but also by these youngsters walking about like so many angels. War's reality was in those wards.

Exposure to Saigon and its environment was important, but I needed to know more of the situation in the hinterland. Some provinces were reasonably secure, but most of the country was dominated, even in the daytime, by the enemy, now called the Viet Cong. No trains ran and no through highways were open. Access to the rest of South Vietnam was only by air, but Air Vietnam, the government airline, was overbooked and unreliable, and Air America was unacceptable on principle because it was widely reported to be operated by the CIA.

The young men of International Voluntary Service came to my rescue. All Americans needed in those early war days was some official-looking travel orders, and they could go to any U.S. airbase, submit the orders for a cursory glance, and a pilot going that way with excess space would be pleased to take them along. I had no such orders, but IVS cut me some—an official looking, properly worded document complete with a bit of wax and the official IVS logo, identifying me as an important U.S. relief worker in need of any assistance that could be given to him. I used it for the next two months, and as an American was able to fly widely around the country.

My first venture was a trip to the highland city of Pleiku, in a sparsely settled province north of Saigon, inhabited largely by tribal Montagnards living in stilted huts, and 75% controlled by the Viet Cong by day and 90% at night. There had been ugly massacres not far from the city, and it was unsafe to venture far afield.

The mood in Pleiku was tense because it had just been involved in a massive military operation to open up the highway from the coastal town of Qui Nhon to reprovision the city. Two large convoys had gotten through, but it had required 5,000 troops, heavy armament, and three weeks to accomplish.

My host was the U.S. Operations Mission representative—one of only four American civilians living in the province. He confirmed the dominance of the Viet Cong in the region and spoke of the plight of the Montagnards, long despised by the Vietnamese and living on the ragged edge.

I drove with Tom Sturtivant of IVS to visit an agricultural training school that he had started four kilometers outside of the city. This was well beyond the secure perimeter for Americans, but Tom was so trusted and respected that he could move into the countryside with reasonable safety and even dared to spend nights at his school. Being with him, and seeing the depth of his caring and his commitment to serve all who sought his help, strengthened my faith that even the hardest of hearts can be softened. Tom's life offered concrete evidence that there are other ways than fists and guns to deal with enemies.

The same inspiration came from young volunteers from the Vietnamese Youth Association, who were my guides on a visit to Vietnam's Delta, the rice bowl of Southeast Asia. Its 15 provinces, bisected by the Mekong River and laced with canals, are all less than ten feet above sea level and subject to annual flooding.

Like the VYA projects in other parts of South Vietnam, the projects in the Delta were in rural hamlets, most of them Viet Cong controlled. The AFSC was making funds available in support of their work. I was eager to see it first-hand, despite its setting in places normally inaccessible to Americans.

I felt safe enough with the VYA because of a phenomenon that baffled Westerners—military and civilian—throughout the war: the uncanny amount of information about local conditions, anticipated air strikes, and other war-related topics available through unknown sources to Vietnamese but not to foreigners. These insights, in addition to the good will engendered by VYA's work, gave me confidence each morning in my host's assurance that the itinerary planned for that day would be safe.

Only once did I find myself at risk. We had skirted rice paddies down in the Delta for perhaps two kilometers to a small canal where the students were rebuilding a war-destroyed bridge that gave access to hamlet paddies. When we reached the site the leader took one look at me and became agitated. "What's he doing here?"

My hosts explained I was an American Quaker in Vietnam to help its people and had no connection with the "other Americans."

"He must leave at once. Our arrangement with the 'black pajamas' [the VC] is that they will permit us to rebuild the bridge, but if any American shows up here, he will be shot." I was immediately given a black shirt and a conical hat to disguise my identity and started back over the paddies with two companions. It was a long two kilometers, but no shots were fired.

Still shaken from that adventure, I went for a walk in the village that evening and found a little bistro where I could get a cup of tea. Sipping it, I noticed a young American soldier at an adjacent table with his head in his hands, weeping. I sat down beside him and asked if I could help. He looked up—I judged he was maybe 19—and between sobs and gulps of whiskey, he blurted out his story. He was a draftee, new to Vietnam, and that afternoon had flown his first combat mission on a helicopter gunship. On the way back to base, they had crossed a "free fire" zone—alleged VC-occupied territory—where he was ordered to shoot anything that moved. A woman with a baby on her back was working in her paddy, and the poor lad had done as ordered—he killed both with a burst of fire. "I seen the kid fly six feet in the air and splash into the paddy. He was just a little guy. I killed them both. They never hurt me . . . Mister, I killed them . . . I killed them . . . that little kid . . . my God, my God . . ." His head fell to the table again, and the tears flowed. I put my arm over his shoulder and gently patted his back. After a few minutes, I suggested we walk together in the cool evening until he quieted enough to get back in his jeep. We did so. I never knew his name.

Later I made a second trip to the Delta, this time to Can Tho, under the auspices of the U.S. Information Service. Their connections made it possible for me to visit a Choi Hoi center, where Viet Cong defectors were sent for re-education. Through an interpreter, I had a long talk with two tough, wiry little men, both veterans of years in the swamps and jungles as guerrilla fighters, living on a weekly ration of baked rice cake and equipped only with their weapons. They had enjoyed none of the support services available to both ARVN and U.S. forces, but their morale was sustained by a strong officer network, regular indoctrination, training in guerrilla tactics, and familiarity with the terrain. They told of lying motionless for hours under the muddy waters of Delta canals, weighed down by rocks and breathing through hollow reeds. Often they would feel their way slowly along underwater rock trails, the reeds moving as if by the current, to shelter in caves with submerged openings where they could wait for nightfall.

What motivated them? The certainty that they were driving out a hostile invader and liberating their country. Why had they defected? Because they were exhausted from years in the swamps and jungles, with little human contact. (Later I heard rumors that some Viet Cong used Choi Hoi centers for R & R, and on release returned to their units.)

While there was no way to verify their stories, those two men underlined the difference between the contending armies. Our side had overwhelming power, modern weapons, and every kind of support service. Their side had nothing but motivation and commitment—and turf that was theirs. But it would prove to be enough.

A trip north to the old imperial city of Hue, close to the 17th parallel, was notable mainly for the further evidence it provided of the Viet Cong control of South Vietnam's countryside. Only the city and its environs were secure, although during daylight hours I was able to join the Hue branch of the Vietnamese Youth Association in a seminar and work camp near the coast, and visit an IVS project making bricks and building charcoal kilns 40 kilometers to the south. En route, we passed a freight train—the only one I saw in Vietnam—moving slowly southward, its locomotive pushing two cars in front to detonate any explosives placed on the track. ARVN troops were evident, filling potholes in the road, repairing destroyed bridges, and guarding those still passable, but it was clear from the burned forests and the bombed villages that it was the U.S. Army and Air Force that were doing the fighting.

Hue was instructive, the return to Saigon an adventure. A pilot agreed to take me, but with a stop en route to resupply a Green Beret outpost in Bao Loc, a village well up in the highlands. The landing site at Bao Loc was a gravel strip on a former French tea plantation. The strip was on a mountain ridge, and the gravel was coarse enough to cause a tire to blow as we landed. The plane careened wildly and tossed me and a dozen ARVN soldiers from our bucket seats. We skidded to a halt, with one wheel shattered and 13 passengers scared but unhurt.

The field was empty save for a small shed to which we were soon ordered by a Green Beret from the Bronx, equipped with a bullhorn. He told us under no circumstances to venture among the tea bushes. This was hostile territory. They had radioed Hue for a new wheel, but if it wasn't parachuted in by 7 p.m. we would have to be billeted overnight at the commando base. He didn't want to alarm us, he said, but the Viet Cong had blown up the bridge on the edge of town the night before and were rumored to be attacking that night.

None of this was reassuring to Quaker ears, since the Green Berets were our toughest fighters manning the most dangerous outposts in Vietnam. It was even less reassuring when he asked passenger Cary to meet him in the corner of the shed

and told me that in the event of a sleepover I would be billeted with him.

When we met, his first question was: "Cary, how well do
you shoot?"

"Not very well," I said. "I'm a Quaker."

"A QUAKER . . . jeez . . . 120,000 Americans in this (exple-
tive) country, and I've gotta draw a Quaker . . .(silence) . . .
(frowns) . . . Well, never mind. I've laid on a party. Poker
starts at seven. The girls arrive at eight. If we're lucky,
the Viet Cong won't make it 'til 10." This scenario was un-
settling. I could handle the poker, but after that . . .

It was a long afternoon, spent mostly in beseeching the
Lord if possible to postpone other chores and expedite the
shipment of one airplane wheel. He did. At 6:35, a tiny para-
chute floated down into the tea bushes. Viet Cong or no Viet
Cong, one American and a half dozen ARVN soldiers raced
to retrieve it. Willing hands, working like an auto race crew
at a pit stop, helped install the wheel. At 6:55 we roared off
without gunfire, leaving behind my Bronx friend with an extra
girl but freed of a nonshooting Quaker.

Back in Saigon, the relatively mild Phan Huy Quat government had been replaced by the flamboyant General Nguyen
Cao Ky. Angry at what he regarded as an apathetic city, Ky
had cracked down with a 10 p.m. curfew, tanks in the streets,
no night clubs, no newspapers, public executions, and silent
religious groups, with harsh penalties for infractions.

Every Tuesday afternoon there were briefings at the U.S.
Embassy, where government and military spokespersons reported to the media on the war's progress. I usually attended.
Their tone was upbeat, with emphasis on enemy body counts,
improving security and military successes, reassurances to be
passed on to city desks and TV stations in the States. But in
Vietnam cynical reporters, many of whom had extensive field

experience, referred to these events as "the Tuesday after-noon follies." The information given was from province chiefs whose self-interest dictated sugarcoated reports. Most had fallen from favor in Saigon and had been sent to the field. Their reports had little relation to reality.

This judgment of the Saigon briefings was confirmed on a visit to Song Be, 120 kilometers north of Saigon, with a delegation of U.S. religious leaders. I had arranged their itinerary at the request of the Fellowship of Reconciliation and joined them on an Embassy plane to the site in Phuoc Long province where a major battle involving heavy casual-ties had taken place in May. Lectures were given by province officials and military commanders about the battle and the role of the U.S. in Vietnam, its moral commitment to the freedom-loving Vietnamese, and the brutality of a ruthless enemy. They sounded hollow to me, remembering that the U.S. had spent the previous decade in helping the French to deny them freedom.

Behind the military and diplomatic optimism, conditions were worsening. The war was driving thousands of Vietnam-ese from their villages, creating a refugee problem. In Phu Quoc, near the Cambodian border and the site of large rubber plantations, half of the 60,000 people who lived there had fled. There were stories of children dying in the jungles. Heavy bombing had wiped out rubber production. What would become of either the refugees or the 4,500 plantation employees and their families was not known.

Another refugee area was around the coastal city of Qui Nhon. I flew there to see how bad conditions were, thinking there might be a role the AFSC could play in easing the suffering. Conditions were pitiful. A hundred thousand refugees were living in scattered camps in the province, with 3,000 more arriving each week. Most refugees that I saw were women and children. Shelter was makeshift, and rice shipped north from the Delta fell short of the need. Rations had been cut. Several camps were being provisioned by air for security reasons, but the biggest problem was idleness: no work, no schools, no recreation, no nothing. The mood was despair: nowhere to go, homes destroyed, families scattered, lives in ruins. I flew south to Nha Trang, where the Mennonites had a hospital, to discuss the possibility of their joining the Friends in a joint refugee program in the Qui Nhon area. Security would be a problem. Only three camps were reasonably secure. Several were inaccessible.

During my time in Southeast Asia I made two visits outside Vietnam, one to Cambodia and one to Laos, both to look at the region through a different prism.

Cambodia was officially nonaligned, but it had long been an enemy of Vietnam. At the time of my visit, diplomatic relations were maintained with Hanoi, but not with either Saigon or Washington. There were so few Americans living there that appointments with European and Asian diplomats were easily made. I found them virtually universal in their admiration for Prince Sihanouk, who dominated the country to such an extent that information from other government officials, even ranking ones, didn't amount to much more than government handouts.

The source of diplomatic admiration for the prince was the consummate skill with which he played off Hanoi and Washington against each other. Both courted his support, but the balance he managed to maintain between them was keeping his country at peace and was seen as pure Machiavelli.

This view was best expressed by the dean of the Phnom Penh diplomatic corps, the Australian ambassador. He called Sihanouk "the most articulate chief of state in the world, and one of the ablest." Like most of his colleagues, he was sharply critical of U.S. policy, which had split Vietnam and tried to make its south a western bastion—a policy that he felt lay behind "much of the grief that currently agonizes this part of the world." He said to me, "Mr. Cary, there have been three disasters visited upon Southeast Asia since the end of the Second World War: John Foster Dulles, the CIA, and *Time* magazine, in that order!"

This view was reflected in the press, where the news coverage was different from that found in Saigon. Only in Phnom Penh, for example, could I read about the growth of antiwar sentiment in the United States. That news would not get published in Saigon.

My final report was drafted in Saigon early in August, before departing for home. It began with a pessimistic assessment of the situation in both the military and civilian sectors, which I thought had been getting worse during the months I had been in the region. Viet Cong dominance meant that the population, all too aware of the inability of the Army of the Republic of Vietnam (ARVN) to protect them, were withholding support, either in fear of Viet Cong reprisals or out of preference for the Viet Cong. This problem was compounded by many ARVN casualties, worsening morale, and high desertion rates. In my opinion, the problem with the ARVN forces was not lack of training but lack of will. If the war were to be fought much longer, U.S. troops would have to fight it.

Nor were the problems less in civilian sectors. Rice production in the Delta—the rice bowl of the world—was so affected by war and heavy Viet Cong taxes that the rest of the country was now importing 600,000 tons of rice per year to feed itself. The number of refugees had increased by 100,000 since May and now numbered more than 400,000. Contributing to this total was the "no sanctuary" policy of

U.S. forces, which called for hamlets to be attacked without warning and leveled with fire and bombs if Viet Cong forces were thought to have sought safety in them. Worse, certain Viet Cong-held areas had been designated "open target" areas where aircraft could dump unused ordinance before landing. These tactics were the most shortsighted and costly, in terms of public disaffection, of all our war policies. The military appeared to think only of body counts.

To quote from the report:

> From the foregoing, it will be easily understood why the suffering of the Vietnamese population is appalling. They are the hopeless, forgotten victims of a war that for them has raged for 25 years. They feel no stake in the issues . . . are caught in a vise between two sides who try to control them by terror . . . One can only feel a profound sense of moral outrage at the whole situation and cry out to stop this madness, but still the fighting and killing goes on . . . Every day it continues constitutes a sin against God and man.

The report concluded with four proposals for AFSC service:

1. A refugee program in and around Qui Nhon (Binh Dinh province)
2. Youth volunteers to work in the Vietnamese Youth Association hamlet program
3. A program of social welfare training
4. A prosthetics program based in Saigon, to make and fit artificial limbs for civilian war victims

Number 4 was chosen, though based in Quang Ngai in the north. The program established a brilliant record of service to all comers throughout the long years of the war.

These months in Southeast Asia, with their first-hand exposure to the suffering and devastation of a poor rice-paddy country, made me a passionate participant in the antiwar movement in the U.S.—from its relatively lonely beginnings in 1965, to its powerful outcry in the early 1970s that forced the Nixon administration to begin withdrawal from our Asian adventure.

During these years I helped plan and marched in ever larger demonstrations, drafted AFSC position papers, waited on Washington officials, wrote letters to editors, spoke at public meetings across the country, and on several occasions committed civil disobedience, leading to short accommodation at local jails.

These activities played a major role in my life for almost a decade. I report on only two that stand out. The first hinted at how differently the history of the region might have played out. It occurred at a luncheon meeting in the Senate dining room, with several voluntary agency executives, peace activists, and antiwar senators. We met to consider how the private sector could responsibly increase the effectiveness of the peace movement at the grass roots. Among the participants was Oregon's Senator Wayne Morse. I sat next to Morse at lunch, and in the course of our informal conversation the question of President Kennedy's views on Vietnam came up. It elicited the following story from Morse (content accurate, specific quotes my best recollection):

> Late in 1963, I received a call in my office from the President. He said he wanted to talk to me about Vietnam and could I arrange to see him. I said, "Mr. President, my time is your time. When would you like me to come?" He said, "How about this evening at eight?" When I arrived, he began

the conversation: "Wayne, you've opposed our involvement in Vietnam from the very beginning,
and I'd like to hear directly from you your reasons
and your present thinking about the situation
there. The recent coup, the killing of Diem, and
his replacement by the junta was, at the least,
premature. Events threaten to slip out of control,
and I have a nasty feeling that I'm being set up for
another Bay of Pigs. I'm now being urged to
send more military advisors, and I need to step
back and look again at our commitments. Are we
on the right track?"

We talked for nearly an hour. The President
listened intently but made no substantive comments regarding my arguments for withdrawal.
Finally, about nine o'clock, he said: "Wayne,
I can't take more time tonight, but we must talk
again, soon, at greater length. I have to go to
Dallas tomorrow, but as soon as I return, I'll
call you and set up another visit." Of course,
he never called, but I am personally persuaded
that John Kennedy would have ended U.S.
intervention.

The second event was the most unusual of my public ap-
pearances in church basements, college auditoriums, peace
conferences, and other forums denouncing American military involvement in Vietnam. This one occurred late in the
war and involved a major event at the Richmond, Virginia,
Convention Center, featuring General Maxwell Taylor as the
speaker. General Taylor, one of the nation's most distinguished
military leaders and a frequent presidential emissary to
Vietnam, had only recently returned from Saigon. He was

scheduled for a status report before an audience that was anticipated to number as many as 1,500.

Antiwar sentiment had by this time reached significant levels around the country, and peace activists in Richmond persuaded event planners to include a war opponent on the program as a way of assuring a more lively discussion. I was invited to fill this role and quickly accepted. It was by far the best opportunity I'd ever had to speak to such a large audience in such a newsworthy setting.

General Taylor had a different response. When he learned of the revised format, he rejected it and announced that if the proposed format were retained, he would not appear. I was disappointed, but I understood his position. As a national figure, he had nothing to gain and everything to lose by taking on an unknown Quaker in such a setting. Changes were made. The general would get top billing and make his speech. I would be permitted to comment on it, but there would be no rebuttal and no exchanges of any kind between the two of us.

This format put a heavy burden on me because, not knowing what General Taylor would say, I could prepare nothing and had to rely wholly on notes taken in the course of his address, a demanding assignment before such a large and distinguished audience with ample media representation. In the event, however, he included such standard arguments as our defense of freedom against a North Vietnamese invasion, the role of training and equipping ARVN forces to take over the fighting, the exhaustion of the enemy, and the bright prospects for a successful U.S. withdrawal, that I had plenty of room to respond with vigor. It wasn't a polished performance, but I thought I acquitted myself reasonably well. The general remained for my comments, but left immediately, and I never had the opportunity even to shake his hand.

Part Three

HAVERFORD COLLEGE
1955-1981

Eleven

<figure>⟨decorative ornament⟩</figure>

CHANGING DIRECTIONS

I N 1969, THE PRESIDENT OF HAVERFORD COLLEGE was looking for a vice president for development. Stephen Cary's name was under consideration, even though he had little fund-raising experience and was at the moment in jail in Washington. It was a turbulent time for a Quaker college, and its president thought that Cary's Quaker background might make him a helpful member of the College community. He got the job.

A more important question than professional experience or whether I was in or out of the slammer was why I was considering leaving the Service Committee in mid-career, as head of its U.S. programs and sometime-emissary to distant corners of the world. Why give up activism for the cloister?

The reasons had deep roots. Over many years a growing involvement in Quaker education had suggested to me that this was an area where I might be able to make a contribution. It began with a shared interest with Betty Cary in Germantown Friends School, where she served on the staff of its Lower School—teaching, substituting, and undertaking endless administrative chores for many years—while I served on its governing School Committee, including 15 years as its presiding clerk.

I had played a role in a decision dating from the 1950s to keep the Germantown Friends School in urban Germantown rather than accept a generous invitation to move to rural Fort Washington, outside Philadelphia. There were two

Betty and Stephen after being honored by the Germantown Friends School Committee. They are standing in front of the lower school building later renamed the Cary building. Betty holds granddaughter Cary Anne Kane.

reasons for this decision. The first was the importance of remaining close to Germantown Friends Meeting, which had founded the school in 1845 and nurtured its Quaker character for more than a century. The second was a sense of obligation to stay as an anchor and a source of stability in a troubled and changing Germantown community.

The decision to stay has had an impact on the school ever since. Its urban location has been an asset by means of which students can participate in the surrounding community and experience directly some of the stresses and dysfunction of crowded urban life. Using this asset with enthusiasm while taking account of security imperatives has been a constant challenge.

In my tenure as School Committee clerk, I worked with the head of school to articulate and give witness to values that find expression in Quaker thought: nonviolent resolution of conflict, decision-making by consensus, honesty in all matters great and small, recognition of individual worth at all levels in the school family, a minimum of rules, and a maximum of self-discipline. Many school catalogs talk about "educating the whole person," but Friends schools work hard to create a value-oriented learning environment that makes catalog words come to life. I articulated this to Germantown Friends School parents:

> We want your children to be exposed to the eternal values that illumine our Judeo-Christian heritage. But we will not bind their conscience. What we hope for is that all may learn to search for themselves and to judge for themselves that which is good and that which should be rejected— or made good. To the extent that we are successful in adding this capacity to the intellectual growth

we seek in the classroom, a Friends school will achieve its twin goals of nurturing mind and spirit.

G.F.S. pursues this goal through a combination of a minimum of rules, a maximum of independence, outreach into its urban environment, academic rigor, the silence of a Quaker Meeting of Worship each Thursday morning, and frequent settings where timely issues of peace and justice are explored.

This combination assures a lively learning environment and a spontaneity risking the appearance of chaos. During the troubled Vietnam years, for example, in the absence of any dress code, license overcame liberty. After one passage through the Upper School and an encounter with a young man clad in a blanket, I wrote to the headmaster, reminding him that the school had a more serious purpose than sponsoring a daily Halloween parade, and suggesting that he needed to crack down on headgear, footwear, miniminiskirts, and blankets. The next day he read my letter to the school assembly, to the acute distress of two students who dismissed their father as a prude and a dork—and so advised him. Family relations were strained, but the dress bar was raised.

During these same years, I became involved in higher education as a member of Haverford College's Board of Managers. This was before the days of nominating committees, limited terms of service, representation of constituencies, and all the other complexities of current board selection. Requirements at Haverford were simple: membership in the Society of Friends and a vita (preferably local) that appealed to Haverford's president, who invited the prospect to his office and extended an invitation.

I went through this routine in the fall of 1954 and appeared at my first board meeting in November. It was an organizational meeting with two agenda items: a welcome to new member Stephen Cary and an inquiry by chairman Emlen Stokes as to how to commemorate Fred Strawbridge's 54 years of board service. I noted that to match Fred's tenure I would have to make it to age 93.

The Board of Managers at the time was composed entirely of white male Quakers—a far cry from the high-powered, cosmopolitan, gender and racially diverse Board of today's Haverford. I met the requirements. The one distinctive quality I brought to my new post was a significant lowering of its average age level, and I settled easily into my role as a listener among older and weightier Friends.

Looking back on my 14 years of Board service, during which the selection process gradually moved into the 20th century, I have nostalgia for the simpler, older patterns, even as I recognize the absence of any term limits to keep some members from staying beyond their prime. One distinguished old Friend, well into his 80s, enlivened an early meeting with a long monologue about an affair between a former Haverford administrator and a waitress at the Blue Comet Diner. Board chair Stokes tried hard to gavel him down, but the rapt interest of us Board members gave a different signal. We heard it all. Board members with deep pockets met financial short-falls or the costs of special projects, but we weren't heavily involved in budgeting, property matters, business operations, or academic development. Contact with faculty was limited to an annual all-male banquet.

In these respects Haverford's governance in mid-20th century reflected an earlier and simpler era. But its Board had great strengths. They may not have contributed much to the College's academic excellence or to the modernization of its operation, but they made important contributions to that quality above all others that makes Haverford distinctive—its Quaker character—contributions to which I sometimes wonder whether today's more cosmopolitan Board will rise.

In those troubled times of cold war and McCarthyism, Haverford College's record in resisting hysteria, supporting human rights, and standing for democratic values in the best Quaker tradition was courageous, and sometimes even unique among American institutions of higher education. A few examples:

1957. Should the College apply for and accept research grants from the Department of Defense?

The question came to the Board because two Quaker values impinged on each other: commitment to freedom of inquiry on the part of faculty suggested one response; commitment to the Friends peace testimony suggested another. A complicating factor was the Department of Defense requirement that all grant applications had to be made by the institution and not by individual researchers.

In light of this requirement, the Board was clear that it would be inappropriate for the College to apply for any grant that had military implications. Haverford's Quakerism had to take precedence over its commitment to the faculty's freedom of inquiry. Faculty could pursue such grants only through another institution, and carry on the research off-campus.

A more difficult question was whether the College would apply for research grants from the Department of Defense that had no military significance and no security or classification restrictions, as was the case with many DOD grants.

Discussion leaned toward approval to accommodate freedom of inquiry until a disturbing analysis of national research support was introduced. This analysis showed that more than 50% of all U.S. academic research was funded by the federal government, and more than half of that by the Department of Defense.

The Board saw this concentration of funding sources as a threat to concepts of freedom of inquiry and to testimonies of the Society of Friends. It was a sign, the Board felt, of military influence encroaching on American life in general and on higher education in particular.

These considerations led to a Board decision that the College should make no applications for research grants from the DOD, regardless of their character. At the same time, it made two decisions in support of freedom of inquiry. A fund was established from Haverford sources to lessen the potential loss of faculty research funds arising from the Board's decision, and one concession was approved: our faculty could carry on nonmilitary research on campus with DOD funds obtained through other institutions.

> *1958. Should the College accept the conditions set by the National Defense Education Act to enable its students to qualify for low-interest government loans to help meet tuition costs?*

The problem was that all applicants had to sign a disclaimer of membership in subversive organizations, or any support for the overthrow of the U.S. government. Friends saw this provision—part of the McCarthy era's "loyalty" obsession—as having an intimidating impact on personal inquiry. It was seen as a part of the mindless anti-communism of the period. President Hugh Borton recommended that Haverford refuse to participate. The Board agreed, and Haverford became one of the few institutions to forgo the economic benefit of federal loans in order to stand against the witch-hunting climate that undermined our nation's free society. We sought other ways to help needy students.

1962. Should Haverford accede to pressure in the wake of the Cuban missile crisis to participate in a national Civil Defense program calling for the designation of shelter areas and stocking them with emergency provisions and equipment? Specifically, would the College permit civil defense authorities to make a survey of our buildings as potential shelters against atomic fallout, and if so, could they be used by the general public or only by campus residents?

The Board declined to authorize the requested inspection, noting that "shelter" in a nuclear war was an illusion serving only to calm cold war fears with bogus assurances. The decision was accepted without public objection, and indeed, the folly of such programs soon led to their quiet death.

1964. Perhaps the most difficult issue faced by the Board of Managers was whether a student should be penalized for bringing disrepute on the College because of unpopular and controversial activities.

The issue arose during the early days of American military involvement in Vietnam, when a Haverford sophomore, the recipient of a City of Philadelphia scholarship, was identified as a leader in a movement to provide medical aid to the Front of National Liberation, our country's Vietnamese enemy. The project provoked widespread outrage and a demand, led by veterans' groups, that the Philadelphia Board of Education withdraw the scholarship and Haverford College discipline the student. The climate was so poisoned that even the young man's innocent and bewildered family in a Philadelphia suburb was harassed and terrorized. The College was caught in an unfavorable public spotlight.

A special meeting of the Board of Managers was called. President Borton reported that, after reviewing a range of options, he was recommending that the College attend a public hearing at the Board of Education looking into the matter and make a strong statement defending the right of free speech within the law, no matter how unpopular. The young man in question was in good standing, thoughtful, and well informed on the background and current scene in Vietnam. His scholarship should not be withdrawn and Haverford contemplated no disciplinary action.

The president asked for Board support and suggested that, if approved, the College's position on the matter would carry the most weight if it were backed with the authority of the Board of Managers. A draft statement reflecting his position was approved for presentation at the meeting of the Philadelphia Board of Education. I was part of the College delegation that attended the hearing. Veterans' representatives and their supporters in city government were vocal and angry, but the Board chair remained calm. The president's reading of the managers' statement and his response to questions were impressive, not only because of their content but also because of the quiet conviction with which they were presented. Reason prevailed. The scholarship was not withdrawn. No disciplinary action against the student was taken.

These Friends school and board experiences and the impact the College had made on me as an undergraduate stimulated thought as to whether I wanted to stay longer with the American Friends Service Committee or explore a career change into education.

Two concerns had made me restless at the AFSC. I was troubled by the burden that extended absences and frequent evening and weekend commitments placed on my ever-uncomplaining and supportive Betty, with three young children and a household to care for and a full-time job to carry. It was a burden that had bothered me most when I left her for three months to explore relief needs in war-torn Vietnam. I had traveled in the midst of violence where the front could be anywhere and she knew little of my whereabouts. Was that fair to her?

I admit, too, that I thought I'd contributed as much to the AFSC as I could. I had been passed over three times for its top post, probably because circumstances had forced me to devote too much administrative attention to one program area at the expense of other areas, which raised questions about balanced commitments. In Quaker culture, one doesn't campaign for leadership posts, but I had been disappointed to be shut out. Could I continue my involvement in peace and justice issues through another avenue of Quaker service?

Haverford had immediate appeal. Perhaps it could contribute—perhaps I could help it contribute—to the easing of a problem that had long plagued the AFSC and its sister organizations in their worldwide operations: finding staff with the gifts of the reconciler. Twenty-five years of activism made me aware of the need. I had found myself in the midst of violence, as in Vietnam or Central America, or sometimes in its wake, as in Europe in 1946, or in the Middle East. I had been where oppression was heavy, as in Pinochet's Chile, the Soviet Union, or the deep South as the civil rights movement stirred.

These settings showed me what destroys community and what builds it. I had seen our workers fail, and been a part of failure. We could feed and clothe a community. We could build houses and repair irrigation systems. We could be a reassuring presence. But we couldn't reach to the hatred, the fear, or the despair that shrivels the soul and raises barriers to rebirth.

But I'd also seen miracles, where those who came to help, or who rose up out of the ruins of their own land, were able to reach to the heart—to the inner recesses where people live—to root out hatred, reestablish trust, and open the door to reconciliation.

What made the difference? Not competence. Competence had been present. It made order out of chaos. It knew how to analyze problems and set priorities. It knew what buttons to push. It saved lives. But a life saved is not a life released from hatred or the other legacies of violence or repression: that required other qualities of character.

The first is integrity—transparent, persistent integrity—because it is the first casualty of the arbitrary exercise of power, whether to oppress, to enlarge itself, or to wage war. In these settings, integrity flees—to be replaced by manipulation, deceit and lies, initially self-serving, but yielding in the end to cynicism and alienation, as we in the United States have learned through the deceptions and lies in Southeast Asia, Watergate, and the Iran Contra affair. Without integrity there can be no rebirth of the trust on which community depends.

Second, there is the capacity to listen and feel compassion when circumstances make these qualities hard to come by. Voices are strident, suspicions run deep. Stress often makes people behave in outrageous ways, especially when there are cultural differences and alienation. To rise above such circumstances, to be able to listen and to care, is a gift. It opens the door to compassion, and compassion makes it possible to walk in another's shoes—the greatest gift of the reconciler.

There is the need also for an abiding faith that human beings can respond to other stimuli than fear, threat, and naked power—faith that remains strong even in the face of rebuffs. To sustain such a faith requires roots running deep, roots that for me have their grounding in the Cross itself, as Joe Havens illumined for me long ago in that Trenton coffee shop.

I believe that those who possess these qualities, far more than the captains and the kings and the power brokers, represent our best hope for the future. For years I had seen the Friends Service Committee search for such persons for its far-flung programs. They are in short supply.

So, against a background of unrest at the AFSC, my experience at Haverford had appeal. I had seen its Board stand bravely for principle, and I knew the kinds of students drawn to it. I had personally felt the impact of its Honor Code in fostering integrity, and I had seen its lively concern to create the caring campus community that its great president, Isaac Sharpless, had spoken of a century ago.

Of all the institutions I knew, Haverford had the most promise of producing graduates with the qualities I had found important in an angry world. Should I leave an agency that so badly needed such persons and join one that offered the prospect of producing them?

My answer was yes. In the summer of 1969, I joined the Haverford community as its vice president for development. It wasn't a retreat to the cloister, but a challenge to add to campus life in a caring community. Haverford became my vocation, activism my avocation.

Twelve

—===➤◆◆◆◆===—

On Haverford's Second Rung
1969 - 1977

HERE WERE A NUMBER OF WEEKS between the old and the new. I spent them on Cape Cod, weighing the future, often alone on the water.

I had, in fact, two jobs. Officially, I was to be Haverford's chief development officer, charged with restoring and adding to the College's material resources, which I knew to be shaky. There was enough interest in my returning to the College that my lack of professional fundraising experience in a field increasingly complex in its demands was not thought to be a major problem. I had much to learn.

My second job, probably as important in President John Coleman's mind as the first, and one to which I was drawn and better prepared, was to support him in his efforts, during a turbulent time, to energize the Quaker values that were at the center of Isaac Sharpless' vision for the College.

For years I had felt that American higher education was giving too little attention to a unique opportunity: the chance to reach beyond honing the intellect to influencing the values by which students would live their lives.

The college setting is an ideal one. Students are independent for the first time, under our care for years when they are most open to new ideas and new directions. Their values *will*

181

be shaped, for better or worse, by the learning environment
a college provides: the ethos of dormitories and classrooms,
of recital halls and athletic fields, and of the lives they see
reflected in the campus community—presidential, professo-
rial, secretarial, janitorial.

Capitalizing on this opportunity beyond the rhetoric of
catalogs and pamphlets was important to me. I knew something of the qualities of character needed to heal a troubled
world. I knew, too, that influencing values isn't easy. They
aren't taught like chemistry. They cannot be forced. They
are shaped slowly over time, best caught by contagion. Subtle
differences divide exposure from dogma and example from
pressure. At Haverford, there had been some conscious effort to understand these subtleties and to create a learning
environment that reflects the values its Quaker leaders
thought important: integrity, openness, peaceful resolution
of conflict, sacredness of human life, respect for conscience.
At the center of its campus life for almost a century had been
a student-run Honor Code governing academic and social
conduct that was one of the most comprehensive and effective in the nation.

Evidence of this tradition was on display in campus set-
tings and College publications in a mantra familiar to all
Haverfordians: the words of President Isaac Sharpless to the
Class of 1889 at their graduation:

> I suggest that you speak truth and do righteousness
> as you have been taught, wheresoever that teaching
> may commend itself to your consciences and your
> judgments. For your consciences and your judg-
> ments we have not sought to bind, and see you to
> it that no other institution, no political party, no
> social circle, no religious organization, no pet

ambition, put such chains on you as would tempt you to sacrifice one iota of the moral freedom of your conscience, or the intellectual freedom of your judgments.

That speaks for the moral witness of Haverford College. Could I contribute to its future strength? Over the next decade I would try to do so—an exciting decade lived against the backdrop of war in Southeast Asia, the growing pains of multiculturalism, and a painful conflict with our sister institution, Bryn Mawr College.

My fundraising and later my financial management responsibilities were on company time. My concern for Haverford's learning environment was on my own.

On the first, ill prepared as I was, I found a setting even more difficult than I expected. Haverford's alumni body, heavily weighted in the service and academic arenas and inadequately researched in terms of donor potential, hardly conveyed a Wall Street aura. Save for mention of estate planning, there was no reference in development literature of deferred giving, though it was rapidly becoming the engine driving capital campaigns. Operations were in the red, and in an accounting department whose cost centers did not relate to budget lines, deficit sources were difficult to identify.

These shortcomings weren't helpful for meeting the challenges of inadequate physical facilities, problems of deferred maintenance, and pressures of an expanding student body. Fortunately, there were bright spots. Haverford had alumni whose lives had been touched by the College in ways that left them deeply loyal and ready to open their wallets in the face of needs.

My development staff was another asset. Mary King was my secretary the day I arrived at Haverford, and she was my secretary the day I retired. But Mary was never my secretary. She was my right arm, my confidant, my defender through every stupidity, the source of my reputation as an organized administrator, and the basis for fresh definitions of loyalty and good humor. The only time in ten years that she disappointed me was one day when I returned from lunch to find her arguing with other staff about the sexual identity of three streakers who had raced by in front of our office. I told her that if she couldn't reach a judgment on that, I'd explain it to her.

Behind Mary came Charles Perry, Bill Balthaser, and John Gould, among others. Perry ran a prize-winning annual giving program, the lone jewel in Haverford's development crown, while Bill Balthaser's fertile brain spawned imaginative fundraising ideas daily and lit my path in pursuit of capital funds. John Gould, Ph.D. historian turned alumni director, organized support events in major cities and enlivened weekly staff meetings with humor, smothering conflict. It was Gould who invented a famed mythical alumnus, identified as Ferd Farkle, '00, who quickly became the standard for judging how a Balthaser idea would play on the hustings.

We needed humor. Chairing staff meetings that regularly featured clashes between Perry's Quakerism and Balthaser's imagination was an art form mastered with Gould's help. A case in point was the day that Bill came up with a proposal for an annual-giving theme based on the famous World War I recruiting poster featuring a stern, finger-pointing Uncle Sam barking at the reader: "Uncle Sam needs you!" Bill's version was complete with a professionally prepared poster replacing the figure of Uncle Sam with an equally stern and finger-pointing figure of revered and awesome Haverford president William Wistar Comfort, known universally as

"Uncle Billy," and had him barking to potential donors: "Uncle Billy needs you!" Predictably, Friend Perry was outraged. The idea was preposterous. Haverford's alumni weren't doughboy prospects. I sided with Perry.

Balthaser, however, wasn't through. The following week a new poster appeared, this time featuring a gentler Dr. Comfort, his finger pointing less imperiously from an elbow position. Still no sale. Version three arrived in week three, with Comfort equipped this time with black, broad-brimmed Quaker headgear and a finger barely raised above desk level. This one passed muster, barely. Peace prevailed: Uncle Billy was Haverford's poster boy for the next year.

Meanwhile, capital campaigns began to take shape. First was the overhaul of Barclay Hall, the treasured residence of Haverford's freshmen for a century. A great granite pile, its exterior conveyed a sense of stability like Gibraltar. Its interior, on the other hand, was like a Dickensian almshouse, thanks to generations of water fights, bowling balls rolling down its long corridors, and livestock illegally lured to its upper floors. Its floors were splintered, its lights hung from frayed cords, and its walls were adorned with graffiti, especially adjacent to third floor windows, where artillery teams were provided with data offering angle of elevation for inner tube slingshots capable of hurling water bombs across campus to land on unsuspecting philosophy majors exiting the library. To bring this gem back to standard cost four times its original cost, but since virtually every alumnus since 1878 had once lived in it, the funds poured in, and its rebirth was my first triumph.

Other projects followed: a new dining center, three additional dormitories, and improved campus lighting. These successes led College authorities to deem me competent enough to add business management to my portfolio.

I was given a loftier title: vice president for finance and development.

I now needed a financial associate. We circulated a job description, and to my surprise an in-house candidate appeared in the person of Assistant Professor of Economics Samuel Gubins. Sam was brash, enthusiastic, articulate, and confident that he was what I was looking for. Unfortunately, he lacked practical experience, which made two of us, so I turned him down. Next morning he was waiting in my office. He told me I'd made a big mistake. He knew what was financially wrong with the place. He was a quick study. He wanted the job, and if I were smart, I'd give it to him, and I wouldn't regret it.

I did, and I didn't. Sam Gubins made me look like a genius. He moved budget preparation to the campus from the treasurer's office in Center City. He persuaded the Board of Managers to provide funds for an outside firm to install a new accounting system. He reorganized the Accounting Department. He tied centers to budget lines. Within a year every department received monthly information relating expenditures to budget. We still had a deferred maintenance problem and an endowment weakened by the demands of an expanding student body, but the red ink disappeared and the budget was balanced.

Even sterling associates couldn't save me from stupid mistakes. The most serious was poor and neglected oversight of the Security Department which, when it became my responsibility, was understaffed. Its patrols not only were carried out on foot because carts might damage the grass, but also followed a regular rather than random route—a handy arrangement for area thieves. These unimaginative policies had made the College an easily accessible warehouse for these gentlemen, who were making off with everything from grandfather clocks, pianos, and Persian rugs to a full range of electronic equipment lifted from student rooms and faculty offices.

I met this crisis less than forcefully, and compounded the error by tolerating, for compassionate reasons, extended absences of the department chief, who was seriously ill. Dis-satisfaction among his leaderless staff became acute and led to a drive for unionization. Jolted awake, I found myself in a self-made dilemma: though politically long supportive of workers' rights to unionize, I regarded unionization in the Quaker arena as a nonissue because we reject adversarial con-cepts and seek instead to find unity in conflict situations. Now at Quaker Haverford the luxury of living with Quaker theory was overtaken by the reality of non-Quaker conflict. The nonissue was suddenly an issue.

I asked to meet with the dissidents. I told them, first, that their complaints, relating to work schedules and departmen-tal disorganization and benefits, were legitimate. Second, the source of these problems was supervisory neglect, for which I was responsible. Third, having been a union supporter all my adult life, I would be a hypocrite to stand in their way now just because the action was in my Quaker backyard. I promised I would not do so if they felt that was their only recourse. Finally, I thought that in a small workplace like Haverford, with its traditions, we could work together to meet our problems. Would the department give me a month to try? They would, and with colleagues helping pull my irons out of the fire, we opened up lines of communication and reached agreement. The unionization drive was suspended, but remained open as an option.

At the same time, I was trying to involve myself in cam-pus life, usually informally, usually in support of presidential initiatives, and often through joining in faculty and student events. I met with newly elected Student or Honor Council members to talk about consensus decision-making in the Quaker way.

The Vietnam War dominated those early years. Opposition and sometimes outrage, fueled by the ever-present threat of the draft, gripped the campus. My direct experience in Southeast Asia and my AFSC involvement in the antiwar movement made me a useful colleague, but it was the president who set the agenda. Jack Coleman was a brilliant wartime leader for Haverford, marvelously creative in defusing crises, in providing constructive outlets for student anger, and in giving public voice to paths toward peace.

Shortly before my arrival, for example, antiwar students circulated a broadside announcing their intent to burn the campus flag. This initiative was promptly followed by a second, from other students, promising to circle the flagpole and beat up anyone intent on lowering the flag. No sooner was number two in circulation than a third appeared, this time from Quaker-related students who proposed to stand silently between the belligerents.

Aware of the delight of the media at the prospect of such a donnybrook, especially on a Quaker campus, and the public relations disaster that would result, Jack Coleman appeared at the flagpole on the morning when the burning was to take place. He made a little speech, identifying with the would-be burners' concern, but proposing that instead of a flag burning they have a flag laundering. The symbolism would be the same, the flag would be clean, and nobody would take offense. The dissidents agreed. Crisis averted; peace preserved.

Jack's next initiative, for which I shared in the planning, called for a candlelight march from three campuses—Bryn Mawr, Villanova, and Haverford—converging in front of the

Bryn Mawr draft board for speeches and rousing music. The turnout was huge, the flickering candles stunning, the press and TV coverage extensive.

For each new escalation, for each new evidence of a rising boiling point, we tried to think of diversions to keep the College on an even keel. Jack chose such a point to draft a moderate letter to President Nixon calling for the withdrawal of U.S. troops from Vietnam, and circulated it to 125 presidents of the nation's most prestigious private colleges and universities, inviting their signatures. Within two weeks, he had 98 acceptances, and the letter was sent and released to the press. It was a front-page story. On the evening it appeared, Coleman returned from a meeting to find a single long-stemmed rose in a Four Roses bottle on his porch, with a note attached reading, simply: "Thanks, Jack. Haverford students." It is possible to channel anger, to turn it in constructive directions. What it takes is leadership, shared concern, and integrity.

Haverford College's most imaginative response to the wartime crisis, however, came when it was most needed: the moment without parallel in American educational history when hundreds of American campuses exploded in fury in the wake of the Kent State and Jackson State College killings and the U.S. military incursion into Cambodia. Across the nation, more than ever before, higher education came close to a standstill with classes and final exams canceled and libraries deserted, replaced by mass meetings and angry demonstrations that often erupted in violence and the trashing of buildings. Hundreds of thousands of young men and women revolted against an unresponsive government in Washington.

Haverford College was no exception. It, too, was paralyzed, swept by spontaneous outrage, on the edge of spilling into the streets of neighboring Ardmore. Fortunately, its student body president, a charismatic, ribald, articulate, and popular Alabamian named Stanley Murphy, warmly admired by both me and the president, appeared in Jack's office with an idea as big and audacious as the upheaval.

> Let's take the whole campus to Washington for a day next week: Board of Managers, administrators, faculty, students, staff, groundsmen—anyone wanting to go—and blanket the Congress and Executive branch with Haverfordians intent on constructive dialogue on the Vietnam crisis.

Coleman was skeptical. Planning, logistics, lining up appointments, organizing at the Haverford end, and all within a week. Could it really be done? He doubted it. Murphy insisted that students would respond. A bold challenge needed a response big enough to keep 700 student hotheads busy and out of trouble. We had to admit that, if anyone could pull it off, Murphy could, so Coleman bought in.

There followed an extraordinary week. The campus community was organized by Congressional districts, with individuals assigned to call their senators and representatives to ask them to reserve meeting rooms for seminar discussions. Others phoned for appointments in the State Department and executive offices. There were orders for buses and box lunches. A final meeting in a Washington church close to the Capitol was planned and ten senators invited to address it. There were regular campus-wide meetings presided over by Murphy. At one, he ruled that if Haverford were going to Washington, it would do it Washington's way. Jackets and ties, haircuts, trimmed beards, and neat appearance were to be the order of the day, and there would be an inspection before anyone boarded a bus—a revolutionary requirement in that era. He set up a barbershop to be open 18 hours a day, where the services were free. At another meeting, he invited discussion of points to be covered, warning that booing would not be tolerated and that he had bouncers scattered around the auditorium who were prepared to throw out anyone who was disruptive.

My assignment was to circulate among planning groups and report on progress. Once I checked into the barbershop and there was Murphy himself, on the phone to an aide of his Alabama representative, with his southern accent in full cry: "Oh, yes, ma'am, it sure is, it's church-related." I made a face. He threw the phone book at me. He got his appointment.

The big day arrived. By 7 a.m., 25 buses were lined up along College Avenue. The chief inspector of wearing apparel, Ed Zubrow, a Vietnam veteran, had deployed his troops on both sides of the boarding area to insure against end runs, and by 7:30 some 750 Haverfordians from managers to groundsmen were on their way.

Washington was impressed. Officials, hard-pressed to contain disruption—and often trashing—on the nation's campuses, were delighted with Haverford College's response. Appointments were kept, issues were debated. At the final church convocation, nine of the ten invited senators appeared. During that meeting, President Coleman took a phone call from an old colleague at MI, Secretary of the Treasury George Shultz, expressing annoyance that he hadn't been informed of Haverford's plans and inviting Coleman to send ten students to join the Shultzes for dinner, which he did.

I was proud of Haverford. No other institution in the land had as creative a response to a highly-charged crisis. No one who was part of that week will forget it. The impact was on the spirit as well as on the intellect.

Vietnam was not the only issue that rocked the campus, challenging Haverford's values and the relevance of its Quaker tradition. There was another matter on which we earned low grades in the early 1970s, have tried to do better for 30 years, but still have far to go: the challenge of multiculturalism. Jack Coleman had not anticipated the crisis of Vietnam when he became the College's president, but he had come determined to lead in opening Haverford's doors to a more diverse student community, especially through enrolling young men of color. The civil rights movement had stirred such interest nationally, and the new president found a receptive Board and supportive faculty.

I shared Coleman's enthusiasm and eagerly encouraged the Admissions Office to widen its recruitment outreach. We launched the new policy with a set of easy—and painless— assumptions. All we had to do was to identify young men capable of Haverford level work, and then welcome them on their arrival on campus. All would be well.

All was not well. Many of the newcomers began to drop out, some with good grades, some with poor grades. And most of those who remained felt dissatisfied and alienated. Protests mounted, skillfully crafted into patterns in the Quaker tradition: silent vigils in front of buildings but not blocking access, broadsides listing demands, and a single centerpiece sign reading THINK. From the black students' perspective, grievances were obvious. We should understand them without being told. They wanted a "safe house," a place of their own in which to meet, minority affairs staff in the dean's office, minority faculty members, and curricular changes.

These problems were facing other campuses across the country, but at Haverford, and certainly to me, as an active Friend familiar with Quaker history, they should have been understood more quickly. For 300 years, Quaker reliance on continuing revelation—the belief that new fragments of God's will and wisdom are always available to further enlighten the always imperfect behavior of the human family—had shaped our own conduct and our outreach into the wider world. Nowhere had this been more true than in our Quaker perception of right relationships with those from different cultures and different stations in life, most notably with the black community in our own land. Originally Friends were advised to be kind to their slaves. They then perceived that a concern for freedom of worship should be matched by concern for freedom of the body. This led to leadership in the abolition movement, from there to the paternalism of schools and jobs for the newly emancipated, and most recently to the insight of working with minorities as equals integrating them into mainstream society.

Now our students were telling us it was time for a new advance: they felt alienated from the Haverford white mainstream and were not drawn to become part of it. In our well-intentioned policies, we failed to see how centuries of isolation and discrimination had produced profound differences in culture and commitments—differences in entertainment tastes, in diet, in music, in interpersonal relations, in lifestyles. What was needed at Haverford—and in the wider world—was an amended culture, one that was an amalgam, drawing on the strengths of both and creating together a new, shared mainstream.

It is a difficult goal, even on a small college campus, much more so in wider American society. The gaps are great, their bridging difficult, but we know where we want to go.

Beyond the stresses of the war and the cultural climate, my Haverford years saw a third campus conflict impinging on our Quaker tradition: the issue of coeducation, and the heavy stress it placed on our close relationship with neighboring Bryn Mawr College. Through the decade of the 1970s, Haverford's interest in the admission of women students, and Bryn Mawr's opposition to it, grew in intensity. The conflict threatened a relationship virtually unique in American higher education. The two institutions, sharing high academic standards, a mile apart but with distinctive pedagogical approaches and campus lifestyles, offered their students a rich mix of curricular opportunities. Was coeducation an issue important enough to risk destroying an exciting, pioneering, and growing relationship?

It was a difficult time for me. On one hand, I was a colleague and ally of President Coleman in his support for Haverford coeducation. On the other, I was a Haverfordian with deep family roots in Bryn Mawr that went back into my childhood. It was a mix where I was sometimes in a negotiating role and sometimes in the cross hairs of hostile fire.

Both institutions had strong reasons for their positions. At Haverford, both faculty and students found mixed classrooms richer educationally, and its Admissions Office was increasingly unhappy about having to turn away hundreds of inquiries each year from qualified young women who wanted to be fully a part of the Haverford scene. Even more troubling, there were data on the collegiate preferences of high school males, showing that 80% preferred a coeducational institution; of the 80%, 60% said they would not consider entering one that was single sex. These data had major implications for Haverford's applicant pool. We wanted to admit women for the right educational reasons before being pushed to do so to maintain quality enrollment.

On the other hand, from Bryn Mawr's perspective, the status quo, involving a growing dormitory exchange program and ever-increasing cross-course registration, was providing Haverford with de facto coeducation and removed any reason for it to admit "its own women." Preserving the single-sex status of both was an ideal situation for Bryn Mawr. By keeping restricted access to courses of special interest to women, it could offer the advantages of a single-sex setting to women who wanted it for valid personal and educational reasons, while at the same time assuring other students access to a predominantly male environment at Haverford, a mile away. Why would Haverford want to destroy this situation by embarking on a course that threatened Bryn Mawr's admissions and might harm the growth of bi-college cooperation?

Haverford's response was that the status quo could never bring full coeducation to its campus. Bryn Mawr's first year students stayed on their own campus and returned to it to complete their majors in their last year, leaving only the two middle years when there were substantial numbers of women in Haverford's classrooms and dormitories. Haverford's Admissions Office could hardly speak of coeducation to potential freshmen because they wouldn't find much of it when they arrived.

The conflict grew, with Haverford pressing for more integration of academic departments, more Bryn Mawr courses open to its students, and even cross-majoring. For Bryn Mawr, opening these doors depended upon ending further discussion of admitting women to Haverford.

Concerned with the peaceful resolution of conflict as part of Haverford's Quaker character, I was caught between counseling patience and living with my emotional commitment to the support of Haverford's case. For President Coleman there was an added complication: the cautious two-steps-forward-one-step-back approach of a Board of Managers reluctant to jeopardize relations with Bryn Mawr and influenced in some cases by their Bryn Mawr wives.

Presidential recommendations for full coeducation were regularly rejected or modified—one year to permit single-year exchanges between Haverford and several women's colleges, another to accept female students as sophomore transfers but not as freshmen. Frustration grew, and finally in the winter of 1976–1977 the dam broke. At the January 1977 Board of Managers meeting, when the Board again rejected a Coleman recommendation, the president resigned.

This shocked the Haverford community, throwing the future into limbo and putting coeducation still more in the spotlight. But whatever the impact on the community, the impact on its vice president for finance and development was greater, because in late March the Board invited me to become acting president for the 1977–1978 year while a search for a new chief executive was carried forward.

I was honored by the offer to lead the College, even if briefly. My term was to be for a year only, and I would not be a candidate for longer service. An in-house candidate would be unfair to others and an unnecessary complication for a search committee. I thought these reasons valid and accepted the offer under its terms, thrilled with the chance to use the pulpit of the presidency to articulate my vision of a college deeply valuing both its academic rigor and the quality of its learning environment.

Thirteen

A Year on Haverford's Top Rung
1977 - 1978

THE YEAR AS HAVERFORD'S ACTING PRESIDENT may have been my happiest.

Heading a small liberal arts college that one knows and cares about is a wonderful job, with opportunities to set the tone for its campus, to articulate its mission, and to interact with its alumni, its resident community, and, above all, its students. Living with the gifted young, with their enthusiasm, their idealism, their brilliance, their openness to new ideas and challenges, is a gift. I savored it to the full.

I knew what I wanted for Haverford College, and now I had a year to speak to it and to build toward it from the best of all vantage points: as its President and spokesperson. Every door and forum would be open to me, its problems mine to comment upon, its decisions mine to influence.

I knew my strengths and weaknesses. I had seen the College from every perspective: from the worm's eye view of a student, the bird's eye view of a board member, the distant view of an alumnus, and the eyes-open view of an administrator, serving under a great president during turbulent times. And I was committed to the Quaker values that were so distinctive a part of its tradition. Most important among my weaknesses was that I wasn't a scholar, now heading an institution of nationally recognized academic strength. I had no classroom teaching experience in a community where teaching excellence was highly valued.

An opening Collection, with students and faculty back on campus, would be my first test. It was, in those days, an important occasion, with the auditorium packed to the window sills, where the president was expected to give a state-of-the-college speech and a summary of his hopes for the coming year.

I wanted to make a good start, and spent much time planning my speech. It began in traditional fashion, reviewing the campus summer and the issues I anticipated would be important in the year ahead. I highlighted the new role of women. After almost a century and a half of gradually eroding male dominance, the College now had, for the first time in its history, admitted women as degree candidates, even though it still limited them to transfer students in the upper classes. Seventeen had accepted admission.

To help these newcomers, and their Bryn Mawr sisters living at Haverford, understand what was expected of them, I read publicly for the first time a Minute that had been adopted by the Haverford faculty:

> The Faculty entered into consideration of the prospects and advantages of female students being admitted to the required exercises of the College, should way open for this. They were united in the belief that if young ladies performed regular recitations and took their meals in company with the other students, it would have a natural and marked tendency to improve the faithfulness of all the students in their studies, the probity of their demeanor, and the general self-respect, refinement,

and moral earnestness of all. The experience of colleges generally, not excepting our own, leads us to acknowledge that the constitution of a family school cannot neglect to fall in with the divine constitution of the family, without fostering those unwholesome states of mind and feeling which are the penalty of all monastic exclusion from natural society. It is therefore approved that the Managers be informed that the minds of the Faculty are now prepared to favor the admission of female students to the recitations and other public exercises of the College, as full members of the College, these girls being placed under the charge of a competent female principal.

This Minute was dated May 30, 1870. It offered evidence that Haverford had been waiting 107 years for the age of women. Even for Quakers reluctant to act with unseemly haste, the Board had had ample time to make up its mind, and had finally moved, even if cautiously.

I then turned from the topical to my hopes for the year ahead, based on the qualities I had found so important in healing broken communities in the wake of war and oppression. I spoke with feeling of my years amid the suffering of Europe in the bitter years of 1946 and 1947, and of subsequent immersion over a quarter of a century in the violence of Vietnam, the Middle East, and Central America, the frightening oppression in Pinochet's Chile, the Soviet Union, communist Poland, and Bull Connor's deep South. Those who could bring new life and reconciliation in such settings were our greatest hope for a better future.

I had come back to Haverford eight years earlier because, of all the institutions I knew, the vision that Isaac Sharpless

Cary Family Archives

Addressing the Haverford community in front of Founder's Hall (1978).

had given it, its Honor Code, and the sense of community it sometimes achieved, gave it the greatest promise of producing young graduates who could make this kind of contribution. I still had that vision.

Against that as a backdrop, I spoke of the values I hoped to strengthen during my short term as interim president:

> May we at Haverford this year use well our academic studies, drawing on the scholarship and the companionship of great teachers, to become a community of learners, growing in competence. May we also become a more caring community, trusting each other a little more, growing in honesty, and in knowledge of ourselves.

Once over that opening hurdle and grateful that my words were well received, I turned my attention to business. High on the agenda was convening a meeting of the Academic

Council, the senior faculty committee which makes recommendations on major academic issues facing the College, including questions of appointments and tenure. I made clear how heavily I intended to rely on their judgments. It was hard for me to imagine a situation where I would act counter to their recommendations, but because it could happen, I promised not to act until I had called a special meeting to reexamine with them the issues involved.

There were, in fact, no crises with Academic Council. I had to convey one decision of nonreappointment to a faculty member, which was painful. It was for her a tearful encounter, but we remained—and remain—friends.

I decided to continue, and at some points expand, President Coleman's policy of meeting weekly with important campus constituencies, including the Student Council, the Minority Coalition, and the key staff of the Haverford-Bryn Mawr *News*. I promised an open door to any department or office with a problem or a grievance, and assured Bryn Mawr President Harris Wofford that negotiations on bi-college cooperation and other thorny issues would be carried out across a table, not through broadsides hurled across Montgomery Avenue or through mobilizing Haverford's power blocs. President Coleman had tried to follow the same policy, but the intense feelings generated had sometimes caused a breakdown.

The regular campus meetings with constituent groups were valuable. They were consultations where I shared my thinking and my problems and asked about theirs. Sometimes we trusted each other with off the record discussions, and there was no time when either side breached the trust that "off the record" implies.

This was particularly important in my relationship with the *News*, where mutual trust paid big dividends in the accurate communication of my views and concerns to the campus. The *News* is student-run and free to publish what it wants to, and often it was in a position to hurt me. It never did. When the editor had questions about whether his take on our weekly interview was the one I intended to convey, he called me to check my intent. The editorial page might dissent, but the paper accurately conveyed my views in its columns. This saved me from costly misstatements and led me to share with him a measure of confidentiality unlike any I've shared with any other public journal. The *News* contributed heavily to any successes I achieved, and I owe its staff a major debt.

On another front, I inherited from Jack Coleman warm relationships with members of the grounds crew and maintenance staff. Once a year they invited the senior administrators to a party in the skating shed, always a highlight of the social season. One of the groundsmen's cousins was a butcher, and the menu always included the finest steaks, lamb chops, and sausage, with homemade wine produced in the cellars of Italian groundsmen. Chief of this group was Tom Porreca, who became such a warm friend that years later, when I was running for Judge of Elections at Haverford's local polling place, Tom persuaded 12 of his Italian neighbors to switch registrations and vote for me. I won the election by ten votes.

Sometimes Betty and I had students to dinner to talk about problems that vexed them or me, or just for fun on an open evening. One day before Thanksgiving, a student with an architect father appeared in my office with a professional blueprint of a "cat ramp" that he proposed to build to enable his cat to enter and exit his second floor dorm room at will. This being an unusual challenge, I told him I'd think about it and give him an answer the following Monday. We had

Stephen Cary on the campus of Haverford College.

invited ten stranded students for Thanksgiving dinner. I fixed the price of their meal as a vote on the "cat ramp" question. We had a secret ballot, which resulted in a vote of 6-4 in favor of approval. It was never built. The student expected Haverford's maintenance staff to do so. I didn't need a secret ballot to reject that proposal.

Another student dinner was less successful. Several guests were so consumed with laughter that they punched the table extension with such ferocity that the whole piece broke off and landed on the floor. I carefully repaired and reinstalled the extension. Betty was skeptical of my competence, but I assured her the table was sound. The day after, we hosted a half-dozen of the College's most distinguished alumni at dinner before a concert. All went well until the salad course, when there was a nasty ripping sound and the extension made a second visit to the floor, this time splashing salad dressing over the gowns of the ladies seated to my right and left. Betty had something to say to me afterward about this, but for the moment she reacted with aplomb. Recalling Lewis Carroll's Alice facing a similar crisis, she said "Mad Hatter's tea party!" pulled out her extension, and dragged the tablecloth with all its settings two places in her direction. Guests reseated themselves at more durable locations. The besmirched ladies were most gracious.

A crisis came in November. It arose out of an offer from the Triad Foundation to fund a Middle East studies program jointly at Bryn Mawr, Swarthmore, and Haverford. Early discussions among the three presidents considering this generous proposal were well underway when I learned that the source of Triad's funding was Adnan Khashoggi, a notorious Saudi Arabian arms merchant widely known for his free-wheeling dealings providing arms to the highest bidder in the powder keg of the Middle East.

The more I looked into the matter, the more troubled I became. Indictments, allegations of pocketing bribes as "commissions," and labels by the *New York Times* as "the biggest arms dealer of them all" were part of the public record. I concluded that everything the man was engaged in was counter to what Haverford College and its president stood for. We could not be part of the deal.

I reported this decision to the other two presidents at our next meeting, promising that Haverford's withdrawal from further negotiations would be done as gracefully as possible in order to minimize its impact on the Foundation and the other two potential recipients. Swarthmore also decided to withdraw for curricular reasons, leaving only Bryn Mawr actively pursuing the grant. The *News* supported the decision, but it stirred up controversy with unidentified Bryn Mawr sources suggesting that Haverford had succumbed to pressure from its Jewish alumni, a charge without foundation. Bryn Mawr's position was that most money was tainted to a degree, and the prospect of receiving it without strings and putting it to good use should govern.

As late as February 1978, there was a public debate on the subject between President Wofford and me, sponsored by Haverford's Student Community on International Affairs. There was still no agreement between us on the weight to be given "tainted money," but we met at least one more time for a private discussion. At that meeting I asked Harris whether Bryn Mawr would accept a grant for a program in Women's Studies offered by Larry Flint, the publisher of *Hustler*, notorious for its borderline pornography. When he hesitated, I said: "That's how difficult it would be for Haverford to accept a grant from one of the world's most conscienceless arms dealers. It's as much against everything that Haverford stands for as *Hustler* is against everything that Bryn Mawr stands for." That's where the matter rested. Bryn Mawr went its way, and Haverford and Swarthmore their way.

Throughout the year, discussion of bi-college cooperation continued. Counterpart departments met regularly to discuss their relationship. There were enough areas of agreement by February 1978 to warrant a progress report to both communities, signed by their deans and presidents. All but three departments had submitted reports reflecting plans for future cooperation. None had chosen to go all the way to a single major, nor had any chosen to broaden their differences. These reports together validated the Cooperative Plan's terms, letting students majoring in any department represented on both campuses choose to do so at either. All major programs were now open equally to students on both campuses, a step toward what had evolved into the nation's closest partnerships between distinctive and independent institutions of higher education.

This was a gratifying development considering that agreement was reached despite the continuing controversy over Haverford coeducation. Bryn Mawr had hoped that there could be a two- or three-year moratorium on further discussion of the subject to test the impact of cross-majoring on bi-college relations, but Haverford negotiators had no way to make such a commitment. It was a tribute to the strength of the partnership and Bryn Mawr's largeness of spirit that a major step on academic cooperation was agreed upon without that pre-condition.

There was a second crisis in the early spring. Haverford had invited David Rockefeller, chairman of the Chase Manhattan Bank, to meet with a prominent group of alumni and address a convocation. He accepted, agreeing to speak on a topic for which he was well qualified and one of interest to economists and businessmen: "Does the U.S. owe the world a stable dollar?" It seemed a subject unlikely to provoke controversy, but those of us planning the event forgot for the moment that Chase Manhattan was one of the major American enterprises still doing business with the apartheid regime in South Africa.

Others in our community were not so forgetful. The Student Committee Against Racism quickly announced plans for a demonstration. Leading the protest were Mawrters resident at Haverford, which annoyed me, considering that Bryn Mawr had just received a major grant from the Pew Foundation while Haverford's application had been turned down, because, according to rumor, it was too liberal.

To meet this crisis, I did what President Coleman had done in similar situations. I asked the protesters if I could come to their next planning meeting. They agreed. I told them their event would be a new experience for me: the first time I'd been on the receiving end of a demonstration instead of the planning end. From this new perspective, I wished they weren't going ahead, but I'd be a hypocrite to try to persuade them not to. Instead, I had come to their meeting to advise them how to mount an effective protest.

My advice was to be respectful. References should be to "Mr. Rockefeller," not "Rockefeller." Their presentation should be thoughtful in tone and not strident and accusatory, aimed at provoking reflection rather than anger. Since they hoped Mr. Rockefeller would listen to what they had to say, they should listen to what he had to say rather than be obstructive or walk out. Signs could be visible, but not so large or numerous as to be offensive.

Before a packed auditorium, some of my advice was followed, some was not. Their presentation had balance in its criticism of both the College and Chase. There was no obstruction, but protesters lined up in front of the stage silently walked out when Mr. Rockefeller was introduced.

There were, unfortunately, less appropriate developments that marred the occasion. I anticipated that the Minority Coalition might plan its own protest and was in regular communication with its presidential contact, Momidoo Foon. He assured me up to 24 hours before the event that no demonstration was planned. This remained my understanding until I was escorting Mr. Rockefeller from my office down to the Roberts Hall stage. I had told him that a respectful protest on the South African issue would occur before his speech.

When we reached the stairway landing I was accosted by a small group of black students who announced that they had a statement they planned to read. I said I would not recognize them. I had been told that no Coalition statement was planned, and it was too late now for a change of mind.

After a tense moment of Quaker silence, with my anxiety level high, I invited the protesters massed in front of me to make their statement. They did so in an acceptable manner. At its conclusion, four black students leaped to the stage, in attack mode, and read a statement harshly denouncing the bank, David Rockefeller, and Haverford's racist administration. I acknowledged neither their presence nor their legitimacy, but proceeded directly to the introduction of Mr. Rockefeller. He had faced this kind of situation before and brushed off my apology, but I learned later that he had been annoyed. From other sources, I concluded that the unruly students had hurt their own cause, and I remained certain that Momidoo Foon had not been aware of their plans.

While that crisis was unfolding, I was invited by seniors to be part of their Class Night Show. This annual event had a long tradition, with each class presenting a production of its own composition—sometimes a series of skits, sometimes a musical review, sometimes a satire mocking the College or a neighborhood event. The shows were all well rehearsed, and the house was always packed.

My role was in a musical review, dancing with an ensemble, and then stepping forward to sing a solo of a current hit tune, "Love Me like a Rock," but with homegrown lyrics under a new title: "When I Was the President." No one on campus was less qualified for such a role, but I could hardly say no. The performance lacked distinction, but because it was so unpresidential, it was well received. At the end, as our ensemble bowed, I felt such a relief that it was over, and so buoyed by the tide of laughter that for a moment Haverford was Camelot—a magical moment in a magical year.

Shortly after this event, a group of students, headed by the *News* editor, came to my office to ask if I would be willing to have them mount a campaign to have the "acting" half of my title dropped and become the recommended choice as the College's next president. The campus had been closely following the search committee's efforts to identify a successor to Jack Coleman since the previous fall. Four candidates had been brought to campus, each for visits of two or three days, but none had caught fire. The Committee was embarked on a second round of interviews, with no one yet invited to the campus.

I said I was honored by their interest, but could not encourage it because of the terms of my appointment as interim president the previous spring. I had to honor that agreement. I had greatly enjoyed my year in office, and left them free to take whatever action they wished, but it would have to be on their own initiative.

Chapter Thirteen

Several weeks of campus discussion followed and led to the formation of a Students for Steve Committee. The group met on several occasions with Professor Marcel Gutwirth, the faculty representative on the search committee, who said the committee was adhering to the earlier agreement that Steve Cary was not a candidate. That could change, he said, but the students should understand that popularity, while a factor, could not be a decisive one.

A *News* poll indicated that a substantial majority of students thought I was qualified to be the College's next president, yet not enough faculty and administration responded to make a statistically reliable poll. That probably reflected doubt whether a college of Haverford's academic distinction should have a nonscholar as president. It also coincided with an announcement that Tulane's provost, Robert B. Stevens, a distinguished lawyer and scholar of English birth, had been invited to spend two days on campus. He proved a man of wit and academic accomplishment, and made a good impression.

Early in March, Board Chairman John Whitehead called me from New York and asked me to join him for dinner the next evening at a Center City hotel. At the meeting, he told me that it was the judgment of the Search Committee that after 20 turbulent years, with the campus preoccupied with a succession of activist issues—the civil rights movement, the Vietnam War, multiculturalism, and South Africa divestment—it was time to return the focus to more quiet academic pursuits appropriate to Haverford's primary role as a leading American liberal arts college: the provision of a rigorous quality education. To lead the transition, the new head should be a scholar of distinction. For this reason, the Committee had reached a decision to present Robert Stevens' name to the next meeting of the Board of Managers as Haverford's tenth president.

He and the Committee appreciated my contributions as interim president and hoped that I would remain at the College to strengthen the new administration, where the incoming president would need help. Robert Stevens was not a Quaker and was only marginally familiar with this dimension of the College.

I assured John that I understood the bases for the Committee's decision, arrived at by Haverfordians qualified to make it. It was a decision fully in keeping with the terms under which I had been asked to serve a year earlier, and I promised I would do everything I could to welcome the Stevenses and make the transition smooth.

I tried to follow through on this promise, but it was difficult. I had not anticipated how the outcome, fair and logical as it was, would turn out to be the greatest disappointment of my professional career and would leave me devastated. No one except Betty and our children has, I hope, ever known this side of the story, because it ought not to have been my response.

What lay behind it? Certainly it wasn't anger or resentment, because there never was any. It was due instead to closing the door on a dream that had been my passion: the opportunity to help a Quaker college move closer to its goal of having an impact on the values of its students as well as their intellect. The Search Committee saw me as "popular"— an asset but rightly a peripheral one. What it didn't share, without my experience living in the midst of strife and injustice, was the urgency I felt that the values reflected by a campus community were as important as its intellectual climate. That had surely been at the heart of Isaac Sharpless' vision for Haverford, and it was hard to accept that I didn't have the qualifications to contribute to his goal.

Of course I had my biases that led me to underestimate the need for a renewal of academic focus, because of a growing sense, a hint, that the dream I harbored was attain-able. I had begun to feel that I had stumbled on a way to enter into the lives of students whom I loved and to make a difference: a combination that mixed heavy doses of fun and humor with the articulation of values important in my life, but without lapsing into the atmosphere of piety and religiosity that is alienating to the young.

Finally, I had hoped that I could stay on for three years, until age 65, when I would retire and the search for a "permanent" president would resume. With those three years, I would have time to find out whether my dream was having an impact on the campus. It would be time enough for some-one younger to take over and move the College closer to becoming a college where academic strength was matched by a moral commitment every bit as strong.

With that option gone, and the need to hide pain behind a cheerful façade, life lost much of its customary joyousness. Without Betty to talk to and lean upon I couldn't have man-aged. She was a constant source of support, despite the fact that my year in office had not been for her the joy it had been for me. She had had two jobs, one at Germantown Friends School and one as College hostess.

I didn't help her much with that second job. The president's home needed alterations to increase its graciousness, to ease circulation and the interaction of guests. Some interior painting and removal of squirrels occupying the space be-tween floors would help. The absence of dampers for our seven fireplaces increased our costs of heating. And it would have been helpful if the College could have been asked to provide flowers for special occasions instead of Betty having to col-lect them herself from campus sources.

Instead of helping her with these concerns, reminders that this was only our temporary assignment led me to turn a

Cary Family Archives (photo: Walter Holt)

*Stephen received an honorary Doctor of Human Letters
from both Swarthmore and Haverford Colleges.
Here, President Robert Stevens awards the Haverford degree.*

hurtful deaf ear to them. The year had not been the partnership I had promised her. But none of this kept her from
thinking of ways to lift my spirits. On the day the board for-
mally acted, we left the campus for a picnic at the Brigantine
bird sanctuary. On our return I was cheered to find a note
pushed through the mail slot from Drew Lewis, the only
board member to stop by the house after the board meeting
to thank me for my tenure. It was a special note because Drew
was the board's most conservative Republican, later a member of Ronald Reagan's cabinet, and far apart from me in life
and in politics. But I respected Drew for his integrity, his
corporate leadership as CEO of the Union Pacific Railroad,

and his devotion to Haverford. We had forged a friendship. His gesture buoyed my spirits.

Commencement was my final appearance as president. It was undistinguished, marred first by rain and later by a poor address given by the mayor of Cleveland, who was more concerned about the outcome of an impeachment vote that morning in Cleveland than on enlightening Haverfordians on how to govern a major city.

At the end, there were a few words from me about how to deal with conflict, and words of thanks to so many for making my year so much fun, and to the *News*, and my colleagues for helping me to avoid some blunders, and forgiving those they couldn't prevent. I thanked the Class of 1978 for letting me into their lives—the greatest gift that one can give another. I hoped that I in turn had let them into mine.

At my request, instead of applause, the program concluded with Quaker silence, a time to reflect on how each of us could contribute toward a more caring College and a more beautiful community.

I stayed on at Haverford. It may not have been right to do so. I may have made life more difficult for the new president, who saw me more as a threat than as a friend.

I came back in time from depression to cheeriness, especially after being made chairman of the National Board of the American Friends Service Committee, a post I held for 12 years. Life usefully continued!

Part Four

REFLECTIONS
AND
CONCLUSION

Fourteen

REFLECTIONS AND CONCLUSION

SO MUCH FOR THE ADVENTURES OF A LIFE. What have they left me with?

First, a different but more compelling view of the man of Nazareth, one arising less from the constructs of theologians and more from a historic figure who lived long ago in the Holy Land. I do not want to challenge the beautiful biblical accounts, but it is Jesus' humanness that has brought him into my life. He challenges me as one man to another, facing the problems I face, struggling with the temptations and the vexing difficulties, swimming against a hostile and violent tide, but doing so with such grace and faithfulness and courage that he earned his place as the son of God.

This source of his sonship, won rather than bestowed, is powerfully appealing. Why is it fair to ask me to reach for his faithfulness and to follow in his footsteps if he had a godly head start? I have to believe Jesus and I had the same start, and this is what makes him my brother and my guide, why I turn to him in times of trouble, why he is the standard by which I measure my own faltering performance. It's a difficult standard.

He made that clear when he spoke to the multitudes from a mountain top. His words make painful reading, but I believe he meant what he said. His words are no more than an authentic reflection of his life's witness. He asks of us no more than he asked of himself. And we can't hide behind the excuse that our world and our devils are more terrible than his. Jesus' world was also brutal. His country was under military occupation, dissenters were crucified, and his terrorist, named Herod, was as cruel and ruthless as ours. For 2,000 years, theologians have tried to rationalize his teaching without discarding the teacher. I can't be part of that effort. I must follow his path as best I can.

The Religious Society of Friends is my home. Three aspects of Quakerism hold me there. First is its foundation, which rests on human perfectibility, not on a human sinfulness redeemable only through God's grace. Our Quaker perception of a Light Within through which God's will can be known directly opens the possibility that new truth can be perceived, even if in fragments imperfectly understood, and ever inching us toward the perfection to which God calls us. He gave us choice. The human family is redeemable. The City of God can be built within history.

For Friends this is more than pious speculation. It has substance in evidence accumulated over three centuries of a growing understanding of right relationships with other peoples and other cultures, of a broadened definition of violence, of deeper insight into institutionalized evil and the power of nonviolence, and a clearer grasp of the requirements of reconciliation.

Second, our optimism about human potential leads Friends to focus attention on our responsibilities in this world, rather than on preparing ourselves for the next one. In the words of William Penn: "True Godliness don't [sic] drive men out of the world. Rather it drives them out into it, in order to mend it." Friends have tried to mend the world. We have no creedal rules to which members must subscribe to get a leg-up on salvation. Instead, we are challenged to examine the quality and faithfulness of the lives we are now living.

This challenge is an internal one, based on the presence of a Light Within calling us to seek and do God's will at all times and in all settings.

As a Friend I am expected each year to measure my performance against this inward standard by responding to a set of searching queries relating to every area of my life, a process that is a compelling source of discipline.

Third, Friends are seekers. Ours is a religion of search, not of arrival. I like that challenge. I like the call to be open to others' truths, to be ready to learn from them, and to have no illusions that mine is the one true faith to which all others must subscribe. Here, the witness of John Woolman, the humble 18th-century Quaker tailor, lights my path when he writes in his *Journal* about a visit among the most despised people of his time. "A concern arose to spend some time with the Indians, that I might feel and understand their life and the Spirit they live in, if haply I might receive some instruction from them."

How beautiful world history would be if this were the mantra of the faithful! My roots are Christian, which I'm pleased to share at any time. But I have met believers of other faiths whose lives reflect such beauty and grace that my need is to learn from them. I feel no call to press them into my mold.

This view of Jesus and my commitment to Quakerism led me into pacifism. That, too, has grown with the years. A half-century in the service of a Quaker agency has shown me what love can do. I have seen it tested in strife and suffering, and out of that cauldron I have learned some of the qualities of character needed to reach out to the angry and the bitter and to reconcile enemies. Its witness hasn't changed the world, but it has changed me.

I've come to know the human spirit at its most beautiful and at its evil worst. This has let me share more fully the joys and the pain of others, to savor life more deeply and joyfully. I have grown through:

- the love and gratitude of poor villagers of Italy's war-ravished Abruzzi toward a young man who brought back to them integrity;

- the depth and power in a spontaneous Meeting for Worship when exhausted young relief workers learned that their efforts had helped win the Nobel Peace Prize for the Society of Friends;

- the gentle voice of Margarethe Lachmund, the courageous German Quaker, as she assured me that the living, daily presence of God in her life allowed her to speak the truth in love even to the Nazis;

- the sense of belonging in a muddy waterhole in a Massachusetts forest in 1942;

- the anguish of a young GI unable to erase the image of a baby blown from the arms of its mother in a rice paddy;

- the fortitude of a lone Pole in 1946, congealed with cold, as he began to rebuild his home;

- the silent, gnawing fear that stalked Santiago's poblaciones in Pinochet's Chile;

- the awareness of the depth of human wickedness when I looked down at the crushed skulls of six murdered children in Cambodia's killing fields;

- the beauty of a moonlit night off the coast of Patagonia as a school of Antarctic dolphins played joyously with our vessel.

These images, beautiful and terrible, leave me with no illusions about the evil abroad in the world, but they assure me too of the goodness and beauty of which the human family is also capable. They light my hope for the future.

These gifts flowed out of my decision 60 years ago to refuse to fight in the "good war." I was troubled then that I had no answer to Nazi wickedness. I have one now through the Society of Friends and other peaceful voices, an answer set forth in 1918 and offered month after month, year after year for two decades, beginning even before the shooting stopped in 1918. One of its early voices was that of a letter written to the *Philadelphia Public Ledger* by Henry Cadbury, a 20th-century Friend and biblical scholar. His letter appeared on October 12, 1918, a month before the armistice ending World War I:

> As a Christian and a patriotic American, may I raise one cry of protest in your columns against the orgy of hate in which the American press and public indulges on the receipt of peace overtures from the enemy. Whatever the result of the present German request for an armistice, the spirit of implacable hatred and revenge exhibited by many persons in this country indicate that it is our nation that is the greatest obstacle to a clear peace and the least worthy of it . . . Every concession on the part of the enemy is counted as a mark of weakness and is made an excuse for more humiliating and unreasonable demands . . . Surely it behooves us at this hour, when not retaliation of the past but the assurance of a safer and saner international

fellowship, is the world's greatest need, distinguish-
ing justice and mercy from blind revenge, keeping
ourselves in the mood for moderation and fair play.
A peace on any other terms or in any other spirit
will be no peace at all, but the curse of the future.

This letter was more intemperate than most of what Henry
Cadbury said or wrote. But his condemnation of war hysteria
and his prescient judgment of the future were beacons of
reason at a time when reason had fled. Predictably, however,
its publication produced such outrage that even Quaker
Haverford College suspended him. (The College was spared
a final decision on dismissal when two months later Cadbury
announced that he had accepted a tenured appointment at
Harvard, where he went on to enjoy a 30-year career as a
distinguished Professor of Divinity.)

Haverford's Board of Managers showed little courage in its
response to Cadbury's voice. But the Society of Friends
adopted his call for "moderation and fair play," beginning
with the acceptance of Herbert Hoover's invitation to feed
children whose lives were threatened by the blockade of
Germany continuing long after the shooting ceased. When
Americans were in no mood to "reach out to the Hun,"
Friends mounted a food program reaching more than
one million German children a day for two years. They established Peace Centers in German cities, lobbied against
the vindictiveness of Versailles and its demands for repara-
tions, and tried to ease the suffering of the German people in
the period of wild inflation in the late 1920s.

Such voices went unheeded. Americans were more concerned with the Red Scare and with "a return to normalcy"
than with pressing our allies to move past vengeful German
policies. The result was bitterness and despair among the
German people—a mood that spawned Hitler and assured

him a following. As Henry Cadbury had predicted, the victors' peace became a curse.

Generosity toward a defeated enemy was the Quaker answer, shared by other peacemakers. But as war clouds gathered in 1939, it was popular to ask Quakers for their answers to Hitler, and when responses were unsatisfactory, to dismiss us as irrelevant. A different scenario makes clear that it was the question and not the response that was illegitimate. Suppose the Quaker path had been followed since 1919, but Hitler had still arisen and was threatening the world in 1939. Suppose in this crisis Friends turned to the military and looked for its answer. Would not the generals have been justified in answering: "Your question is illegitimate. For 20 years you haven't listened to our advice. We can't help you now. It's too late." Wouldn't that have been a fair answer for Friends to have made in 1939?

This rational argument in support of my decision more than 50 years ago to stand aside from military service has some merit. But ultimately, what governed that decision was not an intellectual exercise. It sprang from a deeper source— a source that the Quaker philosopher Rufus Jones described at the outbreak of World War II:

> If there should be no spiritual volunteers in this crisis of human history to bear testimony to the truth and splendor of this brave way of life for which Christ lived and died, then the final victory of arms by the successful bombing of cities and sinking of fleets, and destruction of armies can hardly save the faith of the ages . . . When the priceless jewel of the soul is at issue, you do not argue or hesitate, or halt between two opinions. You say: "I cannot do otherwise. God help me. Amen."

Out of a life of frequent dissent, I am committed to a view that has little popular support, but that invites reflection. It rests on the premise that nonviolence is fundamental to a better future. Its roots are spiritual but powerful secular arguments support it.

The role of military power in providing security has been fundamentally altered in the last 50 years. The formula that nations used to provide stability in an imperfect world has been to create a force sufficient for defense against aggression, behind which the parameters of justice and peace were to be strengthened. That was the dual aim of America's Containment Policy in the wake of World War II. Its components of strength and peace building were to be balanced.

It hasn't worked out that way, as a glance at our nation's 2002 budget makes all too clear. It allocates $380 billion to the power to kill and less than $10 billion to address the problems of hunger, poor education, disease, and the environment on whose solution peace ultimately depends. This staggering imbalance has arisen, not by design but because, in a nuclear age and a polarized world, the demands of security are open-ended. They so preempt our hearts, our energies, and our resources that there is little left over for meeting human needs and narrowing the gap between rich and poor. Justice denied becomes the seedbed of violence. Instability deepens despite the trillions squandered on amassing power, and we find ourselves more insecure than ever in our history. Might, even unlimited might, can never again provide security.

Nor is deepening insecurity the only price we pay for our readiness to follow the path of violence, however much we clothe it in the language of justice and freedom.

Simone Weil, the French essayist, in her treatise, *The Iliad, or, The Poem of Force*, wrote this about violence:

Its power of converting a man into a thing is a
double one, and its application double-edged. To
the same degree, though in different fashion, those
who use it, and those who endure it, are turned to
stone.

This happens to powerful people and nations. In subtle
and insidious ways, exposure to violence conditions an acceptance of agony ever more easily. We who are powerful
lose the capacity to feel horror, which is itself the ultimate
horror. Think back to the sense of outrage that swept our
land when Mussolini's pilots dropped bombs on Abyssinian
peasants, and again when the Luftwaffe attacked Rotterdam.
But somewhere between Rotterdam in 1940 and Dresden in
1945, the outrage disappeared. There was hardly a ripple when
60,000 men, women, and children perished in the senseless
bombing of that beautiful city—to say nothing of the too
easy acceptance of the worse horror of Hiroshima and
Nagasaki. The same lack of concern continues to insulate
us. How many were troubled by burying alive thousands of
Iraqi soldiers by rolling our tanks over their desert trenches?
And how many are troubled by the deaths of 5,000 Iraqi
children every month as a result of U.S.-supported sanctions?
We Americans, living in a culture of violence, are becoming
numbed by violence.

When feelings of compassion are drained from a people,
and when violence is no longer troubling, nations become
deaf to the needs of others beyond—and even within—their
own borders. An arrogance of power blossoms. The British
succumbed to this in their imperial past. The Soviets visited
it even on their own people. Now it is Americans who are its
most dangerous victims, pursuing policies of violence and
neglect as we please, with little attention given to the

opinions or interests of others or to international agreements that no longer appeal to us.

This is not because of evil intentions, any more than other nations had them before us, but because we, like they, are trapped by our own power. The virus of violence, always latent, has in a nuclear age assumed a new dominance. It engulfs our culture and numbs our hearts. The crisis of our time is not the clash of ideologies or the aggression of rogue states, but the illness of the human spirit.

How can the illness be cured? We can hope for the emergence of new leadership of the stature of Gandhi and Nehru, Arias and Sadat, Mandela and King and the Dalai Lama, who have not succumbed to the arrogance of claiming that "we" are good and "they" are bad. Those leaders' spirits were fed not by the politics of power, but by the politics of caring and conciliation.

Or we can hope that "people power" will rise again as a source of change. The relatively stable world of cold war came apart in unexpected places and unexpected ways through a series of sometimes erratic, sometimes organized resistance to despotic authorities—massive but nonviolent. Unarmed men and women in Manila, in Warsaw, in Dresden and Vilnius, in Prague and Budapest, in Tirana and Moscow, and more recently in Belgrade took to the streets, blocked the path of tanks, faced down troops, and forced the collapse of oppressive regimes. Even where nonviolent resistance failed, as in Tiananmen Square and Rangoon, that resistance keeps tyrants on the defensive.

Those relatively recent events in history made me hope that there was a real possibility of nonviolent social revolution. Modern communication brought images of nuns confronting tanks in Manila, and thousands in the streets in East Berlin and Moscow, into the world's living rooms. We saw angry citizens rising to exert a different kind of power. I thought that never again could it be claimed that liberation could come only from the barrel of a gun.

My hope was premature. The allure of "people power" proved transient. Nonviolence as a relevant method of social change has yet to find significant acceptance. But the history is there, and new opportunities will open. New and mighty expressions of unarmed revolution will arise.

Yet the time is too late and the threat too great to simply wait for new leaders and new uprisings. Those who care about peace and justice must add individually to a spiritual liberation. We have to think more clearly about the price we pay for breaking the human tie and acquiescing in violence. Where are the restraints on savagery? What does our readiness to fear those who fear us, to hate those who hate us, to kill those who would kill us, do to our spirits?

If, out of this searching, we want to cleanse our own spirits, we can say a personal "no" to immoral claims of power wherever they appear and whatever the cost, remembering that it has been the "no's" of the few, daring to put principle ahead of convenience, that have been the seed of the advances in human liberation over the centuries.

Most of us cannot do great things to expand justice and build peace. But we can cure our own spirits, and that is the stuff of peacemaking. It swells a movement. It puts us in the prophetic tradition. It brightens hope. On August 20, 1945, barely two weeks after Hiroshima, an editorial in *Life* ended with these words:

> Our sole safeguard against the very real danger of a reversion to barbarism is the kind of morality which compels the individual conscience . . . The

individual conscience against the atom bomb? Yes.
There is no other way.

At the end of my life . . . there is no other way.

Stephen loved to travel and planned the many adventures of his later
years meticulously. Here, on his last major excursion, he joined
friends bare-boating in the South Pacific.

Photographs*

*Captions in quotes were found on the backs of photos.

*An 11-year-old Steve stands in the upper left between his parents,
C. Reed Cary and a seated Margaret Morris Cary. Grandmother Sarah
Comfort Reeves sits in the middle, with sister Barbara Cary Curtis and
Comfort Cary Richardson on the floor. Also in photo are members of
the Cadbury family, including his mother's sister Rachel Cadbury
on her mother's left.*

230

*12-year-old Stephen with sisters
Comfort (8) and Barbara (14)*

*With Betty and two of their
children, Anne and Charles
Reed, in 1954. (Dorothy was
born in 1957.)*

Housing built after the war in Finland. (1947)

"There were 199 applications to this trade school in Toulouse, but only 73 places." (St. Lazaire, France, 1948)

"The men in this picture received brain injuries during the war and have been pupils in a tailoring school run by the AFSC. Here they are shown wearing new clothes which they made themselves." (Finland, 1948)

"Shoemakers employed at the neighborhood community center in Frankfort after the war."

233

*Taken shortly after one of the two treks to the
Himalayas Stephen undertook after turning 60.*

*Betty Cary carrying a skeleton across campus for a visit to
the Germantown Friends School kindergarten. Betty has
worked in the elementary school for 50 years.*

Stephen with family
Top row, l to r: *Phil Kane, Anne Cary Sampson, Charlie Cary, Dorothy Cary holding Cary Anne Kane, Hugh Sampson, Debbie Cary*
second row: *Elizabeth Sampson, Stephen G. Cary, Betty Cary, Margaret Sampson*
bottom row: *Abigail Cary, Katherine Sampson, Stephen Cary.*

The Cary Family at Cape Cod

Top row: *Elizabeth Sampson, Stephen and Betty, Hugh and Anne Sampson*
Middle row: *Katherine and Margaret Sampson*
Lower left: *Debbie Cary, Stephen Cary II, Charlie Cary and Abigail Cary.*
In front: *Dorothy Cary, Cary Anne Kane, Phil Kane and Sarah Kane.*

SELECTED SPEECHES AND WRITINGS

A Response to September Eleventh

As a Quaker, a pacifist, and one of the 9 percent of U.S. citizens who dissent from our country's current response to the September 11 attack, many friends belonging to the 91 percent majority have asked me to explain my position. Piecemeal answers are time-consuming and unsatisfactory, so I have drafted this fuller statement that I can share with all interested.

It goes without saying that I share the view of all in the U. S. that what happened in New York and Washington was an unspeakable crime. I, too, want the perpetrators identified and brought to trial—preferably under international auspices. Those are givens.

There are two roots to our national anguish, either painful in itself, but together responsible for causing a level of shock as deep or deeper than Pearl Harbor. The first is our sadness over the terrible loss of lives and the pain we feel for those whose days will never be the same. The second is the harsh recognition of a new national vulnerability. For 300 years we have been secure behind our oceans. For 300 years we have been in control of our fate. The coming of the atomic and missile age actually ended that happy state of affairs a half-century ago but did not seize the nation until September 11, when it came like a bombshell. Citizens of the U. S. knew then that our world would never be the same. It was a stunning shock.

This article appeared in Friends Journal, *March 2002* © *Friends Publishing Corporation.*

The question we face now is how to respond to this new reality, and this is where the 91percent and the 9 percent part company. How do we differ? As I understand it, the 91 percent, under the president's leadership, hope to regain control and restore at least a measure of invulnerability by building alliances, tracking down evildoers, and military action. In his words, "It is America's mission to rid the world of evil. We must root out the terrorists and stamp out terrorism, and we will do so." It is a new kind of war, against civilian populations, and not fought by opposing armies. Our military response will be measured, designed to flush the guilty from their hiding places, and punishing enough to persuade those who harbor them to turn them over. The war's end is indefinite, but it will be long and will continue until the threat of terrorism is eliminated. The U. S. will stay the course. Justice will prevail.

The people of the U. S., traumatized by events, find comfort in a new national unity, based on a fervent patriotism that finds expressions in showing the flag, singing "God Bless America," arranging for 40 million children to simultaneously recite the pledge of allegiance, and congratulating ourselves on our role as the champions of justice and the torchbearers of freedom. This outpouring is reinforced by the full weight of the government, the media, and the entertainment, sports, and corporate communities, and leads to unquestioned backing of the bombing of Afghanistan as the opening phase of the new war.

There is a need for comfort in trying times. The decline in partisan bickering and the coming together of our diverse society are welcome. But acquiescence has a downside in the current crisis because it silences dissent and the serious discussion of alternative policy directions. From my perspective, this is a dangerous state of affairs because the path down which we are going is likely to lead to more terrorism rather than less, and to decrease security rather than rebuilding it.

Why? First, because retaliation, whether identified as "punishment" or "justice," does not teach the enemy a lesson or lead it to change its ways. Retaliation stiffens, angers, and invites counterretaliation. If we have not learned that over the last half-century in the Middle East and Northern Ireland conflicts—to name just two of many settings where the tit-for-tat game has been on daily display—I don't know where we've been. Retaliation as a way to prevail against an enemy has, short of annihilation, been a failure. Has any benefit really accrued from the daily bombing of dirt-poor, starving, and chaotic Afghanistan? Has this really reduced the threat of terrorism?

Second, we will likely see more terrorism because our bombing will increase alienation and, in many countries, especially throughout the Arab world, add to hatred. It is already doing so. Polls taken in Turkey and Pakistan have shown that a shocking 80 percent of Turks and a majority of Pakistanis oppose our bombing, and a dangerous number even supports bin Laden. It is just this hatred that produces the fetid soil from which the terror masters recruit their troops. (Compare: the rise of Hitler in an embittered Germany in the wake of a vindictive Versailles.) If we succeed in capturing bin Laden, there will be plenty of others prepared to take his place. Increasing hatred assures more terrorism. In sum, I believe the president's "crusade against wickedness" will fail.

What is my alternative? How seriously should I take the instructions for dealing with enemies given to me by Jesus, whom I claim to be my guide, my brother, and my master? There is no doubt about where he stood. He made it clear in the greatest of his sermons when he preached to the multitude from a mountaintop: "And why beholdest thou the mote that is in thy brother's eye, but considerest not the beam that is in thine own eye? . . . Thou hypocrite, first cast out the beam out of thine own eye; and then shalt thou see clearly to cast out the mote out of thy brother's eye" (Matt. 7:3–5).

Reflecting on these words is not a popular exercise for Christians these days. Brushing them aside has been made easier, first, by the efforts of theologians who for 2,000 years have found them too uncompromising and have looked for ways to temper them without repudiating their preacher; and, second, by claiming that Osama bin Laden is a new and more terrible devil than the world has ever known, who must be dealt with differently.

Neither of these rationalizations is satisfying. I believe Jesus meant what he said because his words are no less than a faithful reflection of the vibrant witness of his own life. Nor can I accept the convenient bin Laden argument. Jesus' world was at least as brutal as our own, his country under military occupation, and its terrorist differing from ours in name only. His name was Herod, and his al-Qaida was his army.

These reflections have made me think about motes and beams. What are the beams in our American eyes that make people hate us? And if we can remove them, won't that lessen hatred and reduce terrorism? Human beings do not fly civilian airplanes into buildings to kill 3,000 innocent people without harboring a depth of anger that makes them easy targets for a bin Laden to persuade them that, in doing so, they will become God's martyrs. We in the U. S. live with illusion if we do not recognize that there are millions, especially in the Arab and Muslim worlds, who harbor this kind of feeling toward us. Doesn't it make sense in such a circumstance to ask what options are open to us to ease this dangerous situation? A few voices are doing so, but I have yet to hear a single word on the subject from any government source.

Indeed, to the contrary, President Bush has been widely quoted as saying that he, "like most Americans," is "amazed that people would hate us, because I know how good we are." With all due respect, I am appalled at the shallowness of such a comment from the most powerful man in the world.

I think there are things we can do that would point us in a new and more hopeful direction. I identify them in what follows, in the hope that they will provoke thought.

AID TO OTHERS

We need to take a fresh look at our outreach to the world's poor, its hungry, its oppressed and illiterate, its sick, its millions of refugees. We think of ourselves as generous and caring. The reality is otherwise. The U. S. is by far the most miserly of all the world's industrialized nations in the percentage of resources it allocates to nonmilitary assistance to the underdeveloped world. I think we should be troubled when we glance at our current budget: $340 billion for the power to kill; $6 billion for the power to lift the quality of life of the poor and dispossessed, on whose succor peace ultimately depends.

WORLD ARMS TRADE

Shouldn't we reexamine our role as the largest player in the worldwide trade in arms? We justify it on the grounds that it helps democratic allies defend themselves against aggressor nations, but often they are dispersed on the basis of two other criteria: (1) the ability to pay or (2) the recipient's qualification as the enemy of our enemy and therefore entitled to our weapons. It is this armament that frequently ends up in the hands of tyrants and is used to oppress their people or attack their neighbors. A poignant current example: Afghanistan, where we armed the Taliban because they were fighting the Russians, but who then used our largesse to seize power, with tragic results. The arms trade is great for Lockheed, but a curse to the world, and a source of slaughter from which hatred is spawned.

SANCTIONS AGAINST IRAQ

Shouldn't we be concerned about the 5,000 to 6,000 Iraqi children who die every month because of U.S.-supported sanctions? Aren't these lives just as precious as those so wantonly destroyed on September 11? The sanctions are of course aimed at Saddam Hussein, but after years they have left him stronger than ever, and they are being ignored by many nations, including close allies. What purpose are they serving to justify the added burden of hatred they provoke?

THE ROLE OF THE CIA

Whatever it may have accomplished that we don't know about, what we do know should raise the grave concern of all in the U. S. Particularly egregious has been the CIA's role in arranging coups that overthrow governments we don't like, even popularly elected ones. The list is long—Guatemala, Chile, Iran, Cambodia, to name several. Do we in the U. S. have any awareness of the millions of human beings slaughtered by the regimes we installed in their place or opened the way for? I have personally seen the tragedies we wrought in three of those examples—Chile, Guatemala, and Cambodia—and it is an appalling record. Our readiness to interfere in the internal affairs of other nations poisons our image, especially when others see the firestorm that erupts here when foreigners mess in our affairs, even when through relatively innocuous illegal contributions to our political campaigns.

U.S. POLICIES IN THE MIDDLE EAST

This is the most sensitive and difficult concern for me to raise, but because it is probably the most important source of hatred of the U. S. throughout the Muslim world, where the greatest threat of terrorism is centered, I have to speak to it despite my full support of an independent Israel. The problem is the perceived 50-year imbalance in our stance in the Israeli-Palestinian conflict.

I speak to this issue on the basis of three visits to the West Bank and Gaza during the last 20 years, and six weeks living in Jerusalem, with instructions to focus on meeting with Likud officials to better understand their point of view. There are a number of factors that underlie Arab anger:

(a) The harshness of Palestinian life under a half-century of brutal Israeli military occupation—brutal not because it is Israeli, but because any occupation in a hostile environment is brutal. Neither people in the U. S. nor, indeed, many Israelis, have any idea of what the daily life of a Palestinian is like and has been like for 50 years: arbitrary cutting off of livelihoods; daily encounters with checkpoints often involving long delays; land seizures; unfair allotment of water; summary trials in military courts; sudden shutting down of schools and colleges; blowing up of homes; thousands trapped in squalid refugee camps since 1948. I wish U.S. and Israeli policymakers could spend two weeks living with a Palestinian family; they might better understand the rock throwers.

(b) Massive military aid to Israel. This is justified as necessary to assure its security in a hostile environment, but U.S. weapons, from heavy tanks to helicopter gunships, kill Palestinians at a ten-to-one rate and give Israel over-whelming superiority in the brutal game of mutual re-taliation. This adds to Arab anger and robs us of the neutrality required of a broker in peace negotiations.

(c) The Israeli settlement program. Deliberately designed to honeycomb the West Bank to make a potential Pal-estinian state geographically impossible, and involving the seizure of large blocks of land without warning or compensation and the eviction of all who live on it, the program has always been a massive obstacle to any mean-ingful peace settlement. Yet for over 30 years the U. S. has made only the most modest protests and has made it financially possible by large grants of nonmilitary aid that have served annually to free Israeli funds for its construction program. Some years ago, I was sitting in the office of Mayor Freij of Bethlehem when he pointed across a valley at a settlement under construction and said, "Mr. Cary, I have friends whose family has lived on that land for 700 years. They were just told to get out. We could do nothing. Do you blame us for being angry? I can promise you one thing: the Israelis will never know peace until this sort of injustice is ended. You Ameri-cans could have stopped this program, but you weren't interested in doing so."

(d) Highways crisscross the West Bank to assure easy passage between Jerusalem and the settlements. Cars with Israeli license plates can reach most of their destinations in 20 to 40 minutes, while Palestinian cars take several hours because of holdups at military check-points.

(e) I've mentioned water. I do so again to underline that, because it is in such short supply throughout the region, its allocation is a major issue. Israel controls all water resources and, in the eyes of Palestinians, its allocation is so unfair that it is a source of bitterness, of which they are reminded daily.

(f) Terror. We rightly condemn and give full press coverage to Palestinian terror—the blowing up of Israeli buses and the tossing of bombs into marketplaces—but where has been the outrage, or even press mention, of the Israeli practice of many years of forcibly removing Palestinian families from their homes and bulldozing or dynamiting them because a relative has been accused of being a terrorist? Isn't this cruel retaliation against innocent people also terrorism?

Or, to cite a more recent, specific example of terrorism: the assassination of Israeli Tourism Minister Rehavan Zeevi. You will remember that a few months before his killing the Israelis assassinated two radical Palestinians (in what they labeled "preemptive strikes") by blowing up their cars from helicopter gunships (U.S. provided). The Palestinian response: nothing—not, alas, by choice, but because they had nothing to respond with. In contrast, the Israeli response to the Zeevi killing: heavy tanks (U.S. provided) sent into ten Palestinian towns, at the cost of 25 Palestinians lives—all in territory turned over, at least in theory, to the Palestinian Authority. I don't justify assassination under any circumstances, but there's hardly been a clearer example of the imbalance of power—courtesy of the U. S.—that is such a bitter source of Arab anger.

The Arrogance of Power

Throughout history, great powers and empires have always been tempted to go it alone, to pursue their own interests without regard for the interests of others. England was the victim of this mindset throughout the 19th century. In the 21st, are the immense wealth and power of the United States taking us down this road? Some troubling evidence:

(a) Our stance toward the United Nations. We call on it when it suits our purposes, but ignore or denounce it when it doesn't. We don't pay the dues we solemnly committed ourselves to pay because some things about the organization displease us. This petty behavior badly hurts our image around the world.

(b) We walk away from treaties we signed and ratified, but which we no longer want to be bound by. A current example is the Anti-Ballistic Missile Treaty, the cornerstone of arms control for the past 20 years.

(c) Ignoring, vetoing, or reneging on a whole range of negotiated agreements that enjoy the overwhelming support of the world community, but which we don't like because they may limit our freedom of action. Examples: the Kyoto agreements on global warming, the Nuclear Test Ban Treaty, the elimination of land mines, the Law of the Seas agreement, the establishment of an international war crimes court, and the regulation of international trade in small arms.

Wouldn't a more generous, cooperative role in the community of nations, instead of readiness to go it alone because we are the superpower that nobody can challenge, help to change our image and lessen anti-Americanism around the world?

Earlier, I spoke of identifying and bringing to trial the perpetrators of September 11 as "a given," but I haven't mentioned the subject since. It is still a given, but it has a different priority with me than with the nation's 91percent.

Blasting Osama bin Laden and his lieutenants from their caves or killing them on the run will satisfy the widespread desire for vengeance, but its price is too high and its contribution to easing the threat of terrorism too low. Destruction of a starving country and blowing up Red Cross relief depots, hospitals, and residential areas—however unintentionally—only add to the anger that is the root cause of terrorism.

I give priority to pursuing other avenues that promise to improve the international climate to the point where diplomatic and legal initiatives can produce the culprits for trial and punishment. Biding our time will prove less costly than dropping megaton bombs.

I have wanted to give some sort of answer to the many friends who are troubled by bombing and retaliation but ask, often plaintively, "But what else can we do?" My suggestions are of things that in the long run would seem to me more likely to free us from terrorism and restore security than rooting out bin Laden by twisting arms to build temporary military alliances, meeting violence with violence, and bombing poor countries.

In making my case, however, I have two problems. The first is how to speak forcefully on so many issues without coming across as anti-American and/or anti-Israel—perceptions bound to produce more heat than light. It's also frustrating because I am as devoted to our nation as any flag-waver. My aim—and my definition of patriotism—is to help a great country become greater, and more worthy of its dreams.

My second problem is the impression I may convey that the United States is the only one responsible for bringing terror on itself, which is patently not the case. We are one player among many. Other countries, including nations in the Arab world, are guilty of sins of omission and commission that have contributed to the present poisoned atmosphere, and which must be addressed. My position is only that we are complicit and should undertake our response to September 11 where it is easiest and most important to do so—where our own house is out of order and where we can ourselves do things that will contribute to easing the world's sickness.

We must move beyond the naive but satisfying illusion that "we" are good and "they" are evil—that the devil always lives somewhere else: now in Berlin and Tokyo; now in Moscow, Hanoi, and Beijing; now on to Belgrade and Kabul; but never in Washington. The devil lives in the hearts of all God's children, and until we take responsibility to try to lift up that which is good in us and cast out that which is bad, the scourge of terrorism will continue to torment us.

On Becoming a Pacifist in 1940

I GREW UP IN A PRACTICING QUAKER HOUSEHOLD and was educated under its auspices for all of the 16 years it took me to make my way from kindergarten to a B.S. degree. With that background, even General Hershey might have expected a 4-E request, but though I owe him a great deal, for me it didn't come easily. My Quakerism in 1940 was still largely subliminal. Fortunately I met Joseph Havens in the Trenton Y where we were both living, and Joe was an articulate and convinced pacifist engaged in nightly debates with two Air Force-bound Cornellians. I joined in these proceedings and in two weeks I had debated myself into a pacifist position from which I have never retreated.

I became a CO largely for religious reasons, though I had a strong sense of outrage, dating from family dinner conversations during the 1920s and '30s, that the vindictive policies of the Allies had made Hitler's rise possible, and that humane policies long urged by Friends and others would have avoided the whole terrible tragedy. But much more important than these political considerations were my belief in the sacredness of human life and my interpretation of the central message of Jesus of Nazareth.

I discovered, when the time for choice came, that Friends' understanding of the relationship between God and man had a powerful personal meaning for me. If each of us has the capacity to communicate directly with the Divine, we must

---

Stephen gave this talk at numerous venues and panel discussions.

each have something God-like in us, and this makes all human life sacred, not to be destroyed for any reason or under any circumstance. Further, I found strong reinforcement to this personal conclusion in the life and teachings of Jesus. I believed then, as I believe now, that the central message of Christianity is that love is the overcoming power in the world, and that Jesus' life, and certainly his death, was a mighty witness to his own commitment to that message.

Other Christians may argue from selected scriptural passages that Jesus would have been prepared to kill to advance his Kingdom, but I can't. For me, the whole spirit and tenor of his life and his final acceptance of death on the cross make such an argument utterly untenable; whatever others may be able to do, I could not, and cannot, reconcile Christianity and war. I became a CO—with no illusions that it offered a short-range response to Hitler's evil, but a feeling, too, that the military response was no answer either—unless one thinks that 40 million dead and a continent in ruins qualifies as an answer.

I have never been troubled by the charge of "realists" that pacifism is irrelevant in a violent world. Faith does not depend on relevance, but beyond that, it has always seemed to me that minority views *are* relevant in a democratic society. They serve as a pole of discussion and influence policy to the extent that their arguments are persuasive and their voices strong. How else is a war-less world to come about save by the individuals bearing witness to a different way?

Pacifism: Relevant Witness or Pipe Dream?

I N COMMENTING ON THE PACIFIST BELIEFS of Friends, I should make clear at the beginning that they claim no easy answers to the problem of evil in the world. For more than three centuries the Society has held to its peace testimony because, for Friends, it seems to flow inescapably from the life and spirit of Jesus, and especially from the circumstances of his death. This religious perception, and their own experience, has persuaded them that nonviolent resistance, in combination with persistent good will, has the power to change the minds and hearts of other men: to lift up in them the good and diminish the evil. But it is only a faith, always imperfectly expressed, and the reality of evil is so great that Friends should be modest in the claims they make for faith, certainly in the short run.

Against this background, I'll comment on two levels: first, in relation to pacifism as a personal witness, and second, about its relevance politically.

In the first area, I would argue that there is ample evidence that such a commitment can be a practical philosophy for an individual life. The path of nonviolence is not an easy one, and it is always inadequately traveled, but for those who seek to follow it the results can be satisfying and joyous, with a clearly constructive impact on those touched by their lives, and sometimes even on great events,

Written for Germantown Friends School Bulletin *12, no. 3 (Spring 1974). Stephen (GFS '33) was at the time vice president for finance and development, Haverford College.*

as for example in the instance of Gandhi and the freedom of India.

I believe it is the quiet rebels, the men and women of conscience, standing courageously alone and peacefully affirming, at whatever cost, the truth as they see it, who have lifted humanity out of barbarism. So it was with Socrates— and with Martin Luther King. These spirits, far more than the captains and the kings, have purchased human dignity and human freedom with their own blood, not with the blood of their enemies. For them, the choice has never been simply to kill or be killed, but rather to seek the third option that is always available to those who have the courage and the imagination to discover and follow it: the option of quiet, unflinching adherence to what one perceives as right. Death may be the price, but so may it also be for the fighter, and which approach is more likely to make an opponent re-examine his premises? Put in Christian terms, if Jesus had chosen to fight at Gethsemane as his followers urged, would the impact of his death have shaken men's hearts in the same way as his acceptance of the Cross? I think not. In the championing of a cause, there is profound power in the willingness to accept suffering oneself rather than inflict it on others. In that lies the relevance of a personal commitment to nonviolence.

One further comment on the personal side: We know that violence destroys the enemy; do we consider enough what violence may do to us? Simone Weil, in her remarkable essay on the *Iliad*, writes these words:

> Its power of converting a man into a thing is a double one, and its application double-edged. To the same degree, though in different fashions, those who use it and those who endure it are turned to stone.

Are Americans, in their blind faith in the power of violence, being turned to stone? If not, how else explain what has happened to us between our moral outrage over Mussolini's bombing of the Abyssinians in 1937, and our easy acceptance of the infinitely more barbaric American attack on Southeast Asians in recent years? I believe we must individually turn away from violence, lest we one day find ourselves faced with the ultimate horror: our inability any longer to feel horror. How far down that road have we already gone?

POLITICAL RELEVANCE

On the matter of political relevance I will make only two points. The first is that I know of no way society can be changed—or the scourge of war ended—save by the slow process that begins with the individual changing himself. At the outset he is, in a political sense, wholly impotent, but as others join him and the weight of their argument and the loudness of their voices increase, they become a relevant minority, whose views temper and influence decisions in the direction of their concerns. Could anyone deny, for example, that the gradually swelling chorus of opposition to Vietnam— and in terms of *that* war it was a pacifist chorus—had a profound impact in compelling our government to bring a halt to U.S. involvement in that obscenity?

The second thing I want to say is that when the non-pacifist chooses a particular moment of history that suits his purpose, and then points his finger at the pacifist and says "You're irrelevant," he is unfairly loading the dice. The usual challenge is in terms of Hitler poised for attack, with his legions at the ready and Europe's appeasers cringing before him. Obviously, when such a flash point comes, the pacifist has no answer. Neither does the non-pacifist, despite his facile claim to the contrary, unless one thinks that 40 million dead, a continent in ashes, and countless millions wandering homeless and hungry over the face of the earth are acceptable outgrowths of rational human conduct.

Perhaps the results would be better if the pacifist were allowed to take the photograph of history at a point of *his* choice, which is as inappropriate an exercise as the one so often engaged in by the non-pacifist. If so, my photograph would not be of the world of Adolph Hitler, but of the world of Versailles. Looking at *that* moment, I suggest it is possible that if the allies in 1918 had dealt with a defeated Germany with generosity rather than with vindictiveness, and had helped her economically in the 1920s instead of letting her people go hungry and suffer through a terrible inflation, the course of history might have been quite different. The Germans would have had no cause to turn to Hitler in the first place.

The Quakers called for such an approach in 1918 and thereafter, but they were not heard, and the world, having pursued quite different tactics in the interim, is hardly justified in turning to the Quakers in 1930 and saying "You see, you're irrelevant, your philosophy is impractical." The point I want to make here is that pacifism is not a tactic to be turned to when all else fails. (Imagine, for a moment, how well the Pentagon would fare under reversed circumstances!) It is a way of approaching problems, a way of dealing with emerging conflict through means that in their very nature build community rather than destroy it, a way of overcoming hatred by refusing to hate. In that sense, I assert both its soundness as a philosophy and its relevance as politics.

ADVICE TO STUDENTS
ON ACTS OF CIVIL DISOBEDIENCE

As I began to think about my talk this morning, I was amused by the thought that I might entitle it "Sophocles and Me." Of course he rather outshines me as a writer and dramatist, and Thebes in the 5th century BC isn't quite the same as Philadelphia in the late 20th century AD. We do have a common interest in civil disobedience as an instrument of social change, which remains as great today as it was 2500 years ago.

Civil disobedience is, of course, the central theme of his great tragedy of Antigone: the first great literary treatment of the subject. His drama is stark; a brave but wholly powerless Antigone is driven by conscience to act on the demands of a higher law in defiance of the massive power of the state. She does so peacefully and by herself, hiding nothing, readily admitting her guilt in dramatic confrontations with King Creon, and accepting without question her sentence of death.

One person, one act of defiance, one death, but because of her steadfastness, and her beautiful attitude, she wins in death the heart of the city, and looses a chain of events that bring down the king and engulf him in a horrible personal tragedy.

I would suggest to you that Antigone's triumph is also the triumph of the great spirits throughout history who, like her,

---

This talk to the tenth grade at Germantown Friends School was given in November, 1998.

have witnessed for justice and widened the parameters of human freedom.

Indeed, as I view history, it is the courage, the stead-fastness, the quiet defiance to established authority by brave men and women, often at great personal cost, far more than the captains and kings and the power brokers and massive military battles, won and lost, who have given us our most precious freedoms — of speech, of worship, of assembly, or other civil liberties — so much that contributes to the qual-ity of our lives — which we usually take for granted.

This is not to say that issues fought out by armies on great battle fields have not sometimes contributed to these great causes—as in forcing the Magna Carta on King John, for example. But I revere more the long labor of those who stood up for human dignity and freedom and were reviled for their civil disobedience. Many are heroes today: the Hebrew prophets, Jesus of Nazareth, the martyrs, those imprisoned or burned at the stake, the 40,000 Quakers jailed for ministry in the 1600s for the right to worship in their own way, those like William Penn, whose defiant response to his jailer who had offered release if Penn would agree to keep the peace was: "I will stay here till I rot ere I yield one iota of the free-dom of my conscience." Or in our own day I revere the Gandhis and the Kings who translated religious witness into positions of power. And let us not forget those brave nuns and the citizens of Manila who blocked Marcos' tanks, or those who did witness in Warsaw, Vietnam, Prague, Budapest, Rangoon, and Beijing where peaceful civil disobedience contributed so much to the collapse of communism. All these actions were the stuff of freedom.

But, I must now say, that disobedience has as great a potential for mischief as it has for good. It is a dangerous witness and unless carried out with controlled and limited circumspection, it can indeed undermine communities, as its critics loudly maintain, by weakening respect for law. Law is the backbone of a free society, and we all have an obligation to live within it. Any decision to violate it must be carefully thought out, and carried out in a controlled framework with rigid discipline.

Absent these controls, civil disobedience can be a disaster— as it was in this country in the 1920s. Then, many thousands of Americans defied the law and were civilly disobedient during the period of prohibition. Bootleggers and speakeasies got booze any way they could for selfish gratification. In the roaring 20s the respect for law was at the lowest ebb in our history.

In this light, with these pitfalls, I want to give my rules for undertaking civil disobedience:

• It is the last, not the first, recourse.

• Its purpose must be at the community level and not gratification of personal interest or gain.

• It absolutely must be respectful and nonviolent. Its aim is to persuade, not to defeat — to encourage thought and self examination in others. Violence angers; violence closes minds; violence does not spur thought. Moreover, authority knows how to deal with violence.

• The perpetrator must accept the punishment that established society exacts in good spirit. This acceptance too is essential; it contributes to discussion.

These four guidelines are absolutes; if these are not met, civil disobedience should not be undertaken.

Two other considerations must also be weighed.

- There is a need for openness. Antigone never hid what she did or why. Openness is part of the attitudinal approach which persuades, but it is not always possible, as for those who hid Jews during World War II.

- It should not interfere with the rights of others to act as they think right. Tactics of obstructions are dangerous— but in my opinion under rare conditions they are justi- fied.

Sophocles did not deal with the issue of other options for Antigone, but her purpose was not selfish. I should point out to you how truthfulness and goodness follows the acts of civil disobedience in the stories. Antigone acted wholly in a peace- ful way. She did so openly and accepted the punishment.

You can tell that I'm a passionate believer in the power inherent in civil disobedience, and bow low in admiration to Antigone and all who have followed her.

THE QUAKER MANDATE

In the year that king Uzziah died I saw also the Lord sitting
upon a throne, high and lifted up, and his train filled
the temple.
Above it stood the seraphim: each one had six wings; with
twain he covered his face, and with twain he covered
his feet, and with twain he did fly
And one cried unto another, and said, Holy, holy, holy, is
the LORD of hosts: the whole earth is full of his glory.
And the posts of the door moved at the voice of him that
cried, and the house was filled with smoke.
Then said I, Woe is me for I am undone; because I am a
man of unclean lips, and I dwell in the midst of a people
of unclean lips: for mine eyes have seen the King, the
LORD of hosts.
Then flew one of the seraphim unto me, having a live coal
in his hand, which he had taken with the tongs from off
the altar:
And he laid it upon my mouth, and said, Lo, this hath
touched thy lips; and thine iniquity is taken away, and
thy sin purged.
Also I heard the voice of the Lord, saying, Whom shall I
send, and who will go for us? Then said I, Here am I;
send me.

---

*Transcription of a talk given in the final session of Philadelphia Yearly
Meeting, March, 1979 and subsequently printed in the* Friends Journal, *November 15, 1979 (titled "The Quaker Proposition."). Stephen
at the time was a member of Germantown Monthly Meeting, vice
president of Haverford College, and chairman of the Board of
Directors of AFSC.*

I begin with these words from the sixth chapter of Isaiah because they fall, I think, with particular poignancy on Quaker ears, and maybe especially on our ears as we enter this day into our fourth century in Philadelphia Yearly Meeting. For we Friends, in perceiving that there is a Light that lighteth every man, lay on ourselves a special obligation to follow the Light that is given to us so directly. We are called to be God's instruments in service. Many of us, I think, remember from our earliest days those famous words of William Penn: "True godliness does not turn men out of the world, but enables them to live better in it, and excites their endeavors to mend it." That is the Quaker Proposition to which I want to talk this afternoon: our personal obligation to mend and how we should try to carry it out.

It is not a new question in this Yearly Meeting, nor in any gathering where Friends meet to consider their faith and their responsibilities. Indeed, I remember another Yearly Meeting in this room, a long time ago, when we were all very much exercised about a particular racial conflict, and someone rose in the body of the meeting and expressed the hope that Clarence Pickett might go to that particular scene and attempt to bring the angry parties together. The meeting responded warmly to this suggestion until Harold Evans, who was sitting way up in the balcony, in the far corner of the meetinghouse, almost in the last row, rose to speak, and in that beautiful voice, which so many of us can hear still, said, "Here am I, Lord, send Clarence." And after a pause . . . "Friends, have we nothing to say for ourselves?" That's all he said, and he sat down. I've never forgotten the impact of Harold's statement.

That's why, earlier this month, when those troubled young students from Haverford and Bryn Mawr came to me and said they wanted to tell Friends about our failure to rid ourselves of all the elements of racism on our campus, my advice was: "Yes, of course, go and share your concerns, but don't ask the Yearly Meeting to solve our problems, because the answer is not going to be found at Fourth and Arch Streets, or even in the resources of the Chace Fund, however welcome they would be. Nor will they be saved merely by adding more students to live in our community in its present imperfect state. The answers will be found on our campus in dealing with our own curricular shortcomings and with the attitudes—the thoughtless insensitivity, almost always unintentional, that still lingers in our community, and makes our minority students feel less than full members of it. These are the problems. They are my problems. And all you students whom I love and admire, they are also your problems. Only we can solve them."

So the first response to the proposition is: What can I do, not what can be asked of others to do. But on the heels of the first question comes a second, and I think it is much more difficult: How shall I do it?

This is where I think we Friends are in the most trouble, not so much because we are unconcerned, but because our concern is imperfectly exercised. The world has always needed mending, but in other ages the main hurts we felt in our hearts were those we could see, whose mending was primarily a neighborhood assignment. Of course, we had our traveling Friends who ministered far from home, but theirs was a special instance in a special time. John Woolman rode his horse up and down the coast from Mount Holly, New Jersey because his soul was on fire with the injustice of the slavery that he saw all around him. Vietnam, the Middle East, Southern Africa, and Chile, Communism and Nazism, famine and revolution and poverty in the far corners of the world were not part of his life because he did not own a TV, and his newspaper, insofar as it recorded distant troubles and sufferings at all, did so weeks, months, and even years after the event.

Not so with us. The challenges and the sorrows of every continent pour in on us each day with the evening news. The vast winds of change that affect our world grip and excite us right in our own living rooms. As Private Meadows says in *The Sleep of Prisoners*,

> The frozen misery of centuries breaks, cracks,
>   begins to move.
> The thunder is the thunder of the flood,
> The thaw, the flood, the upstart spring. . . .
> Affairs are now soul size
> The enterprise
> Is exploration into
> God.

We Friends want to be involved in that change, in that rebirth. We long to ease the agony, to achieve the justice, to build the peace.

And because we are Quakers, people everywhere turn to us for help. Not, Friends, because of our special merit, but because our fathers and our grandfathers and our mothers and our grandmothers bore their witness, in season and out, in good times and bad, with a consistency that—for all the individual backsliding—has for our Society been unbroken over the centuries, and has won for us a measure of the world's respect. We are only the inheritors, but our reputation as Friends still makes us wanted and needed. Small wonder, then, that we are pressured by our own consciences into more and more areas of concern. Our faith offers us no relief because it assures us that love overcomes and overcomes universally: its only limits are the imperfections of our own imagination and the inadequacies of our own will in its application.

So, as I look at our service bodies and at the concerned and active members of our monthly meetings, I see them increasingly pressured and harassed, on a kind of accelerating merry-go-round, pouring themselves into ever more disparate—and far flung—concerns, a far cry indeed from the single-minded passion of John Woolman. Indeed, I find myself on the merry-go-round. And in these circumstances time to nourish the roots is hard to find.

But time, Friends, is not really the problem. There is a much worse one, and it lies in the decline of our own felt need for nourishment. This is the age of organization. We join together for greater power and effectiveness; we assemble substantial funds; and thus empowered with money and troops, we come to feel sufficient unto ourselves. The old approach to exercising our concerns, when a Friend asked to be liberated by the Meeting, and the Meeting through its worship and its prayers served as guide, counselor, and support, no longer operates in most of our service enterprises.

Fundamentally, conditions are different. We cannot and probably should not return to the old and simpler practices of a simpler age to conduct the tasks we have charted for ourselves. It is appropriate that we join together and assemble funds and organize our work, but I think, Friends, that, as we do so, we need also to reflect deeply, and to pray earnestly, about another piece of Penn's wisdom: "Have a care, Friends, where there is more sail than ballast." And I would suggest that when we look at the history of our Society or at the contributions of those past Quaker leaders whose memories we most cherish, we will discover that they reflect that care: that it has been when our sails and our ballast have been in balance that we have been at our best.

In all our fervor—in all my fervor—to be doing, have I paid too little attention to the power that lies in being?

Do we remember that it is the spirit of our service, the aura that surrounds it, the gentleness and the patience that marks it, the love made visible that compels it, that is the truly distinctive quality that lifts Quaker service above lobbying, above pressure, above coercion, that inspires the doubtful, and reaches to the heart of the adversary?

All of us in our own lives, in our own day, everyone in this room, have seen truth spoken to power by men and women who radiated this spirit. Memories flood in on us at the very thought: Clarence . . . Rufus . . . Henry . . . and those two towers of wisdom and delight, Margarethe Lachmund and Anna Brinton. And in my own case, my beloved friend Robert DeWitt, who served so nobly as the Episcopal bishop here in southeastern Pennsylvania not long ago. I remember him especially on one occasion in Washington. We were vigiling and fasting for peace in Vietnam with a few other clerics when, all at once, as we stood quietly in worship in front of the White House, the Reverend Carl McIntyre—all six feet six of him—strode up and began to belabor Bob DeWitt. Glaring down at him, challenging in manner, harsh in judgment, angry in tone: "Bishop, I hope you realize that what you are doing is playing right into the hands of the communists." The slight, little bishop looked up at the angry man towering over him. He smiled, and said sweetly, "Carl, our aim is to play into the hands of God." So simple, so gentle, so disarming, so uncomplicated, that the encounter ended right there. McIntyre, though surely unpersuaded, could think of nothing to say, and went quietly off about his business. This kind of spirit, this gentleness, this certainty of the immanence of God's love at work among men is not found in strategy meetings, in manuals, or in organization charts, important as they may be.

We know in our hearts, but we don't very often translate

into our lives, the perception that these are found, over time, only in worship—only in the quiet, never-ending search to discover the immediacy of God's love in our lives. Yet it is the heart of the matter, because it is only by drawing on God's strength that we can cling to the sense of compassion and forgiveness and patience that alone informs our Quaker service with the quality that truly persuades. Friends, if we would stand against the hurricane, we need roots that run deep. I know that for all of us, on those rare occasions when we have found the courage, the will, to put principle above convenience, there is a deep and profound gratitude for a faith that goes beyond knowing.

This is the spirit, Friends, that removes the dilemma that seems so often to vex us in our deliberations: the apparent conflict between our call to confront and our call to reconcile. We were warned the other evening, in our consideration of divestiture, of the danger of coercive confrontation. And it is dangerous. But surely Friends must sometimes confront, candidly and directly. John Woolman did it all the time, and if coercion is making someone feel uncomfortable pressure, then Woolman was coercive as well. But he was also marvelously loving. The miracle of John Woolman is that he was at the same moment able to be both a coercive confronter and a loving reconciler. That is what we have to aim for, too; without love, confrontation produces anger; with it, it provokes self-searching. I think therefore that we torment ourselves unnecessarily in our preoccupation with the conflict between confronting and reconciling. There need be no conflict. Confrontation in love has within it the seeds of reconciliation. This is the spirit, too, that answers for us the question: How far should I go in making my witness? The answer is: just so far as I can continue to feel the humanness of my adversary and exercise toward him the same loving compassion and understanding that I want for myself. It is a spirit that sets limits, just as at the same time it is a spirit that compels, that turns back our timidity, that says "take a stand," when others say "wait, let's be careful, all the evidence isn't in." Thus it both drives and controls. Of the two, I think we Friends in Philadelphia Yearly Meeting are more in need of the drive.

It is the spirit, too, that holds us to a sense of responsibility to the human being who is opposite to us, whoever and wherever he or she may be. For me, Friends, this sense of personal responsibility to the human being who stands opposite to me, while it is limited ground on which to stand, is the only solid ground there is. Once we leave it, once we abandon our responsibility and break the human bond for any other loyalty, any other set of political or philosophical values, no matter how appealing or compelling, the descent into barbarism follows as the night the day.

Finally it is this spirit, too, which sustains us when we are defeated. For we must not think that our Quaker witness is based on a success ethic. Life is too complex, the human response the result of such a variety of forces, that cause and effect predictions are quite impossible. All we can know is that love endures, while that which is gained by force crumbles. Again and again the human spirit has been ruthlessly suppressed, sometimes for centuries, only to emerge quite undiminished when the yoke is lifted. Even in our own country, where we cherish freedom, we all know in our own lives the emergence of that spirit. I recall, for example, David Lilienthal in the hearings before Senator McCarran—tormented, harassed, reminded of the perils of Communism: Did he not believe that this was a terrible problem, did he not believe that the State was in danger, did he not believe we must fight fire with fire? Finally Lilienthal, turning and facing his tormentors and saying, "Senator, this I do believe." And then followed that soaring witness to the freedom of the human spirit that shook the fearful men in Congress.

Or, again, many of us remember, I'm sure, watching on television when Senator McCarthy and the lawyer from Boston, Mr. Welsh, were dueling, and McCarthy launched his vicious personal attack on Welsh's young assistant. Suddenly the articulate lawyer disappeared and in his place stood simply an anguished human being: "Senator, is there no limit to which you will not go to destroy a man?" That was the turning point: the human spirit rising up to augur the defeat of the Senator from Wisconsin in that oppressive trial. But the knowledge of those instances, the certainty of the triumph of the human spirit in history, has to be enough for us to make our witness; we cannot know the outcome of our own individual struggles.

Man's vision of all this is partial; our ability to discover the way is limited, and we are faint-hearted. We make bad judgments. We spread ourselves too thin. We lose our tempers. We get tangled up in our structures. Our list of failures is long. But, Friends, we have to remember, too, that we have had our triumphs. We have sometimes seen hatred exorcized, the estranged reconciled, the depraved reborn, the violent made peaceable, and sometimes in most hateful and unlikely places. And when this miracle has happened, it seems to me that the key ingredient has not been sound planning or scientific knowledge or other special expertise, indispensable as these things are, but the quality of life of the human instrument who has tended to his ballast even as he filled his sails. These witnesses to truth have put first things first.

If we would speak to our moment of history as others have spoken before us, I think our first responsibility is to

Be still, and know that I am God.

Lord, we know that when a man breaks his heart before Thee, he can enter into the gate.

Thou wilt lift him up and give strength to his arm and make him mighty.

Lord, bend us to Thy will, renew us, give us the will to stand for peace, to act for justice.

Give us the strength to persevere, the courage to hope.

And, Lord, make us know the sacredness of all life.

And, finally, give us the faith to believe.

Lord, I believe; help Thou my unbelief.

QUAKER COMMITMENT TO JUSTICE, PEACE, AND THE INTEGRITY OF CREATION

D EAR FRIENDS, it is hard to be a speaker so near the end of the line. We are all tired. So many papers have been presented that none of us is able to absorb much more. For this reason I have largely scrapped my paper and instead will try to be pointed and brief.

What I have to say, partly because of my experience this week, will be directed in large part to the churches of the First World. I really have little I can offer to the churches of the South. What they have said to me here serves to still my voice, for I have heard, repeatedly, a cry of anguish and a cry of impatience. They long for peace, they know the threats to God's good earth, but they are so immersed in the ocean of poverty and oppression that engulfs them that their passion and their preoccupation is with justice. They plead for our help, not our words. Therefore, hearing their plea, I can only ask for their forgiveness and commit myself as a Quaker from rich and complacent America to do more, and talk less.

My task is to set forth the ways which I think the tiny group to which I belong, the Society of Friends, best expresses its ecclesial commitment to justice, peace, and the integrity

Address at a consultation called by the World Council of Churches, Glion, Switzerland, November 1986. It was subsequently published by the American Friends Service Committee as "A Possible Quaker Contribution to the Christian Dialogue Regarding Justice, Peace, and the Integrity of Creation." At the time, Stephen was the chairperson of the Board of Directors of the AFSC.

of creation. I am tempted, of course, to inflict on you a broad explanation of my Quaker faith—but I resist that, and will confine myself to giving just enough background to help you to understand where our expression of commitment comes from.

I begin, therefore, by saying that, as a Quaker, I believe that there is a Light that dwells within each human being on earth, and gives to each of us the capacity to know directly the will of God. It follows for us that the presence of this Light endows each life with a sacred dimension, so that it must not be debased or exploited or destroyed for any reason or under any circumstance. Though God alone knows how far I could find strength to sustain this witness should I be tested, I still hold it as an article of faith. Evil must be resisted—one cannot be neutral between justice and in-justice—but the resistance must be by means that reflect the spirit of Christ.

These things I was taught as a child growing up in a Quaker household, but I later found them richly confirmed by my reading of the Scriptures, where it seems to me that the whole spirit and tenor of Jesus' life, and above all else his death, was a mighty and unyielding witness to his central message that it is love alone that endures, and challenges, and overcomes evil. It is the whole armor of God, with its breastplate of righteousness, its shield of faith, and its sword of the spirit that we must wear, as Paul wrote to the Ephesians so long ago. For me, though I know not for others, Jesus' teaching in this area is simple. It is categorical. It cannot be rationalized.

But it is in my experience over 40 years in Quaker service all over the world—often in the midst of strife and suffering—that this instruction has translated itself into con-viction. Over these years, the power of love has become, for me, *certainty*, and my faith in nonviolence a way of life, beyond disputation. This does not give assurance, dear friends, that I could keep this faith were I to be walking in some of your shoes, but I believe it is the faith to which Christ calls me.

Many times in this service I have seen our workers fail. They have helped to feed and clothe and serve a community, but they could not reach to the hatred, the despair, the self-ishness, or the anger that paralyzed and consumed it. But I have also seen miracles where hatred has been exorcized, the estranged reconciled, the depraved reborn, and the violent made peaceable—sometimes in the most difficult and un-likely places.

Those who performed these miracles came from no one class or group. Some were young, some old and wise, a few were Quakers, most were not, some rose up out of the wreck-age of their own communities, some came from afar to min-ister to need, some were Christian, some were not.

But what distinguished them all was that they dared to believe that human beings could rise above their baser nature, that they could respond to other stimuli than fear and threats and naked power. They reached out in love to the alienated and the despairing, sure that if their faith was visible and enduring it would have the power to confront evil, to reconcile, and to change.

They lived as if this were true, and it became true. The spirit of their service, the aura that surrounded it, the gentle-ness and patience that marked it, and the love made visible that compelled it broke down the barriers, and changed the hearts of the embittered and the angry.

Some of you have asked me, could it have changed all hearts, even those most hardened? I do not know, for Jesus has not given us a success ethic; he assures us only that love endures—forever. Indeed, when Jesus himself tested it, it failed, for the hearts of his tormentors were not softened. They had the opportunity, but their faith then—and alas, our faith now—was in Barabbas, the man of violence, the Rambo who had dared twist the tail of the Roman tiger, and it was for the release of this hero they clamored, while Jesus, the man of love, was rejected, mocked, and crucified.

Of course we Christians know that love didn't fail, that in death Jesus triumphed, that the victory was his, that he lives with us still, teaching his people and opening our hearts. Knowing this, I do not understand why we still stand in the courtyard, still choosing Barabbas—and in my country giving him two hundred billion dollars to spend each year, with each dollar inscribed with the mocking words "In God We Trust." What hypocrisy we American Christians are guilty of! I am sorry, but it seems to me that in our support of militarism we crucify Christ afresh every day.

I am persuaded that there is another way. We have all caught glimpses of it in the lives of men and women such as those I noted a few minutes ago. I believe deep in my heart that those who possess it, far more than the captains and the kings and the power brokers, are the last best hope of the world, and that if we're going to keep from blowing ourselves back to the Stone Age, we church leaders had better nurture such spirits and send them out to serve in the name of a loving God.

For me, placing such people in our service is the first expression of our Quaker commitment to justice, peace, and the integrity of creation, for they represent our approach to mending the world.

The second evidence of our commitment lies, I think, in our particular perception of the interrelationship of justice and peace. We can all unite in the view expressed by many here that there will not be peace without movement toward justice. That linkage is clear—but as a Quaker I raise the question of another more troubling linkage: that which exists between arms and justice, and ask whether it is possible to move significantly toward justice as long as our commitment to seek security through military power so overwhelmingly preempts our hearts, our energy, and our resources.

There is, in our perception, a growing incompatibility between a commitment to armament and a commitment to justice, for our reading of history over the past 40 years is that both cannot be simultaneously pursued in a nuclear age, where the demands of military security are virtually open-ended. Where, we ask, over the past four decades have the demands of justice, so necessary for the achievement of peace, been given priority by nation-states over the demands of military power, deemed so necessary for the achievement of security? The Scriptures tell us that man cannot serve two masters. In this situation we think to do so, but we cannot.

To the extent that this is true—and I think it merits serious examination by the main line churches—it adds yet another imperative for the reconsideration of traditional Christian attitudes toward war. I have already asked how the church can continue to choose Barabbas; I now ask how we can continue to arm him. Both questions provoke a third: Has the time come when the Christian church, if it is truly committed to struggle for justice, peace, and the integrity of creation, must return to its pre-Constantine witness, and break with the war system with its readiness to bless violence to gain its ends? If not now, when? After the missiles start flying?

The third expression of our Quaker commitment to justice, peace, and the integrity of creation is our affirmation of a loyalty to God that reaches beyond our loyalty to any nation-state. Western Quakers suffer under the bonds of cultural isolation. Despite hopeful outreaches into the Third World, we remain far too much a white, western, and middle-class community, not relating effectively to the masses of the world's people. We are far behind many of your communions in reaching out to the broad human spectrum, and we have much to learn from you in this regard. But we have never been bound by the equally limiting bonds of nationalism that it seems to me have shackled many in the established churches. Quakers have tried to be good citizens in their own lands, but we have insisted that our obligation to maintain fellowship with the human being opposite to us, regardless of whether he or she has been popularly classified as friend or foe, transcends our national identity. We have sought to succor all those who suffer on every side in time of war, sometimes to the displeasure of our governments and our fellow citizens—as, for example, most recently during the Vietnam war, when Quakers insisted that Vietnamese lives were as precious as American lives, and sent aid to children in Hanoi as well as to children in Saigon, even at the cost of committing civil disobedience.

I therefore unite with my Peace Church colleague, John Yoder, in saying that this broadened vision of our responsibility to our brothers and sisters is one that the whole Christian community needs urgently to come to. As he wrote in an essay in the *Ecumenical Review*: "There (is) something unspeakably odd about affirming that it is important to maintain the possibility of eucharistic fellowship with fellow Christians whom one is also prepared to kill at the behest of, and for the sake of interests of a particular civil power structure." Indeed, I would go further, as would many in the Peace Churches. We would extend that commitment not to break the human tie to the whole family of man, Christian and non-Christian alike. We would argue that even though it is limited ground on which to stand, it is the only solid ground there is, and that once we leave it, once we allow ourselves to be carried away by any cause, or consumed by loyalty to any idea, or political philosophy, or abstract doctrine, however urgent or compelling, the descent to barbarism follows as the night the day.

Fourth, and last, we bring to the dialogue a history of service in seeking to mend the world that I think is the Society of Friends' most compelling expression of its ecclesial commitment to justice, peace, and the integrity of creation. The two largest Quaker agencies, the American Friends Service Committee and its sister in Britain, Quaker Peace and Service, are tiny by the world's standards, but over many years they have tried, in William Penn's phrase, "to see what love can do," testing their faith in places where conflicts rage and the alienation and the despair and the hatreds are deepest.

Both agencies are structured to reflect the interrelatedness of justice and peace; both embrace at the same time our concern for justice and human rights and our concern for international accord. Speaking now for the American Friends Service Committee, I can say that it is equally important for us to be involved in trying to lift the level of life in America's inner cities and in the *poblaciones* of Santiago as it is to seek accommodations in the cauldron of the Middle East. The American Friends Service Committee is not a peace agency; it is not a human rights agency or an environmental agency. It is all of them together; it feels compelled by its reading of the gospel to try to cultivate the whole vineyard.

Our concern for justice finds many expressions in our own land. For 30 years we have worked to open wider job opportunities for America's exploited minorities. We march to break down the segregated housing patterns that have condemned so many to live in ghettos. We have worked to create unitary, quality education systems in U.S. cities—North and South—since 1950, well before the Supreme Court outlawed segregated schooling. Other programs reach out to the homeless, seeking not so much to provide temporary shelter as to enable them to demand homes and job training—to foster the self- respect and dignity that comes from taking up their own cause. We help Native Americans—our Indians—to cope with problems of ill health, poverty, and exploitation of their resources. We travel with the migrant stream of farm laborers as they seek to secure the rights and services to which they are entitled, joining too in their organizing campaigns, participating in demonstrations, training the participants in nonviolence. We organize women in Appalachia to campaign for the opening up of nontraditional jobs; we work to end the exploitation of women in factories across the U.S. border in Mexico, established there to benefit from cheap labor. And of course it goes without saying that all across the United States our workers call on Americans not to profit from apartheid, to demand that corporate America cease its economic support of the South African regime, and that our government apply strict sanctions against it.

Similarly, we have many programs overseas that try to lift the quality and dignity of life. A program in Guinea-Bissau, where women carry much of the farming burden—as they do so widely in the Third World—trains them in farming methods and brings them together to support each other and grow in self-confidence and dignity. We helped resettle nomads in Mali, whose traditional way of life is no longer open to them. We have worked with Mapuche Indians in Chile to preserve their culture and their communal agriculture, and to help them market their crops through their own organizations.

Our concerns for peace have similar international expression. We aid those who suffer, we seek to understand the roots of conflicts abroad, but our peace focus is in the United States, which wields vast power, often all too irresponsibly. The American Friends Service Committee was—and is— deeply involved in the freeze movement, in campaigns over 40 years to end nuclear weapons testing, in joining and promoting the Pledge of Resistance Campaign that aims to put thousands in the streets, committed to nonviolent civil disobedience, if the United States should introduce troops or otherwise attack Nicaragua.

We have a program where we send International Affairs representatives to areas of conflict, with the responsibility of moving throughout the region, assessing the dimensions of conflict, the climate of opinion, and what measures might offer a chance for peaceful resolution. Such persons serve in Southeast and East Asia, in the Middle East, in Southern Africa, in Central America. Sometimes, as in the Middle East, where we have had such emissaries continually for 35 years, there is an added responsibility to identify the voices of moderation on all sides, and to serve as a bridge of communication among them. In all cases, the experience and insights of these representatives form an important resource for our nationwide programs in the United States aimed at educating the American people with regard to these threatening conflicts—programs whose content is often sharply at variance with the position of our government, but based, we think, on accurate readings of the mood and loyalties of the countryside and the city—so frequently misread by diplomats and generals, and yet in the long run so crucially important in influencing the outcome.

Sometimes, too, our on-site experiences are translated into books. These studies, bolstered by scholarly input, are illu-

279

minated by Quaker convictions about human dignity, conflict, and peace-making, but their language is the language
of the secular world, in keeping with their intention to be
serious studies rather than utopian scenarios of wishful optimism. Most find commercial publishers, and most provoke
serious dialogue beyond the borders of the religious community. Sometimes they are controversial, as when we evoked
the wrath of large segments of the Jewish community in the
United States by insisting in our publication *Search for Peace
in the Middle East* that the Palestinians, no less than the
Israelis, had rights that needed to be recognized.

We have also tried over 40 years to establish contact across
the greatest barrier of all—the dangerous and threatening
conflict between the U.S. and the USSR, seeking to recognize the reality of the threat felt by both, but to strip away
the mythology and the mindlessness of the Pavlovian anti-
communism that so poisons the climate in the United States,
and the equally damaging Soviet fear of opening their
society to outsiders. Quakers have maintained offices in New
York and Geneva close to the United Nations, where we
provide neutral settings to which diplomats may repair to
discuss problems and conflicts.

Finally, in the area of protecting God's creation, we have
long opposed nuclear power development on grounds of
both safety and the wholly unsolved problem of dangerously
polluting waste disposal. We have trained hundreds in
nonviolence in organizing demonstrations against poorly-
located nuclear plants. Other Quakers lobby our Congress
to take action on acid rain, which is destroying the forests
and lakes of New England and Eastern Canada, and Friends
were active in the research and drafting of the Law of the
Sea Treaty, with its provisions regarding pollution of our
oceans.

All these programs—more than 100 of them—constitute, as I said earlier, our strongest Quaker expression of a lively commitment to justice, peace, and the integrity of creation. They are, of course, insignificant on the total scene, but I have described their breadth and range at such length because I want to convey the sense of priority they occupy in our scheme of things in serving the Lord. The $19 million the American Friends Service Committee allocates annually to this work is by far the largest budget of any in the Society of Friends. We place such emphasis on our worldwide service outreach because we believe that it is in witnessing creatively and imaginatively—if always imperfectly—to Christ's love in an angry world that our Christian commitment to justice, peace, and the integrity of creation will be given substance—*as it will in no other* way.

Friends, we surely need the Glions and the projected world convocation in 1991 to help unite and inspire us, but in the final analysis it is in ministering to broken bodies and burdened spirits in the rice paddies of Cambodia, the mountains of El Salvador, and the ghettos of America that our commitment will truly impact the world.

These concerns and challenges and expressions of commitment constitute my view of our Quaker contribution to ecumenical dialogue. As a tiny group entering your deliberations with our Peace Church colleagues, we are ready to share whatever modest strengths we have and gain from your strengths to the end that we all may witness more powerfully to a world grown weary of violence, and a human family brought low by too much cleverness and too little faith.

Address to the Annual Gathering of the American Friends Service Committee, November 17, 1990

Excerpts from introductory remarks by Asia Bennett, Executive Secretary of the American Friends Service Committee:

This is a significant occasion. Steve Cary is moving toward the conclusion of nearly 12 years as the clerk of the AFSC Board and the Corporation. He has had many other leadership roles in the Service Committee, but this has been an especially important one.

When Steve leaves the clerk's role in January he will conclude the most recent chapter in a record of service that spans 48 or so years. Steve was born in Philadelphia, graduated from Germantown Friends and Haverford College. In 1942 his fledgling business career was interrupted by the draft, probably to the great good fortune of the Society of Friends. He went to Civilian Public Service camp as a conscientious objector and then became a CPS camp director for the AFSC. In 1946 he went to Europe as AFSC Commissioner of European Relief with headquarters in Paris. He subsequently served as assistant to Clarence Pickett, as administrator of AFSC's domestic programs, and as associate executive secretary coordinating AFSC regional offices. He was acting executive secretary and associate executive secretary for Information and Interpretation the first time such a

---

Address given on the occasion of Stephen's retirement as Chairperson of the AFSC Board and Corporation.

role was created. In 1969 Steve left the pay of the AFSC for a position at Haverford College, where he retired as vice president in 1981. He then began his volunteer and committee role for the Service Committee.

Over all the years Steve has taken on numerous special projects for the AFSC. Many of these have used his gifts of expression as a writer and speaker and many of them have called on his delight in travel. The record of Steve's travel is extraordinary. I first remember hearing Steve's name in 1955 in connection with a Quaker delegation to the Soviet Union in the depths of the cold war, led by Clarence Pickett with Steve as the energetic staff person. But in each decade from the 1940s to the present the list of his travels reflects events in the world and in places where the Service Committee has worked: Europe, Latin America, Southeast and other parts of Asia, Africa, the Middle East, and just this past week he returned from leading an AFSC delegation to China at the invitation of the Chinese Association for International Understanding. There have been many return visits on AFSC's behalf to various places in the world and lots of additional travel for his own interest and pleasure. I recall a committee meeting where Steve participated by radiophone while sailing around Cape Horn. Of course he has traveled in the United States as well, to visit AFSC regions and represent AFSC in a variety of ways.

Twice his journeys have been short distances but have involved new experiences: when he went to jail for two weeks during the Poor People's Campaign in 1968 and again to protest the shipment of bombs to Vietnam in 1972.

Steve is a prodigious worker—generous with his time and attention, a good colleague, a centered Friend whose tender heart and spiritual depths inform all his interactions. And best of all, I think, is Steve's gusto for life and his uproarious sense of humor.

I once heard the Reverend Joseph Lowery introduced extravagantly and at much greater length than I have subjected

283

Steve to. Lowery responded to that introduction by saying, "I don't know whether I deserve the reputation, but I thank God for the rumor." I now give you Steve Cary, who deserves both the reputation and the rumor.

⟹◈⟸

THANK YOU, ASIA, for your introduction, though it makes me nervous. My recent adventures in China and my homework for this weekend's meetings of the AFSC Board and Corporation haven't left much time for speech preparation. When I finally did begin to address the problem, I found myself flooded with so many ideas that, if they were laid end to end, they'd reach into tomorrow morning.

As I began to look at them, I recalled a wonderful little tale that my friend Red Schaal, the long-time secretary of the Middle Atlantic Region, told me about an occasion when he was introducing Gladys Walzer, a faithful worker for the Women's International League for Peace and Freedom at a peace conference at Cornell many years ago. Red said that in the middle of his introduction he looked down at his notes and Gladys thought that he'd finished, so she got up to speak. Red sat her down until he'd finished. Then she made her speech. Red was very rigid about how much time he allowed, so when Gladys ran overtime he tugged at her skirt to get her to conclude. When she finally did, Red rose: "Friends," he said, "I'm very grateful for Gladys' contribution, but before we have a question period I'd like to note that this occasion is an historic one. I've been running these institutes for 20 years and this is the first time I've ever had a speaker run over at both ends."

I feel this afternoon like running over at both ends. My problem is not what I want to talk about. I want to talk about the American Friends Service Committee, but I'm puzzled about how to do so in the time I've been allotted, and how to do it in a way which brings the Committee and my relationship with it to life. I could of course speak of its range of programs, ever shaped and ever changed by experience, how they have evolved in the light of our expanding understanding of such words as violence and nonviolence, and how they have been influenced by our changing perception of the roots of evil.

Or I could talk about some of the problems that beset us and how I think they might be addressed. This was a tempting approach because I have just read an absorbing monograph written by the director of the Friends Historical Library at Swarthmore College, Jerry Frost, who, after being buried in our archives for some months, has produced a lively paper on the earliest years of Service Committee history, from 1917 to 1924. Reading Jerry's paper has been a source of comfort to me because he's discovered that as early as 1918 the Service Committee was under criticism from important segments of the Society of Friends who were suspicious of its motives and charged it with being too secular, too political, and giving priority to skills over religious motivation in staff appointments. It would be fun to trace some of those problems to the present. But I have decided to do neither of these things. I resist them because I think that, although they might be instructive, they wouldn't convey the sense of excitement and vibrancy that for me characterizes the AFSC. I'd like to say something more personal, something that will help you better understand the American Friends Service Committee and the gifts it has given to me.

I take as my text for this exercise a familiar passage from George Fox's *Journal*, which all of you will immediately recognize. I choose it because my life at the AFSC has served to illumine and make real to me Fox's words, written in 1647:

> I saw also that there was an ocean of darkness and death, but an infinite ocean of light and love that flowed over the ocean of darkness, and in that also I saw the infinite love of God and I had great openings.

Friends, the AFSC has shown me the ocean of darkness, and it's been a gift, which may seem odd. I want to say a few words about some of my encounters with it. I think the first time I really came in contact with the face of massive evil was in that period when I wandered across Europe in those terrible years just after the end of the Second World War. The appalling destruction, the terrible breakdown of community, but most of all the suffering of multitudes of men, women, and children—the bereaved, the homeless, the cold and hungry, the sick—millions existing with their lives in ruin. I recall especially the day in 1946 when I walked alone through the death camp at Auschwitz and stood looking up at the ceiling at the shower heads, which only months before had spewed forth not water but deadly gas to destroy the helpless, naked souls below. One does not forget that kind of exposure to evil.

Or I think of the killing fields of Cambodia. I remember one village where I came upon a half-opened grave, half filled with water. I looked down into it, and there were the crushed skulls of six little children. A lone child's sandal floated on the water . . . Unbelievable, unfathomable evil. . . .

Finally, I remind myself also of those pitiful province hospitals in Vietnam where children, sometimes three to a bed, stared silently at the ceiling, their bodies racked with the searing pain of napalm, or their limbs shattered or blown off by bombs from the battleship *New Jersey*—lying safely in its off-shore sanctuary, hurling death and destruction into defenseless villages 30 miles inland. That, too, was the face of evil.

I don't recount this last because I equate my country's involvement in Vietnam with the atrocities of the Nazis or the Khmer Rouge, but to illustrate what my beloved friend Milton Mayer was fond of saying: "The devil is not a traveling man, living yesterday in Germany, tomorrow in Cambodia, and the day after that somewhere else. The devil is in the hearts of men and women the world over, and if we would deal with the devil we have to exorcize him from the hearts of the human family."

I'm grateful for having had the opportunity to see and experience the enormity of evil because it has served to enhance the sense of awe and wonder that I've felt when I have encountered the ocean of light, for this, too, has been a gift to me from the American Friends Service Committee. It has showed me miracles—miracles where hatred has been exorcized, the estranged reconciled, the depraved reborn, and the violent made peaceable. Through it, I know beyond disputation that there **is** an ocean of light. Community was reborn where there had only been hatred and suspicion. The ocean of light was seeping over the ocean of darkness. . . .

But I would remind you that we have something going for us that we don't often think about. I want to tell you what it is. The scene is Amsterdam. The time is 1947. A Dutch Friend bursts into the room, holding up a newspaper with black headlines, "Quakers Win Nobel Peace Prize . . . honored for relief service." As Friends do on these occasions, we immediately fall silent in a spontaneous meeting for worship. After a time a young woman rises and says, "All I can say is—a little love a sure goes a long way." It does, friends. And that's our hope. Even though we are tiny, and even though there is a vast world to mend, it's important that we keep on witnessing to what love can do.

In that context I'll close with a little story that for me encapsulates what the American Friends Service Committee is all about. It's a story about a man riding along a dirt road in the country, and he looks down from his horse and sees a little bird lying in the dirt on his back with his feet in the air. He's so curious about this that he gets off his horse and walks back and says, "Little bird, what are you doing lying there in the dust on your back with your feet in the air?"

And the little bird says, "The sky is falling and I'm trying to hold it up."

The man bursts out laughing: "Why that's the dumbest thing I ever heard in my life. What does a little bird like you think you can do about the sky falling?"

And the little bird looks up and says, "One does what one can. One does what one can."

Friends, the American Friends Service Committee did what it could in 1918. It was doing what it could when I first encountered it in 1940. It's doing what it can today, and I can assure you it will keep on trying to keep the sky from falling because, despite its feet of clay, despite its sins of omission and commission, despite the fact that it stumbles and falls and that its reach falls so far short of its grasp, it remains for me a lustrous little puddle in the great ocean of light and love. That's why as I leave it after almost half a century I say to all of you in this room, and I say to all Friends everywhere, "Thank God, thank God almighty, for the American Friends Service Committee."

WORLD WAR II
CIVILIAN PUBLIC SERVICE REVISITED

EXACTLY HALF A CENTURY AGO, in the months immediately preceding Pearl Harbor, World War II conscientious objectors began being drafted into Civilian Public Service, the first congressionally-authorized program of alternative service in U. S. history. The program was the offspring of an unlikely marriage between the Selective Service System and the three historic peace churches who were to share in its administration, but whose motivation and goals for the enterprise were divergent and incompatible. As a four-year participant (read *assignee*) in this unprecedented church-state experiment, I recall CPS as part zoo, part bureaucratic battleground, and part school for pacifists.

The agreement between the two parties called for a network of base camps to be established in relatively remote settings, each housing from 40 to 150 men, and administered by Quaker, Brethren, and Mennonite service agencies. Civilian employees of Selective Service were responsible for the assignees during working hours; the churches carried supervisory responsibilities during nonworking hours. Additional work opportunities, called "detached service" in the jargon of the times, were gradually developed, almost always after difficult negotiations and extensive Selective Service foot-dragging. These new assignments provided the men with

This article appeared in Friends Journal *in January, 1992 © Friends Publishing Corporation.*

more significant work experiences in such roles as mental hospital attendants, medical guinea pigs, and, occasionally, more glamorous undertakings as orderlies in general hospitals and as parachutists dropping into remote areas to fight forest fires.

Looked at from the vantage point of 50 years, I see the whole experiment, which involved more than 10,000 men, as an extraordinary paradox. From one point of view, CPS was an ill-conceived venture that scarred, at least temporarily, the lives of too many of its participants. The projected partnership of Christian church bodies seeking maximum service opportunities for young men of conscience with a large and controlling government agency interested essentially in keeping COs out of public view and performing unrewarding work to discourage others from seeking CO status, was inherently unworkable, and, many would say, seriously compromising of church integrity. Although the draft continued on and off for many years after the end of CPS, none of the peace churches has ever sought to renew it.

But from another point of view, Civilian Public Service was an unparalleled success. It became the greatest source of active lifetime pacifists the U. S. peace movement has so far seen. The vitality of the three peace churches and their service agencies, and indeed of the wider peace movement, in the four decades following World War II were significantly enriched by the influx of returning CPS graduates into positions of church and agency leadership. The reason is clear. When thousands of diverse and independently minded young men are forced to live together for years in isolated and restricted circumstances, there is little to do on dull work projects and long evenings but talk and argue—and that's what we did for four years. We argued about whether pacifists should put a lock on the refrigerator when food was disappearing, or how we should relate to a neo-Nazi who was in camp because he didn't want to fight Hitler. We argued about the peace church role in administering conscription, and how we should deal with the attack-on-your-grandmother syndrome.

Out of all this, we honed our thinking and our understanding to the point where many emerged from the war years as mature pacifists ready to invest their lives in peacemaking. Looking at this side of the paradox, it is no surprise that the government, for very different reasons from those of the peace churches, has never shown any interest in renewing the marriage contract that terminated in divorce in 1945, when the peace churches wanted out, and got out.

None of this was foreseen at the beginning. The CPS structure was the outcome of negotiations between three great peace church leaders —Clarence Pickett for the Friends, M. R. Ziegler for the Brethren, and Orie Miller for the Mennonites—with the first director of Selective Service, Clarence Dykstra, a broad-gauge and public-spirited official with considerable understanding of church perspectives. The big mistake made by church leaders in the negotiations was their serious misjudgment of the diversity of the CO community. They assumed it would reflect essentially the religious outlook and values of their own faith communities. Assignees would be eager to work hard on menial tasks to earn the right to more rewarding assignments, and for the same reason would be glad to work without pay.

Some men accepted these challenges, but many did not, and these came to bitterly resent the pay level of $2.50 per month, provided by the churches for "expenses." Large numbers of assignees saw themselves as slave labor and worked accordingly. It was one thing for a well-to-do Quaker with family backing to cooperate with a government that held him in a compulsory work program that paid him nothing for four years. It was quite another for a poor boy with a hostile family and no funds to have to endure the same experience.

In defense of the church leaders, it must be noted that they were assuming a one-year draft and were negotiating with Clarence Dykstra. Had he remained director, Selective Service policy might have been different. He would have been sympathetic to better work assignments and to the use of assignee skills in a wider range of detached service assignments. He might even have been uneasy about the pay issue as the draft was extended to two, three, and four years, lasting "for the duration," as we used to say. But Dykstra was soon gone, replaced by General Lewis B. Hershey, a military figure of reasonable disposition, but limited in outlook and understanding, and fearful of public criticism. The general remained in charge throughout the war, and under him Selective Service administration of the CPS program became narrow-minded, bureaucratic, and self-defeating.

It all began hopefully enough. We were seen by our peace church sponsors as "creative pioneers," by a generally tolerant public as peculiar, and by the military as curiosities. The first Quaker-operated camp was close to Fort Meade in Maryland, and when soldiers had time off they sometimes drifted over to Patapsco to "see what the conchies looked like." One hot August afternoon an assignee who had played football for the University of Pennsylvania was digging a latrine. As he shoveled out dirt, tanned and shirtless, a couple of recruits from Meade stopped to admire the muscles rippling across his back. "See, there's one, there's one! Look at him, look at him!" His friend whistled. "Man, oh, man," he said, "I'd hate to have him hit me with a fistful of love!"

Right there, he put his finger on the central flaw in the CPS structure. Neither the COs nor their church sponsors had a fistful of anything. It was from the start a lopsided operation. The churches paid all the bills, the unpaid men did all the work, Selective Service called all the shots.

I was lucky. I parlayed a knowledge of accounting into an office job at my first camp in Petersham, Massachusetts. This rescued me from the bitter cold of a winter forestry project, and shortly, by default, got me promoted to camp director. From there, with various detours, I directed two more camps, and these posts gave me, over four years, as much of a bird's eye view of the system as it was possible for an assignee at worm's eye level to have. It is, therefore, as a camp director that I report, after half a century, on the CPS scene.

The first point to be made is that a CPS camp was a zoo. To administer one with any order or coherence required a range of skills that began with an ability to walk on water and went from there to more difficult assignments. Lacking any of these qualifications, I administered, but not with either order or coherence. A director had to deal with limited and sometimes ill-tempered government functionaries with one hand, while with the other he coped with assignees whose range encompassed Pulitzer Prize winners and ditch diggers, Ph.D.s and third graders, stock brokers and ballet dancers, fundamentalists and atheists, confronters and cooperators, the sick and the healthy—always under the watchful eye of Big Brother in Washington, D. C., with whom the camp director was obliged to do battle almost every day.

This ill-assorted lot were all thrown together in open barracks with no privacy and sent out to work six days a week on projects that ranged from the made to the tedious to the grimy. One Quaker camp was engaged in draining a swamp, and the men spent their days wallowing in knee-deep mud. Another group weeded endless beds of tiny seed-lings. A third dug water holes to create pools that would be useful in fighting forest fires. I spent four months in a camp where the project was to cut down the saplings along the Skyline Drive in Virginia to open the vistas for nonexistent tourists in an era of gas-rationing—saplings planted ten years earlier by Civilian Conservation Corps boys to prevent ero-sion. One Quaker assignee to this Mennonite-operated camp caused consternation by refusing to carry out an assignment where he was ordered to dab black paint on all the one-inch sapling stumps so they wouldn't be noticed.

Given these problems, one might predict that our per-formance would be less than satisfactory—and one would be right. The biggest work-related difficulty was a philosophical split, especially evident in Quaker camps that drew by far the widest range of assignees, on how we should react to the system. Some were determined to win respect by co-operating and working hard, while others took the opposite approach, dragging their feet to confront government injus-tice with noncooperation and demonstrate that free men could not be enslaved by Selective Service edict. Like Odysseus's Penelope, knitting by day and unraveling by night, the eager cooperators and the conscientious malingerers worked to neutralize each other. The results satisfied neither and angered the work bosses, who complained regularly to the camp director, who in his turn was alternately blessed and cursed by the camp factions, depending on which side of the philosophical fence he came down on.

These skirmishes were troubling enough, but much worse was the problem posed by the sick and infirm. Selective Service's discharge policy was cut from the same cloth as its work policy: one was aimed at getting COs out of sight, the other at keeping them there. As a camp director I could at least understand the policies of draft authorities in most areas, but I could never understand their attitude toward medical discharges, which I regarded then—and regard now—as unfeeling, inexcusable, and cruel.

To begin with, local boards had little understanding of the inflexibilities and stresses of the CPS system, and in their eagerness to be rid of problems tended to hurry men off to camp who were unstable or physically disabled. This wasn't necessarily malicious; many assumed that CO camps, like military bases, could discharge these marginal draftees who were unable to perform their duties. Unfortunately it didn't work that way with us. We had to go through an elaborate discharge procedure that usually took months, during which the morale of the entire camp would be undermined by the presence of numbers of depressed and ill young men, unable to work, unable to leave, lying in their bunks all day long, a drag on themselves and everybody else. Many of these men could manage "on the outside," but, trapped in the inflex-ibility of barracks life, they went to pieces.

Others had more or less severe physical disabilities that should have disqualified them, but hadn't. I remember one man who suffered from such severe arthritis that he had to be carried into camp. It took us three months to get him discharged. Most cases were less severe, but we lacked the range of assignments available to the military, and it was hard to place men in tasks they could handle. Every camp had its quota of these idle men, called "SQs" after their designation (sick quarters) on the daily work charts. They could remain in this category for months, sometimes reach-ing a point of despondency where we had to put a suicide watch on them.

I became so familiar with the government's routine rejec-tions of our discharge applications that I could quite accurately predict when the file was being assembled whether it would succeed or fail. This turned out to be a useful skill; it enabled me to explain to frustrated psychiatrists why their recommendations were being disregarded.

At one camp, I became close enough to our psychiatrist—who was in a hospital 50 miles away to which I regularly drove his camp patients—to suggest to him that he submit his reports to me in draft form. I would undertake to rephrase them with the words I knew would satisfy Selective Service and return them to the psychiatrist, with the understanding that if my amateur revisions in any way did violence to his professional diagnosis he was to change it. He then sent the final product back to me. Working this way as a team, we discharged eight men in six weeks—a record performance which had nothing to do with changes in the patients' condition and everything to do with semantics.

All of this illustrates why Civilian Public Service was unworkable and involved endless battles between parties operating from different premises. Fortunately, however, there was some common ground, which did make it possible for CPS men to make important contributions in areas of need. Most notable was the service given by COs as attendants in mental hospitals. These assignments were unglamorous and invisible enough to satisfy Selective Service, while at the same time they were desperately needed. Conditions in public mental hospitals at that time were unconscionable. All were severely understaffed, and such staff as they had were often incompetent, if not sadistic. Large numbers of CPS men, working in hospitals throughout the country, brought a level of caring and competence into the system that it had never seen before, and were instrumental in founding a national mental health organization that has ever since set standards and given public awareness to issues relating to the care of the mentally ill. This work was undoubtedly the most important and lasting contribution made by World War II COs. They also made valuable contributions to medical science through their role as guinea pigs, where they volunteered for experiments in such areas as nutrition, disease, and survival.

A third potentially valuable program was the training of Friends CPS men at Quaker colleges for relief service overseas. Unfortunately, this program was barely launched at Earlham, Guilford, Haverford, and Swarthmore when U.S. Representative Starnes of Alabama, angered that Europeans and Asians would discover that there were U.S. pacifists, attached a rider to the 1943 military appropriations bill specifying that no funds so appropriated could be used for such a training program. The American Friends Service Committee was, of course, meeting all the costs with private funds, but the Selective Service official who had to sign the transfer orders was an army colonel whose pay, while he signed his name, came from the appropriation authorization. This made the order illegal under the Starnes rider so that all the units had to be closed and the men returned to camp, thus establishing the fact that Congress had its share of small-minded men.

Despite many such disappointments, the CPS experience was a positive one for those who were stimulated by the richness of its diversity and could adapt to the limitations of its unrewarding and unpaid work. For them, the years in CPS were growing years from which they profited. For me, the struggle to give coherence to the tangled web of CPS administration was the most demanding and maturing assignment I've ever had. It yielded rich rewards in life-long friendships—CPS alumni remain to this day a special fraternity—and in teaching me more about human relationships and how to live with the reasonable and the unreasonable than any other four years of my life.

But, on balance, the price was too high. For too many, the experience was negative, and for the three churches, their involvement in administering conscription and being party to putting noncooperators in jeopardy of prison ran counter to their religious commitments and compromised their integrity in ways that should not be repeated.

"Integrity, Trust, Community and Self-examination"

Collection Talk at Haverford College, September 7, 1977

GOOD EVENING—and to all of you who returned today and yesterday—welcome back to Haverford. I think you're going to find the campus pretty much the way you left it—with one glaring exception, which you may already have noticed. The great Shackamaxon elm between Founders and Hilles is gone. The Dutch elm fungus finally choked its vascular system to such an extent that it died early in the summer. For several weeks it stood bare and majestic against the sky, but on the 18th of July it was cut down and hauled off. For all of us who love the campus it was a sad event, because it was our most historic tree.

As for our new students here tonight, I refrain from welcoming you because you've been welcomed so often since Saturday that it's getting maudlin, and after the orientation program you've had under the leadership of Steve Gellman and Dave Hilbert you are by now veteran Haverfordians. But I do want to pause right here and express my appreciation—and the college's—for the job that Steve and Dave and their Customs Committee have done—and while it's dangerous to single out special contributors to a joint effort, I do want to especially thank Ted Bobrow and Jennifer Evanson and

Speech at the opening Collection of the Haverford College community, the year Stephen served as acting president.

299

David Luljak and John Snyder for their contributions. It seems to me what you have done—working behind the scenes in virtual anonymity, and for no other reason than a desire to help new students understand the college—represents Haverford at its best, and I thank you.

I've enjoyed very much observing Customs Week, and I assure you that it's a far cry from the Customs Committee that we had here when I was a freshman. We had one, but its function then was wholly limited to teaching freshmen proper respect for their elders. And I'll have to admit that the Committee made my first week at Haverford a traumatic one. I got nailed my second day on campus for failing to supply a match for a sophomore cigarette. I was called before the Customs Committee and sentenced to walk around the campus for a week with a piece of bread over each ear, held on like a pair of earphones, with a sign on my back that said, "My name is Stephen Cary and I'm a ham sandwich." It wasn't so bad walking around here, but I can tell you it was pretty humiliating at my first Bryn Mawr mixer.

But I got off easy: the chap I was walking with didn't have a match either. This guy was hauled up before the Committee, too, and they took one look at his barrel chest—he was built like an inverted pyramid—and they said, "*That's* the kid for the bearskin." They made him put on this huge bearskin, get up on a dining room table, and sing "Chloe" to the student body. The only thing was, this guy had a spectacular voice, and he brought the house down, but the result was that poor devil had to get in that bearskin and sing "Chloe" every Tuesday night till Thanksgiving.

Well, those days are gone forever, and we have freshmen who by now are thoroughly oriented into the Haverford scene which makes it easier for me since I can now talk to a full house of old hands. And I must say, that in my, what shall I say?—astonished pleasure?—at being at this podium at all, I've given more than casual thought to what I might say.

I know, of course, that brevity is a prized quality in Collection talks. And that's a problem, because verbosity is one thing Haverfordians are good at. Which reminds me of a tale that's told about Haverford's late, great classicist, Arnold Post. Professor Post once had a particularly verbose student who simply talked in class all the time. Finally, midway through the semester when he could stand it no longer, Post interrupted the young man and said, "Sir, verbosity may be your long suit, but I assure you it's not long enough to cover the asininity."

My aim tonight, therefore, is to talk long enough to say some things I very much want to say, and to stop before my verbosity no longer covers my asininity. It's a fine balance, and I may well fall over the edge.

I want to do two things:

(1) Point out four areas of college life that I think are going to be especially important during this transitional year while we wait for our new president to be named.

(2) Say some quite personal words about my view of this college and what I think we should all be about.

First, the areas of my special concern for this year—not in any order of priority:

(1) Relations with Bryn Mawr College

I look for a good and constructive year in our two-college relationship, though not, probably, an easy one. As many of you know, we reached a milestone agreement last spring in the area of academic cooperation—an agreement that goes a long way toward establishing the principle of open access, including the cross-majoring option, and providing mechanisms for examining and correcting, where possible and appropriate, duplication and conflicting requirements.

This year we jointly have the task of working out the implementation of this far-reaching agreement—which won't be easy. Each department at Haverford will be meeting with its Bryn Mawr counterpart to discuss their departmental programs and the structure and requirements of the majors. The aim will not be to force any one or two predetermined patterns on the two departments, but to allow for wide latitude in order to preserve features—sometimes differing features—that a given department feels is educationally important. A collateral step toward more open access will be an examination of courses on both campuses with a view to increasing the number of courses acceptable as satisfying prerequisites and distribution requirements. All of these discussions will be carried on against specified deadlines that insure final decisions by March of 1978 at the latest.

Another step the two colleges have taken is to establish mechanisms for talking together on a continuing and regular basis. I expect to use these mechanisms. And I think it prudent, considering my own capacity to develop a head of steam, to go on public record here tonight to say that there will be no broadsides hurled across Montgomery Avenue from Roberts Hall this year. It's possible there could be some hard meetings, but I hope we can both focus on talking across a table rather than on mobilizing our respective armies. Bryn Mawr and Haverford sometimes *have* conflicting priorities and interests, our lifestyles and educational philosophies have their differences, and these things are both the source of our strength and the source of our troubles. On one hand they greatly enrich your educational experience, on the other they sometimes make intercollegiate relationships difficult. But beyond the difficulties is a powerful bond, and I'd like to say to all Bryn Mawrters here tonight, particularly because most of you don't know me very well, that though I sometimes fight with you because of my passionate loyalties to Haverford, the fighting doesn't really diminish the affection I have for you, because I'm too aware that the richness, the excitement, and the stimulus that come from having a great institution right on our doorstep are for us an asset beyond calculation. I hope that works both ways.

(2) The second area of my concern is closely related to the first: namely, the role of women at Haverford.

For 130 years or more, this place was, regrettably, a male bastion. When I was a student here in the middle 1930s and a young woman appeared on campus, the first one to see her yelled "Fire"—which was the signal for all the residents of Lloyd and Barclay to run to a window and have a look.

I'm glad to say we've gotten beyond that, but there is still a long way to go before we can say that the role and the place of women on this campus is truly equal to that of men. In the last few years we've made progress—in adding significantly to the numbers of women on our faculty and in our administration and in increasing the presence of women in our classrooms.

Of course I'm pleased this year that 17 women have elected to enroll in our upper classes as degree candidates, and I warmly welcome each of them to the Haverford maelstrom. I would also like to say to every Bryn Mawr student who will be living at Haverford this year that we think of you, too, as full members of our community, as valued and as

303

welcome as all the other students on our campus. We have an exciting opportunity this year to see if we can truly integrate *all* our women residents into Haverford's community life, and I want to do everything I can to make that happen.

But I don't know if all of you women realize what's expected of you here at Haverford, and to help you at this point, I'd like to read a Minute adopted by the Haverford faculty on the subject. As far as I know, it hasn't been read publicly before. I now quote directly from the faculty minute:

The Faculty entered into consideration of the prospects and advantages of female students being admitted to the required exercises of the College, should way open for this. They were united in the belief that if young ladies performed regular recitations and took their meals in company with the other students, it would have a natural and marked tendency to improve the faithfulness of all the students in their studies, the propriety of their demeanor, and the general self-respect, refinement, and moral earnestness of all. The experience of colleges generally, not excepting our own, leads us to acknowledge that the constitution of the family, without fostering those unwholesome states of mind and feeling which are the penalty of all monastic exclusion from natural society. It is therefore approved that the Managers be informed that the minds of the Faculty are now prepared to favor the admission of female students to the recitations and other public exercises of the College, as full members of the College, these girls being placed under the charge of a competent female principal.

This helpful Minute, I should advise you, is dated Fifth Month 30, 1870. I think it makes clear what is expected of you, and clear that, as far as the campus is concerned, we've been waiting for the age of women for 107 years. It also confirms that the Managers have had what might be regarded as reasonably adequate time to make up their minds—but then Quakers don't move precipitously. In any event, and be all that as it may, I feel that we're in a happy, challenging situation, and that this year is going to be a bad one for the elements of chauvinism that still plague us. Certainly, I'm going to try hard to make it a bad year for those elements in myself.

(3) My third central concern is in the area of diversity.

This is the year we're going to be tested to see just what we mean by our stated commitment to make Haverford more truly hospitable to culturally and racially diverse groups— hospitable socially and hospitable educationally.

I'm not so naive as to claim that we're going to be able to solve in one year all our problems, rid ourselves of all our hang-ups, or overcome all the frustrations and alienations that our minority students have felt. But I can promise you that we are going to move further down the road. For the first time we don't have to rely on what a former colleague of mine used to call "ad hocery" to insure that these matters get attention. For the first time we don't have to hope that busy administrators or busy minority coalition members will take the needed initiatives to push the matter to the fore. This is because we have begun to institutionalize the concern for diversity at Haverford—the tough negotiations between the college and its minority students that occurred last April have produced machinery and established responsible committees whose charge is to broaden the mix of our administration and faculty. We have added key personnel who are centrally concerned with the strengthening of minority representation on the campus and improving the quality of the Haverford experience for minority students, and indeed, for the whole community.

Finally, I want to promise our minority students that the concerns that you and the college have won't be pushed to the back burner by other circumstances this year. I expect to meet regularly with Karla and to keep in close touch also with coalition spokesmen just as I meet regularly with Jeff Genzer and his council officers. The thing we need to avoid is allowing problems to worsen by neglect, and I'll do the best I can to be accessible and to see that that doesn't happen.

(4) A final area of interest: the College's finances

This is pretty dull stuff for most of you, so I'll be mercifully brief, but it is going to preempt a lot of my time, and you should know where matters stand.

On balance, I bring you a strong and optimistic report on our financial situation:

> (1) Our four-year capital campaign for $20 million, is, after one year, past the 12 million mark. It received a wonderful boost on Alumni Day in May when Bob Collins of the Class of 1952 announced that he planned to give the college one million dollars over the next few years.

> (2) I can also report that our annual giving program in 1976-77 broke all records, with a total from our alumni, parents, and friends of $543,000, and a participation percentage by living alumni at a

phenomenal 64%—quite possibly the highest participation rate of any college or university in the nation last year. Haverford is truly a national leader in this category—and the most phenomenal thing about it is that each of the last seven classes to graduate exceeded 60% participation. I report that for the benefit of the seniors, because I certainly would hate to see that record broken.

The result of all this is that our endowment is up, our term debt at the bank is down, and our budget is balanced.

So it's a good picture, but I don't want you to go away feeling that everything is coming up roses with Haverford's finances. A few years ago, Jack Coleman gave a less encouraging report, and many students somehow got the impression that he had implied—which he hadn't—that Haverford was virtually on its last legs: that the next step would be to close our doors. It took some time to eradicate this preposterous notion; and I don't want what I've just said to be interpreted in the opposite fashion. We still have a rocky road to traverse—no private college can feel secure in these days of inflation and rising costs. We have an *enormous* job ahead of us in the capital campaign: the money that comes in easily and naturally is already here; the real job is still to be done. So all I want to convey tonight is that Haverford has been gaining on its financial problems; we think we have a handle on them to make them manageable, but we don't plan to rest on our oars, and I'll be allocating a *lot* of my time to rowing over the next eight or nine months.

These, then, are the areas I'm especially concerned about—these, and winning back the Hood trophy, and, gentlemen, I want that so badly I can taste it. There will be other problems that arise. In fact, we've already got one that I feel I should mention because it's much on your minds: namely, the campus housing situation.

There *is* more overcrowding than we expected and there *are* more of you living in places where you don't want to live. The situation is not as bad as it was a month ago, nor as improved as I hope it will be a month from now, but it's still a genuine problem that Greg Kannerstein, Donna Mancini, Lita Sabin, and I are extremely concerned about. What happened? Housing at Haverford is a complex and convoluted problem. It's hard indeed to make sound judgments on housing needs under our present room assignment procedures. The plans of students to take time off and to return after leave often remain indefinite until well into August; the relative popularity of off-campus versus on-campus living varies from year to year. Estimates of the numbers of new students aren't available until long after room draw, so that the room draw committee has to guess at how much space to reserve for new students.

All these uncertainties meant that we had to make a lot of guesses, and we consistently guessed too low. The upshot was that the administration did not move fast enough, soon enough, to reserve additional space in Haverford Park Apartments, and some of you are paying the price, which I deeply regret. I regret it especially because I don't think I can entirely hide behind the problems I've listed. They are real, and we're going to be undertaking a serious review of our procedures to see if we can find ways to do better in the future. I have to be honest with you, and say that, after a review of all the memos that circulated in May and June about the housing scene, I think we *should* have seen the warning flags and taken action sooner. After all, that's why the College bought HPA—to have a housing pool available— and we didn't use it well this year. So, the administration carries some responsibility for putting some of you in space you're not happy about, and for this I am deeply sorry. All I can say at this point is that we're going to do our level best to ease your problems and to avoid future crises of this kind.

Let me move now to the final thing I want to do, which is to go beyond the topical and the reportorial to talk to you from my heart about this college you've chosen, and what I think it ought to be. Most of you know, I guess, that Haverford is to me a very special place. I've only been back here eight years, but the reason I came back to Haverford goes back much longer than that, indeed, almost 30 years, to an experience I had that made my whole life different. I'd like to say something about that experience because it leads directly to what I want to say about Haverford.

Late in 1945, I was asked to assume responsibility for overseeing all Quaker relief operations on the European continent in the wake of World War II. So for two years I wandered over the face of the continent—from the northern tip of Norway to the south of Italy, from England to the Soviet Union—visiting relief teams, arranging for the transfer of people, vehicles, and supplies, trying to solve organizational problems, planning new projects, terminating old ones. Because of this experience, I suppose there are few people anywhere who have had the opportunity I did to observe first-hand the price mankind pays for the folly of war.

Initially, I was overwhelmed by the awesome spectacle of a continent in ruins—its cities in rubble, its treasures destroyed, the beauty of its monuments lost forever. Physical destruction was massive, ugly, unbelievable. But worse than physical destruction was the breakdown of community, of social organization: the fabric of society in nation after nation torn apart—services disrupted, government in shambles, men, women, and children reduced to fending for themselves.

309

But worst of all: the unspeakable human suffering, the concentration camps, the homeless, the orphaned, the sick, and the hurt, whole populations displaced, families separated—lonely, hungry, and bereaved—suffering too deep for words, suffering so terrible that I used to ask the forgiveness of God each night for any part I might have played in allowing it to happen. And over it all hung a pervasive cloud of hatred and despair that cast a pall over everything. All I can say about those two years is that no one in this room could have seen what I saw, felt what I felt, experienced what I experienced, without committing his life to the purpose of preventing such a thing from ever happening again.

But beyond the searing experience and the commitment it produced, I discovered something about what is required to confront and deal with the massive problems and the monstrous evils that engulfed Europe in 1946. I saw our workers involved in failure—they helped to clothe and feed a community, but they couldn't reach to the hatred, selfishness, the greed, and the anger that paralyzed and consumed it. But I also saw miracles, where humanity and warmth and caring were reborn, and compassion returned and hatred gave way to forgiveness, and community was rebuilt, and people began again to trust. Many of those who worked these miracles weren't much older than you here tonight. Some were members of our relief units and some were brave souls who rose up out of the wreckage of their lives and their communities.

Their formula was no mystery. They all were possessed of two great qualities. The first was competence—competence to analyze and understand intractable problems, competence to grasp language and social organization, competence to know where to begin, and what buttons to push. Competence was essential, but it wasn't enough. A second ingredient had to go along with it—and that was a special kind of faith, which insisted that human beings *can* rise above their baser natures, that they *can* respond to stimuli other than fear and threat and naked power, and a conviction that this faith, expressed with vast enthusiasm, and persistence, and courage, and humor, and backed with competence, had the power to confront evil, to reconcile, and to change. They lived as if this were true, and it became true. This I know, as Friends say, experientally. I have seen this combination at work, and I believe to the depth of my being that those who possess it are the last best hope of the world, and that we'd better find a way to turn that kind of person out into society if we're going to keep from blowing ourselves back to the Stone Age. The human spirit against the atomic bomb? Yes, there is no other way.

And I have the wild, impossible dream, that this college, because of its tradition, the testimony of many who've been here, the quality of the lives they've led, and the quality of community that once in a great while we have achieved can make that kind of contribution. I had that dream when I came back here in 1969, and I have it still as I start my short stint as acting president.

As far as the competence is concerned, I have no doubt at all. You have come here for a good, solid education, and if you are serious about getting it, and are willing to reach out and become involved in learning and in knowing your teachers, you will get it. Professor Bernstein encapsulated the case for Haverford's education superbly some years ago when a major foundation wrote and asked him for ideas on new and innovative programs to improve the quality of the undergraduate experience. In his response, Dick Bernstein did not deny the usefulness of such programs, but he had this to say about education and about Haverford.

Suppose one were really (no nonsense) concerned with the quality of the undergraduate experience, then where would one put the emphasis? The answer is simple. The best education of young people has always been in an environment where there is free and easy interchange of ideas and talk, where there are manageable and livable communities of common concern. It was true in Greece, true in Cambridge and Oxford, and true at the high points of American undergraduate education (like Chicago under Hutchins). But where does this go on today? Universities make gestures in this direction, but they are little more than gestures. It is in the quality liberal arts colleges that it takes place. Come to see for yourself. Spend a week at a place like Haverford, Swarthmore, Wesleyan, or Amherst. What do these places have that other places don't have? Again the answer is simple. They are still genuine communities, and dedicated to the principle that a college ought to be a community of learning; they practice this. "New creative programs" are a fallout from such places, not the heart of the matter.

So, friends, I *know* we can educate, but what else will you take with you when you leave? Your values will be shaped here, but how, and in what direction? This is not an intellectual issue. There is no curriculum for values. They gradually emerge over time through your interaction with your fellows and through the impact of your environment and your experience, until they are part of you, and you feel them in your bones.

What will the Haverford community contribute to this process? Can we shape it so that we help build in you a restless uneasiness with the status quo, a faith that you can do something to change it, and a commitment to be about the business of doing it, whatever you choose? My belief is that we can.

First, I think our community must be one where our yea is yea, and our nay, nay. Integrity is in short supply in the world. Short cuts and manipulation, and a few lies here and there, seem to offer quicker routes to get us what we want. In the short run they often do, but the price we ultimately pay, as we have learned to our sorrow in this country, is the price of burgeoning cynicism and distrust, and I don't want that for Haverford. I want honesty in all things, large and small, that we may come to feel in our community that honesty is the norm, and discover through it, the joy of trusting each other. That is why our honor system and our honor council have long been, and remain, a centerpiece of our student life. And I want every member of this community, whether technically bound by the honor code or not, to strive to live by it and live up to it.

And the second quality, closely akin to the first, is trust. I think that Haverford should be a place where the first thing a person does when he meets another is to trust him. That's a daring idea; it's an idea that is bound to lead sometimes to disappointment, but I remember an essay that Judge Learned Hand wrote at the height of the McCarthy period, when the country was so paranoid about communism that trust and confidence were everywhere being abandoned and replaced with loyalty oaths. Hand wrote eloquently of this barrenness of the oath mania, pointing out that it is far better to accept the risk of a few evil people escaping detection than to abandon trust because, he said, trust is the *stuff* of liberty—the cement of a free society, without which it cannot exist. May we at Haverford, all of us, therefore be about trusting each other, so that our society will be free, and so that you, who are here for a few years, will leave daring to trust.

Third, I think the Haverford community should resolve to get along together. Conflict arises here as it does in any group. Faculty, administration, and students have interests that sometimes diverge, and the question is only whether we succumb to the easy temptation to accept adversary relationships and create power blocs, and build strength to make *our* interests prevail. For power, and its opposite, powerlessness, are facts of life here as elsewhere. All I can say is that all my capacity, and all my energy, will be directed at avoiding that temptation, and striving instead to be sensitive to the interests of different groups, trying to discover common ground, trying to open avenues of agreement. And I will judge my performance not on the basis of how wisely I use such power as resides in the presidency, but on how I fall back on its arbitrary use at all. I know there are cynics who say it can't be done—that power is the only arbiter in the affairs of men. I don't believe that. For I have seen community emerge in settings far less promising than ours: settings in war-torn Europe, and in the Washington jail, among angry and bitter people, where extraordinary individuals were able to foster community by helping others to submerge difference. Surely we should be able to do as much at Haverford.

Fourth, I want this to be a joyful community, where we revel in the astonishing abilities and the artistry of those around us—in the music of Sylvia Glickman, in the brilliance of a faculty lecture, in the sort of superb teaching that Tamara Brooks treated us to here in this room last Saturday evening, in the artistry of the Zipins and the Cowies and the Lavellis and the Shumans on Walton Field. I don't have those skills, and the opportunity to thrill to them in my friends here is for me the magnificent fun of Haverford. I think we need to cultivate our feelings and our enthusiasms, to learn to be involved, and to live life fully, to the end that you carry with you a great zest for life when you leave, because you'll need it.

Finally, friends, may we learn here in this community the value of self-examination and quiet reflection, and how to measure our lives against the plumb line of our faith. There are many instruments through which we can learn to do this, and each must choose his own, but I commend you—faculty, administration, and students—the quiet peace of the Haverford Meeting House on Thursday and Sunday mornings, where generations of Haverfordians have listened week after week to the wisdom of Isaac Sharpless and Rufus Jones and William Comfort and Douglas Steere, and have taken stock of their lives, and which is still available to all of us who want to test it and sample its value. For me, it is close to the heart of the matter.

So there, in outline, is the Haverford community that I think could shape your lives in ways you'd be grateful for all your days. What I want for Haverford this year is that we use well our academic riches, that we don't waste the scholarship or the companionship of great teachers, that we become a little more of a caring community, that we trust each other a little more, and grow in honesty, and in knowledge of ourselves.

I promise you that all of my energy and my time, and my ability, and all of my heart, will be directed at trying to contribute to the building of that kind of Haverford.

Thank you for listening.

QUAKER VALUES IN EDUCATION

I HAVE TO BEGIN BY SAYING that I stand before you something of a broken man. It was just 46 years ago, almost to the day, that I sat as you members of the class of 1979, utterly at the mercy of a commencement speaker on one of the hottest days of the decade. As he droned on, with no apparent terminal facilities whatever, I made a resolution that under no conceivable set of circumstances at any time or at any place would I ever give a commencement address. From that day to this, I have kept my pledge, but, alas, it is at this moment shattered—whether because advancing senility weakens resolve or because of the persuasive powers of your headmaster, I cannot say.

I remember only two tiny fragments of that occasion so many years ago, neither of which identifies either the speaker or his subject, both of which are lost mercifully in the mists of time. But I do recall one horrendous incident in the middle of his speech, when he quoted from the Gettysburg Address. When he came to the part which says, "The world will little note nor long remember what we say here," I remember a classmate next to me leaning over and saying, "Well, Lincoln blew it, but this guy is right on target!" I had one of those frightful moments of trying to contain myself despite a compulsion to laugh.

The other little fragment has to do with a piece of dry ice that I brought with me to the Meeting House to succor me

---

Stephen delivered this Sidwell Friends School 91st commencement address to 97 seniors on June 8, 1979.

from the dreadful heat. (Now maybe you are not familiar with dry ice. It is frozen carbon dioxide and used to be a very popular refrigerant.) I had the good fortune to be seated next to the nearest thing we had in our class to a ravishing beauty. Being the fine fellow that I am, I shared my dry ice, wrapped in a paper towel, with her. The trouble with dry ice is that when it is squeezed, it vaporizes, and a little pillar of steam kept rising between us despite our best efforts to shift our hands inconspicuously, between which we clenched the ice. Most people thought we were just holding hands and that it was just a case of rather bad taste . . . but not my sister. She came up to me immediately after the ceremony and said, "Stephen, what in the world was thee doing up there? I know Sue is quite a number, but this is the first time I ever saw her actually smoke!"

All of which sets out the ground rules for this particular occasion: No reference to the Gettysburg Address during my speech, and no hand-holding unless you have a piece of ice.

What I want to say begins with what happened to me when, just after my 30th birthday, I was asked to assume responsibility for overseeing all Quaker relief operations on the European continent immediately after the end of the Second World War. For two years I wandered over the continent, from Norway to Italy, from England to the Soviet Union, visiting relief teams; arranging for the transfer of people, vehicles, and supplies; trying to solve organizational problems; planning new projects; terminating old ones.

Because of this experience, friends, I suggest that there are very few people here who have had the opportunity I had to observe firsthand the price mankind pays for the folly of war. Initially, I was overwhelmed by the awesome spectacle of a continent in ruins—its cities in rubble, its treasures destroyed, the beauty of its monuments lost forever. Physical destruction was massive, ugly, unbelievable. But worse than physical destruction was the breakdown of community, of social organization, the fabric of society in nation after nation torn apart, services disrupted, government in shambles. Men, women, and children were reduced to fending for themselves. But worst of all: the unspeakable human suffering— the refugee camps, the homeless, the orphaned, the sick and the hurt, whole populations displaced, families separated, lonely, hungry, bereaved—suffering too deep for words, suffering so terrible that each night I used to ask the forgiveness of God for any role that I might have played in not preventing it from happening.

All I can say about those two years is that no one in this audience could have seen what I saw, felt what I felt, experienced what I experienced, without committing his life to trying to prevent such a tragedy from ever happening again. But beyond this searing experience, and the commitment which it produced in me, I discovered something about what is required to confront and deal effectively with the massive problems and the monstrous evils that engulfed Europe in 1946. I saw our workers involved in failure. They helped to clothe and feed a community, but they could not reach the hatred, the selfishness, the greed, and the anger that paralyzed and consumed it.

But I also saw miracles, where humanity and warmth and caring were reborn and compassion returned, and hatred gave way to forgiveness. The community was rebuilt. People began again to trust. And many of those who worked these miracles were not much older than the graduates who sit in front of me today. Some were members of our relief units; some were brave souls who rose up out of the ashes and the wreckage of their lives in their own communities. Their formula was no mystery. They possessed two great qualities.

The first was competence: competence to analyze and understand intractable problems; competence to grasp language and social organization; and competence to know where to begin and which buttons to push. Competence was crucial, but it was not enough.

A second ingredient had to go with it, and that was a very special kind of faith which insisted that human beings can rise above their baser natures. They can respond to stimuli other than fear and threat and naked power, and a conviction that this faith, exercised with enthusiasm and persistence, courage, and humor, and backed with competence, had the power to confront evil, to reconcile and to change. They lived as if this were true, and it became true.

This I know, as Friends say, experientially. I have seen this combination at work, and I believe in the depth of my heart that those who possess it are the last, best hope of the world, and that we had better find a way to turn out into society this kind of person if we are going to keep ourselves from being blown back to the Stone Age. I have the wild dream— this is why I come back to Friends education—that Friends schools, because of their tradition, because of the testimony of those who have attended them, the quality of the lives they have led, the quality of community that once in awhile they have achieved, can start young men and young women down this kind of path.

As far as competence is concerned, I have no doubt at all. Certainly Sidwell Friends School offers the kind of education that is solid, and if you have been serious about getting it, if you were willing to reach out and become involved in learning and in knowing your teachers, you got it. I know Friends can educate.

But what else do you students take with you as you leave? Your values have been shaped here in your years at Sidwell, but how and in what direction? This is not an intellectual question. There is no curriculum for values. They gradually emerge in each and every one of us, over time, through our interaction with our fellows and through the immediate impact on our environment and our experience, until, for better or for ill, a particular set of values takes hold of us, something that we feel in our bones, and that guides our conduct.

What has Sidwell contributed to this process? Has it given you a restless uneasiness with the status quo? A faith that you can do something to change it? And a commitment to be about the business of doing it, whatever career you choose? I suspect it has, if it has reflected the atmosphere, the climate that I dream of and long for in a Friends school. Has it been a place, for example, where one's yea is yea and one's nay, nay? Integrity is in short supply in the world. Shortcuts, manipulation, a few lies here and there, seem to offer quicker routes to get us what we want. In the short run, they often do, but the price we ultimately pay, as we have learned to our sorrow in this country, is the price of burgeoning cynicism and distrust, and I do not want that for Quaker education. I want honesty in all things large and small, that we come to feel that honesty is the norm and to discover through it the joy of trusting each other. Honor systems and honor councils can become a centerpiece in student life, and every member of a community where such codes exist, whether technically bound by it or not, should strive to live by them and live up to them.

Second, I hope you have found something akin to integrity, and that is trust, a willingness to trust. I think Quaker schools should be places where the first thing a person does when he meets another is to trust him. I remember an essay that Judge Learned Hand wrote in the height of the McCarthy era, when the country was so paranoid about communism that trust and confidence were everywhere being replaced with loyalty oaths. Hand wrote eloquently of the barrenness of the whole oath mania, pointing out that it is far better to accept the risks of a few evil people escaping detection than to abandon trust, because, he said, trust is the stuff of liberty, the cement of free society; without it, it cannot exist. So let us in Quaker fashion be about trusting each other so that our communities will be free, and so that our students who are with us for such a short few years may leave daring to trust.

Third, have all of you who make up this particular Quaker community resolved to get along together? Conflict arises among you as it does in all groups, as faculty, administration, and students have interests that sometimes diverge. The question is only whether we strive for understanding and accommodation or whether we succumb to the very easy temptation to accept adversary relationships, to create power blocs, to build strength that our interests may prevail. For power and its opposite, powerlessness, are facts of life in Quaker education, as elsewhere. This poses difficult problems, but we should resolve that all our capacity and all our energy should be directed toward becoming sensitive to the interests of different groups, toward discovering common ground, toward opening avenues of agreement. I know there are cynics who say this cannot be done. I do not believe that, for I have seen community emerge in settings far less promising than ours, settings in war-torn Europe, settings in jails, among angry and bitter people, where extraordinary individuals were able to foster community by helping others to submerge differences. Surely we should be able to do as much in our Quaker institutions.

Fourth, I hope that Sidwell Friends has been a place where service to others has been right in the middle of the educational process. The place where students, faculty, and administration reach out to help each other and the community outside, because it is in serving others that we discover most surely the capacity to care, and if you remember nothing else of what I say here this morning, I would like you to remember this: *that caring is as important as knowing; without it, knowledge is dangerous; with it, knowledge can be translated into wisdom.*

Caring, my friends, opens us to compassion; it helps us to forbear; it keeps us from hating. Caring also opens us to being hurt, and I must warn you that if you discover the capacity to care, you will also learn that crying is not for children alone, but neither is laughter, because laughing and crying are close together. Both are the rich possessions of the caring human being. Together they lift life from the two-dimensional and the flat to the richness and the depth of the three-dimensional. That is the miracle of caring, and I could ask for nothing more than for this school not only to have shaped and sharpened and disciplined your minds, as I am sure it has done, but also to have moved you to becoming young men and women who care about and revere life everywhere.

Finally, have you learned in these years the value of self-examination and quiet reflection? And how to measure your lives against the plumb line of faith? There are many instruments through which we can learn to do this, and each must choose his own, but I commend again to you graduates the quiet peace of the Meeting house, where generations of men and women have taken stock of their lives and found new strength. It is still an inexhaustible resource, available to all who want to test it and sample its values, and, for me, it is close to the heart of the matter.

And so, love of learning, commitment to honesty, readiness to trust, capacity to live in community together, a caring spirit, and eagerness to seek truth in worship: these are the values that I hope you take with you from this school as you leave for college and for careers. If you have found these values, you will have found rootage that you will be grateful for all of your days.

Your education at Sidwell Friends will not have a price, because it will have been *beyond* price.

A QUAKER VISION FOR HAVERFORD

I DO CARE—I care very much—whether Quaker values still play a role in the life of Haverford College. Indeed, the level of my concern is measured by my certainty that should the day come when they have no role, my interest in the College, which has been a central commitment of my life, would cease.

In saying this, I should make it clear that I am not talking about a role for the institutional Society of Friends. Quakerism as a religion is important to me personally, but the last thing I am concerned about is imposing it on the College or on any member of the campus community.

As long as this distinction between Quaker values and institutional Quakerism is understood, I feel easy about testifying to the continuing importance of Haverford's Quaker dimension. It is important because I believe that these values have something to contribute to the wider world. They are obviously not the special property of Friends—they are embedded in all the world's greatest faiths, but their particular expression in Quaker thinking relates to just those dimensions of the Gospel that are being massively overlooked today and, in my judgment, overlooked at our mortal peril.

Here is a religious group that, because of its particular perception of the relationship between man and God, asserts that human life is sacred, and may not therefore be

---

This article was written for the Haverford College student publication, Chautauqua, May 8, 1987, in response to the question, "Does Quakerism still have a role to play at Haverford College?"

exploited or debased or destroyed for any reason, under any circumstance, at any time. For Friends this is a categorical imperative, and one that our society has lived with, in season and out, for better or for worse, for three centuries. It lies in the heart of Quakerism as it expresses itself in the world. It is what made us pacifists from our beginning. It is what has led us to our concern for human rights, for justice, for the relief of suffering, and to all the other witnesses in the world for which we have become known. Further, it lays exacting obligations on the individual, who, because her own life is also sacred, has a duty to God to develop his talents to their fullest, to act with openness and integrity, to reach out to others, to live in harmony.

When we look at this list of imperatives, and think of them in the context of the age in which we live, their importance is clear to all who have eyes to see and ears to hear. For ours is an age of violence, where life is cheap and where we are so inured to barbarism and human suffering that we lose the very capacity to feel horror, which is itself the ultimate horror. It is an age, too, where duplicity is the stock in trade in governments, where cynicism and greed infect so many of the affluent, and apathy and despair mark the mood of millions of the dispossessed.

What is needed in this kind of world, and needed urgently, is an affirmation, a witness that there is a better way, that human beings can be loving and compassionate and honest, that there is an alternative to violence, and that when we act in these ways there is a chance we can move toward a world of peace because we are creating a world of caring. We need people with this commitment, this willingness to stand up and give witness with their lives that there are other ways of human conduct than the barren exercise of repression and power that seems still to be the world's norm. And we need men and women whose commitment is matched with discipline and creative minds that equip them to put their commitment to work in sophisticated and intelligent ways.

Achieving this combination is the great vision for Haverford College that Isaac Sharpless bequeathed to us. It has been for almost a century a priceless gift, a gift that has made Haverford distinctively different from other fine liberal arts colleges. That this is so is confirmed by countless alumni who have testified that their four years here were for them a moral as well as an intellectual experience. They found at Haverford the learning environment that Isaac Sharpless described in his Commencement address of 1888, which included the famous statement about conscience that hangs over the fireplace in the Founders Common Room, and they have been grateful for it all their lives.

Does today's Haverford continue to reflect the Sharpless vision? Do we continue to be as concerned with the learning environment we provide as with the quality of the academic program we offer? I do not know. Evidence can be cited on both sides, and any judgment is so subjective that I refrain from making one. All I want to do is identify the forces at work as I see them.

Certainly there is some evidence that at least part of President Sharpless's legacy is still with us. The Honor Code, which was born during his years, and which flows directly from the early Quaker testimony that demands a single standard of truthfulness, remains a centerpiece of campus life, creating a climate of integrity that impacts every student who enters the college community.

The effort we continue to make to resolve our differences through seeking unity in the consensus process, and by fostering open debate and wide participation in weighing the issues that engage us, contributes to a climate of harmony and trust and a quality of community that may commend itself to students who have not known it before.

The evident caring of the faculty for the progress and problems of their students, and the evident caring of students for each other in the responsible implementation of the Honor Code, give substance to our claim of being concerned about the worth of each individual and increases the capacity of each of us to be a more caring and sensitive human being.

Not every student will appreciate and own these diverse values. Some may commend themselves to them, others may not, but it is important that exposure and confrontation occur so that choices can be made. We do continue to create a lively, value-oriented learning environment within a far richer and more diverse community than Isaac Sharpless ever knew, and that is to our credit.

But there are other evidences that suggest the erosion of the Sharpless vision, and the erosion is the more serious because it is occurring at the fundamental level of our understanding of Haverford's roots and its purpose as an educational institution. It seems to me, for example, that never in my half-century of association with the College has there been so general a tendency to hang the magic Quaker label on proposals we endorse, and castigate as un-Quakerly those we don't, with, in both cases, little knowledge of what Quakerism is, and little interest in finding out.

The tradition of eloquent interpretation of President Sharpless's vision, voiced by a succession of Haverford leaders such as Rufus Jones and Thomas Kelly and Gilbert White and Douglas Steere, has come to an end. While a number of faculty members continue to feel strongly about the importance of the College's Quaker dimension, none have the time, or perhaps the platform, to articulate it on a regular basis. Nor does our bi-College curriculum, enriched as it is in so many areas, offer an alternative opportunity for students to learn what motivated our predecessors and what their perception of Haverford was. A single course about Quakerism is still listed in the catalogue, but it is not offered this year in Professor Bronner's absence, and no one was concerned enough, or had the time, to teach it.

Nor is there any longer a forum where students are regularly challenged to measure their lives against lasting values. Such challenges may exist in the context of particular courses in philosophy or religion, but these lack the impact of a shared community forum that once was provided by the Tuesday Collection and the Thursday Meeting. With few spokespersons, no instruction, and no forum, is it surprising that students know little about Haverford's heritage and often badly mis-read the substance of Quaker values?

The secularization of all higher education is another factor that affects Haverford. Much of it is healthy, and I certainly have no wish to return to the narrow parochialism that marked an earlier era, but I do voice a note of regret that any reference to spiritual values in discussing the educational process is coming to be regarded as irrelevant or inappropriate. Not long ago, when I was expressing my hopes for Haverford to a prominent member of our faculty and spoke of the twin concerns of Isaac Sharpless, I was dismissed with the comment that "Haverford is not a missionary society." Such a gross misreading of the Sharpless vision is certainly not reflective of general faculty opinion, but it does suggest an antipathy for the discussion of spiritual issues that I believe is growing here, as elsewhere.

Finally, I am disturbed that the increase in teaching loads and the unconscionable burden of committee work and, yes, the increasing pressure to publish, have left faculty so heavily overworked that they have less and less time for the sort of relaxed discourse with students, where values were shared and debated, that once characterized our campus. Students no longer gather every Sunday in Rufus Jones's study or sit around Professor Asensio's weekly supper table, as did their fathers a generation ago. That, too, was part of the Haverford learning environment, and its loss, through no fault of our present faculty, undercuts the quality and depth of undergraduate life. Indeed, were I in a position of authority at the College, nothing would be higher on my agenda than finding ways to lighten faculty loads and encouraging increased involvement with students outside the formal structure of the academic program.

All this adds up to a clouded picture of Haverford's future as a Quaker-related institution and leaves unanswered the question of whether we will retain the special distinctiveness that came to us because of it, or become more and more the clone of other first-rate colleges like Amherst or Bowdoin. I want us to continue to be distinctive. I want us to keep alive the Haverford that Isaac Sharpless gave us because it has meant so much to so many, and because it offers so much to a world torn apart by too much cleverness and too little faith.

So far, we have managed to keep vibrant a number of practices and policies that express his vision, but I wonder how long the plant can continue to produce blossoms if we allow its roots to wither.

WHY QUAKER MEETING IN
A FRIENDS SCHOOL?

W HEN I STARTED TO THINK SERIOUSLY about what to say
to all of you this morning, the first thing that occurred
to me was that we adults ask a great deal of you, You all carry
heavy academic loads, and you have all sorts of extra-
curricular responsibilities—musical, theatrical, athletic,
social, communal, and probably more that I don't know about.
But I don't think we ask anything that's more difficult than
requiring you to come here each week and sit in silence for
40 minutes.

We all live in a world wired for sound, where "dead air" is
the cardinal sin of the electronic media, and silence is everywhere in short supply. You live surrounded by noise. Your
ability—even your preference—to study at full volume amazes
your elders. To move from this incessant cacophony to a place
of silence, and to learn to make good use of it, is a vexing
assignment.

I've been learning about it for more than 70 years, first
entering the world of Quaker silence in this room in 1919
when I was four years old. I'd been nagging my parents
for weeks to bring me to Meeting because my older sister
attended, and I considered it the rankest of sex discrimination that she could come and I couldn't. Finally my mother
caved in and told me I could come on one condition: that I'd

*Remarks at the Germantown Friends School opening September 1992;
they appeared in* Studies in Education: Germantown Friends School
65 *(Spring 1993). Stephen, GFS 1933, was a member of the School
Committee and of Germantown Monthly Meeting.*

sit absolutely still for a whole hour. Piece of cake, I said. So I came and I sat still for five minutes. Then I began to squirm. After ten minutes a gentleman sitting up here in the gallery rose to preach. He opened with a quotation from scripture, pausing at its conclusion for impact, and just at that moment I looked up at my mother and said in a loud voice: "Well, if that man can talk, why can't I?" It was some time before I returned to these premises.

Pursuing the Search for God

Since then I've come to better understand and appreciate Friends' unusual form of worship. The reason we sit quietly together is simple. It relates to the root belief of the Society of Friends that every human being has the capacity to know directly the will of God. God speaks to each of us when we are ready to listen, but because we are all at a different place in our search to know His will, and each has his or her own way of becoming open to listen, Friends needed a form of religious expression that provided maximum freedom to pursue the search. Unprogrammed silence was the obvious choice, affording an opportunity for both quiet reflection and the sharing of insights as each is led. Although not all Friends still follow this pattern, it's been in use for three-and-a-half centuries and has served us well.

It is a form, too, that is especially appropriate for us at Germantown Friends School. We are a diverse community, with a rich mix of faiths—Christian, Jewish, Muslim, humanist—and a special beauty of the unprogrammed silence of Quaker Meeting is that it neither impinges upon nor violates other forms of worship or religious ritual. Each of you is free to use the silence within the context of your own communion if you so wish.

I've noted why Friends worship as they do, but why do we think it's important that you come here each week? The answer goes directly to the question of what GFS is all about. This school, which has been guided by Germantown Monthly Meeting of Friends ever since it opened its doors in 1845, has a dual mission. Its first responsibility is academic excellence: to provide a curriculum rigorous enough to assure that the potential in all of you is translated into competence and that your minds are prepared for college and for life in a world in which knowledge and a disciplined intellect are necessities.

Exposure to Values

Equally important is our second responsibility: to expose you to values that we think are crucial in providing a moral framework for the exercise of competence. These values have particular expression in Quaker thought, but they are not the property of Quakers, for they are buried deep in the teachings of all the world's great faiths. Our aim is to expose, but not to bind. You are free to accept those values that seem right and reject those that do not. GFS is as interested in strengthening your faith in your own communion as it is in defining religious values in Quaker terms.

Over the 60 years since I left this school, I've been testing these two goals, and I find them good. My life has been richly blessed. I've been able to spend large parts of it working directly, if modestly, on the great problems of justice and peace with which the world struggles. It's a calling that has taken me to far places, sometimes amidst violence and revolution, sometimes amidst terrible repression, sometimes where human suffering has reduced me to tears. With such exposure, one cannot escape reaching judgments about what makes for community and what destroys it, what opens a path to justice and what closes it.

Many times I've seen those sent to help fail in their mission. They have been able to feed and clothe a community, build houses, bring water, and run clinics, but they weren't able to reach to the hatred and bitterness that was paralyzing and consuming the lives of its people. But I've also seen miracles, where hatred has been exorcized, despair changed to hope, and trust reborn.

Believing Change Is Possible

What made the difference? All were competent. They knew how to analyze problems; they knew what buttons to push and how to get things done. Competence was essential, but competence wasn't enough. Miracles require more: inviolable integrity, where one's yea is yea, and one's nay, nay, in a world where integrity is in pitifully short supply; compassion, which makes it possible to walk in another's shoes; faith that treasures life where life is cheap; daring to believe that human beings can rise above their baser nature, that they can respond to stimuli other than threats and fear and naked violence. Those who worked miracles lived in the certainty that change was possible, and it became possible.

These are the values to which I hope you are being exposed at Germantown Friends School—in the classroom, in the ambiance of the school, and in this room—because, speaking for myself, I can tell you that I've been grateful all the days of my life for the role this school played in helping me to frame a value structure that has enriched my life.

And it's here, in this room, that you have the opportunity, week after week, to reflect on who you are and what you are, and what you want to be in contrast to what you want to do.

It's a difficult exercise but ultimately richly rewarding. For some of you, it's just beginning. For all the rest of us, it's in mid-course. But wherever you are in your own search, let us this morning make use of the gift of silence. Let us be about shaping our lives to become better able, each of us, to help mend a world grown weary of violence, and a human community brought low by too much cleverness and too little faith.

Quaker Values, Standards, and Personal Responsibility at Germantown Friends School

Germantown Friends School
To: Faculty and Staff
From: Dick Wade
Date: April 15, 1996

Germantown Friends Meeting recorded a minute in response to the "senior prank" on February 7. This action, which rarely occurs, provides us with a wonderful opportunity. The minute, written by Stephen Cary, has been enthusiastically embraced by the School Committee. David West, Clerk of the School Committee, is sending it to our parents this week. We often hear the phrase "Quaker values" used without clarity of what the term means. I am grateful to the Germantown Monthly Meeting for giving us a substantive definition to help guide us in our life together as well as to help us educate our students. I invite administration, faculty, and staff to discuss this letter to see how it can shape our actions. In particular, I hope faculty at all grade levels will consider ways of using the principles contained in this letter in direct discussions with students. I intend to use this letter as a guiding theme throughout the 1996-97 school year.

This interchange between Stephen as clerk of Germantown Monthly Meeting and the School Committee and with the head of Germantown Friends School took place in March and April 1996.

GERMANTOWN MONTHLY MEETING
March 19, 1996

To: David West, Clerk, GFS School Committee
    Richard Wade, Head, GFS
FROM: Stephen Cary, Clerk, on Behalf of Germantown
    Monthly Meeting
SUBJECT: Quaker Values as Perceived by Portions of the
    GFS Community

At its regular meeting for the conduct of business on March 13, 1996, Germantown Monthly Meeting heard a report and engaged in extended discussion of the unfortunate events that took place at our school on February 7 in connection with the senior prank.

We are grateful for the firm response to this incident that was made by Richard Wade, the school's head, and for his thoughtful report to school parents regarding it. Friends fully support Richard Wade in his efforts to achieve wide understanding and strong implementation of the school's carefully crafted policy on drugs and alcohol.

It was clear from the Meeting's discussion, however, that Friends were disturbed by what seems to us to be a dangerous misunderstanding of Quaker values on the part of a significant portion of the GFS constituency. There appears to be a feeling abroad that, because the Religious Society of Friends has no creedal requirements for membership, has a long established and widely known reputation for tolerance, and has a tradition of supporting personal choice, even to the level of civil disobedience, that there is, therefore, no firm or required standard of conduct or rules of behavior to which individual Friends or their institutions are expected to adhere.

Nothing could be further from the truth. In the Quaker faith there is a fundamental and overarching commitment to responsible conduct in every area of our lives—a commitment laid on us by our belief that each can know the will of God directly, and is required to seek and do that will to the best of each one's ability.

Friends see this religious framework as establishing a basis for responsible human behavior that is firmer than any formulation of creedal requirements or secular regulations. Quakers have no creed, but we regularly address a set of queries that challenge us to examine the quality and faithfulness of our lives. Tolerance is not to be confused with license. Personal responsibility and personal choice are important to Friends because they help us to grow, but they are to be exercised under the compulsion of a conscience illumined by the Holy Spirit and tested against the wisdom of others. Rules are necessary in any ordered society. They can be broken, but again, only under compulsion of conscience, never for purely selfish benefit, always openly and nonviolently, and always with a readiness to accept the penalties that established authority imposes on the dissenter. Friends values require living within rules and within law unless all of these difficult conditions are met.

These are not easy concepts to grasp, but they are essential to an understanding of Quakerism and to an understanding of the *modus operandi* of Germantown Friends School. Members of Germantown Monthly Meeting stand ready to help in any way we can to support the school administration in its efforts to convey to the school community the substance of Quaker values and their relevance to the life, the rules, and the practice of Germantown Friends School.

Thank You

PENDLE HILL WISHES TO THANK THE FOLLOWING FOR
HELPING TO MAKE THIS BOOK POSSIBLE:

JACK COLEMAN
NORVAL REESE
JOHN WHITEHEAD

THE INTREPID QUAKER:
ONE MAN'S QUEST FOR PEACE

was composed in Goudy Oldstyle, desktop computer fonts
from the Adobe Type Library. Goudy Oldstyle was designed
in 1915 by Frederick W. Goudy, his 25th typeface and his
first for American Typefounders. One of the most popular
typefaces ever produced, its distinctive features include dia-
mond-shaped dots on the i, the j, and puncuation marks; the
upturned ear of the g; and the base of the e and the l.

This book was composed on a 7600 Power Macintosh
using Pagemaker 6.5. Eight thousand copies were printed in
the United States of America by R.R. Donnelley in 2004. It
was printed on Finch Opaque B/W paper, 606 ppi.

Book design by

Eva Fernandez Beehler and Bob McCoy